The Center Holds

I first met Hayward Alker at MIT. He was brilliant, jovial, and ebullient and I personally have always felt a common bond with him. Though he is sadly no longer with us, his contributions to the field of International Relations will continue to live on. We here at The Toda Institute deeply appreciate his collaboration with us over the years as a peace scholar. We would like to express profound gratitude to him and his wife Ann Tickner for their many contributions to Peace Studies and International Relations. My deepest most heartfelt condolences go out to his family and friends.

Majid Tehranian
Director
Toda Institute for Global Peace & Policy Research
January 9, 2008

The Center Holds

UN Reform for 21st-Century Challenges

Peace & Policy, Volume 12

Kevin P. Clements &
Nadia Mizner, editors

Routledge
Taylor & Francis Group

LONDON AND NEW YORK

First published 2008 by Transaction Publishers

Published 2017 by Routledge
2 Park Square, Milton Park, Abingdon, Oxon OX14 4RN
711 Third Avenue, New York, NY 10017, USA

Routledge is an imprint of the Taylor & Francis Group, an informa business

Library of Congress Catalog Number: 2007033325

Library of Congress Cataloging-in-Publication Data

The center holds : United Nations reform for 21st century challenges / Kevin P. Clements and Nadia Mizner, editors.
    p. cm.
Includes bibliographical references.
ISBN 978-1-4128-0778-4
    1. United Nations. 2. United Nations--Management. I. Clements, Kevin P. II. Mizner, Nadia.

JZ4995.C44 2007
341.23--dc22

2007033325

ISBN 13: 978-1-4128-0778-4 (pbk)

Contents

Preface

Majid Tehranian

The United Nations is in need of repair. We should not wait until the next global tragedy. Twice in the 20th century, we reformed global governance (the League of Nations and the United Nations) during times of duress. We may now be in a position to choose more wisely.

The chapters in this volume attempt to do just that. Ably edited by Kevin P. Clements and Nadia Mizner, the chapters are contributed by a group of renowned scholars who have spent their lifetimes to study the problems of global governance. The world is rapidly changing. The conditions for sound global governance are also changing. There was a time that benign neglect was the dominant policy. Then colonialism came, in which control of the lands in Asia, Africa, and Latin America was considered vital to the interests of Europe and North America. Following two world wars, that doctrine was put to rest. But, the newly independent countries could not fend for themselves. We resorted to decolonization, foreign aid, and spheres of influence. In the meantime, a cold war surged between the capitalism and communist camps. The end of the cold war in 1989 has inaugurated a new era.

Now, the world is deeply divided among five civilizations, including nomadic, agrarian, commercial, industrial, and digital (Tehranian 2007). Professor Samuel Huntington (1996) called this an era of the clash of civilizations. By a clash of civilizations, he means that there is a tension between the West and the rest. Other countries are catching up, sometimes with a vengeance. Russia, China, India, and Brazil are among them. Knowledge cannot be monopolized. For example, in the 13th century, China's industrial secret to produce silk was stolen away to the Byzantium by two Nestorian Christian priests. Similarly, the secret of how to make atomic bombs is currently being spread around the globe.

We need a global governance regime that can limit the damage. The new governance regime would have to be effective and democratic. Since the participants in the global dialogue have increased, the new

1

plans for global governance would have to take a complex variety of interests into consideration. Among such considerations, we may count the following:

- The interests of the states—there are nearly 200 members in the UN system.
- The interests of the transnational corporations (TNCs) who have managed to bring about a global economy characterized by interdependence.
- The interests of an emerging global civil society that is currently represented by the nongovernmental organizations (NGOs).
- The interests of the unrepresented.

There is no easy formula to satisfy all these interests. But, the search must go on before one more major tragedy hits humankind. This book is dedicated to that search.

References

Huntington, Samuel P. 1996. *The Clash of Civilizations and the Remaking of World Order*. New York: Simon and Schuster.

Tehranian, Majid. 2007. *Rethinking Civilization: Resolving Conflict in the Human Family*. London & New York: Routledge.

Introduction: Reform of the United Nations

Kevin P. Clements

The United Nations is the institutional hope for the world's environ-mental, developmental, and humanitarian communities, and the single most important multilateral container for the expression of national self-interest. Insofar as the United Nations represents the people-of-the-world's aspirations for a more just and peaceful world, it retains the capacity to inspire the political imagination of individuals and col-lectives. To the extent that the United Nations is viewed primarily as a "trade union" to represent the "power" interests of 192 state parties, it becomes a source of political cynicism and skepticism. We "the peoples" of the United Nations confront and stand in tension with we "the State Parties." The UN is both of these things, simultaneously. It is a focus for multilateral effort, directed towards the articulation of international responsibility and the alleviation of human suffering, while it is also a site for the expression and protection of national interests.

These two dynamics generate predictable stresses. The protection of national interests often seems more important than the articulation of international responsibilities. In fact, these interests are enshrined in the Charter's principle of non-interference. Article II, Part 7, states "Nothing contained in the present Charter shall authorize the United Nations to intervene in matters which are essentially within the domestic jurisdiction of any state" (United Nations 1945). For the larger powers (both those represented in the Permanent 5 and those aspiring to such membership) this has been interpreted, until the publication of The Responsibility to Protect in 2005, to mean that the United Nations should not obstruct the assertion of power and national interest except in extremis.

The reality is that small and vulnerable nations need a global insti-tution like the United Nations to remind the more powerful states of the importance of emerging international regimes, the rule of law, and global processes that are likely to generate structural stability, justice and peace in the international system. Only the largest states can afford to practice a la carte multilateralism. These states see the United Nations primarily as an organization to advance national purpose. They are willing to transfer issues to the world body when it acts permissively, but will circumvent it when it does not. The United States, under the Bush administration, is the most egregious example of such a state. In recent years, the United States has used the United Nations to try and advance US exceptionalism and unilateralism. Over the past six years, the United States has demonstrated a consistent unwillingness to allow itself to be constrained by international law and has sat very lightly on the doctrine of the "sovereign" equality of states.

The Permanent 5 (P5), and other large states, also see the United Nations essentially as a container for the expression of national interests although they are subtler in their expression of this than is the United States, which feels that it can flout the United Nations with impunity. This position contrasts with the view held by a wide variety of international and national non-governmental organizations, regional organizations, and inter-governmental organizations. By and large, these multilateral groups see the United Nations as the only global body capable of diagnosing and responding to a range of world problems, problems that cannot be dealt with at national levels alone, for example, issues such as population growth, climate change, environmental degradation, development, global threats to health, refugee care, the prevention of conflict, post-conflict peacekeeping, and other humanitarian challenges. These issues are largely addressed by the work of all the specialized agencies of the United Nations, which, unlike some of the central security organs of the United Nations, have made a huge difference to global well-being. Leaving aside the calamitous wars in Afghanistan and Iraq, the United Nations and its affiliates have played a hugely important role in the ending of violent political conflict and in the prevention of further conflict. According to the Human Security Report (2005: 155), the 80 percent decline in the most deadly conflict since the early 1990s can be explained by "the extraordinary upsurge of activism by the international community [including the United Nations] that has been directed towards conflict prevention, peacemaking and peacebuilding."

The United Nations, therefore, must take some of the credit for catalyzing and directing this activism in the face of resistance from more powerful state parties who would rather see it play a secondary role in building international stability.

At age 60, it is clear that the United Nations can do better. This is an opportune time to reflect on ways of developing higher synergies between the twin tasks of pursuing "negative peace," through collective security, arms control, and the peaceful settlement of disputes and "positive peace," through enhanced economic and social development, the promotion and protection of national identity/self-determination, and the safeguard and promotion of human rights.

The outgoing secretary-general, Kofi Annan, sought to promote this in part in his Summit Declaration. In 2005, he stated:

> In the 21st century, all states and their collective institutions must advance the cause of larger freedom—by ensuring freedom from want, freedom from fear and freedom to live in dignity. In an increasingly interconnected world, progress in the areas of development, security, and human rights must go hand in hand. There will be no development without security and no security without development. And both development and security also depend on respect for human rights and the rule of law.

This was a bold attempt to link the security, development and human rights agendas in a holistic, analytical framework accompanied by proposals for higher levels of inter-institutional collaboration and delivery. This agenda, however, did not find favor with some state parties, particularly not with the United States. Its delegation tabled 750 amendments to the rolling text being negotiated between states just two weeks before the Summit began.

Thus, efforts to link development with some of the other initiatives Kofi Annan instigated, such as the report of the panel on High Level Threats, The Responsibility to Protect 2005, failed to materialize. The result of this is that many of the reforms that the United Nations needs to make in order to meet the global challenges of the 21st century remain on hold as the new secretary-general, Ban Ki-moon of South Korea, assumes responsibility for the organization.

Whether the current secretary-general has a real interest in articulating a new vision for the United Nations in the 21st century, or he will focus most of his attention on generating higher levels of bureaucratic efficiency is the question. His background in South Korea suggests that he will likely focus on management rather than pursuing the role of a visionary leader. This may discourage progress on the reform front as the United Nations is clearly at a stage in its development when it is asked to face substantive challenges that require new 21st-century interpretations of the Charter and bold new visions of how to realize the values of the founders.

How, for example, does the United Nations ensure that the interests of the people of the world, most clearly expressed in discourse promoting human security, capture as much attention as the interests of state parties? How will it approach the relationship with the non-sovereign, private, and public actors who are not represented directly in the United Nations but who command power and resources that are often larger and more important than those available to nation-states? How does it deal with state parties who are ineffectively, incapably, and illegitimately treating their own citizens? How can the United Nations enhance its role with regional organizations, and, most importantly, how will it promote a positive and proactive role in relation to all the diverse challenges that are on the current global agenda?

It was in relation to these issues that the Toda Institute for Global Peace & Policy Research organized a meeting of scholars and practitioners on the Reform of the United Nations in February 2006. This volume presents a collection of some of presentations at this conference. The event took place before the United Nations considered its three 2006 landmark documents aimed to reform and streamline different dimensions of the UN organization and functions (namely, "Investing in the UN: For a Stronger Organization Worldwide," "The Comprehensive Review of Governance and Oversight," and "The Panel on System-Wide Coherence"). The February 2006 conference, therefore, focused more attention on a series of meta-themes that participants considered crucial to the United Nations, recapturing some of its original point and purpose as the primary vehicle for "saving succeeding generations from the scourge of war." There were a number of central ideas and themes reflected by the papers, which I shall try to capture here.

The first theme alluded to by many of the contributors was the central imperative of thinking about the United Nations and its reform as though people mattered as much as the interests of states. It was argued that the United Nations, post-9/11, had become far too oriented to the security of states as opposed to the security of peoples. If state parties and citizens emphasized human security, it was felt that this might be a good antidote to narrow concepts of state security. In particular, it was considered important that political leaders and civil society move beyond the politics of fear and that nation-states, multilateral organizations, and civil society organizations become more systematic and bold in mapping current global threats in order to identify those that are probable, dangerous and likely and those that are not. The global War on Terror, for example, has tended to exaggerate the international terrorist threat, the responses to which result in some severe distortions of the global political system (Marshall and Gurr 2005). Thinking about the United Nations as though people matter will generate a greater concentration on positive peace as that framework begins to address the genuine existential fears confronting the majority of the world's peoples in Africa, Asia, and Latin America.

Many recent studies, such as The Human Security Report (2005), focus attention on development, the protection of human rights, environmental sustainability, and the development of effective and capable governance as prerequisites for the advancement of human security. Transforming the United Nations so that human security lies at its core means placing people (individual citizens in all member states) at the heart of both the diagnosis of problems and solutions.

Secondly, there was a strong concern at the conference reflected in different chapters in this volume, that the United States, under the current Bush administration, poses a significant threat to the integrity of the United Nations. Many in the current US administration, for example, believe that the United Nations is inimical to US national interests because it impedes their ability to exercise coercive, pre-emptive diplomacy (Eric Shawn 2006). Whether there is any prospect for effective reform of the United Nations while the current administration is in power in Washington is a moot point. What is absolutely clear, however, is that the United Nations will be diminished consistently if countries such as the United States assert policies of national exceptionalism.

The defense and reform of the United Nations, however, is not just a question of challenging this hegemony. On the contrary, it is absolutely vital that those interested in replacing cultures of violence by promoting cultures of peace have a very clear vision of the world that they wish to see emerge and of the role the United Nations might play in this process. Challenging the post-Westphalian political order and the "statecraft" that accompanies it is one approach to re-evaluating 19th-century concepts of the state and the narrow concepts of militarized nationalism that often accompany such perspectives. We must ask, however, whether the United Nations can be reformed with an unreconstructed United States playing a spoiling role, or whether it might make more progress if the United States were excluded from the organization? The downside of the latter scenario is that the United States would have even fewer restraints on its power. This might lead to a more dangerous United States than one constrained somewhat by emerging norms of international responsibility. The United Nations is undoubtedly stronger with the United States playing a positive role as an active member. The only real question is whether this current administration is capable of playing such a role or whether it has developed such a negative perspective that it will remain defiantly unenthusiastic until the next presidential election in 2008.

Thirdly, it is critical that individuals, civil society, regional and other intergovernmental organizations articulate fresh visions for the United Nations. Without a vision, the people perish. Without a new vision or a restatement of the older visions for the United Nations, expressed by its founders, it is unlikely that it will ever begin fulfilling its idealistic promise. The primary source for such a new vision should derive from internationally oriented citizens and from both public and private multilateral organizations.

Richard Falk, for example, believes it is important to frame visions in terms of horizons of feasibility, necessity, and desirability. In this process it is absolutely critical that space be given for multilateral (public and private) discussions about how to imagine different types of world futures and what role the United Nations might play in their realization.

Only by exercising imagination (see Elise Boulding 1991) can we determine what sort of world we want to bring into existence. We cannot engage in visionary imagining, however, if we allow ourselves to be constrained by the realms of possibility and feasibility; although these are important elements of how to realize specific visions in time and place. It is vital that we learn how to imagine desirable worlds that are nonviolent, inclusive, just, and equal if we are to understand what sort of role a reformed United Nations might play in helping to realize them.

Fourthly, there is a growing recognition, especially by those UN agencies working for "positive peace," of the central importance of focusing policy-related attention on the most vulnerable and the weakest in terms of international politics and economy. These individuals and groups should be both the object and the subject of multilateral endeavor. This is a vitally important principle because it provides a significant reference point for evaluating institutional impact and effectiveness. If the poorest and most vulnerable do not have their basic human needs satisfied and are not actively included in the revisioning processes, there is a high probability that they will consciously and unconsciously sabotage development initiatives in a wide variety of different sectors. In numerous case studies of human development, human security and social harmony, for example, infant mortality rates correlate extremely highly with levels of peacefulness. Focusing on the development of institutions ensuring that weak, vulnerable babies and infants survive, for example, is an important test of whether or not responsible private and public sector agents are genuinely interested in developing ideas of public good and higher levels of social well-being. Similarly ensuring that women's roles in development and peacebuilding are enhanced is also a critical component of ensuring a high regard for the collective good. In relation to women's role in peacebuilding, Security Council Resolution 1325 provides an excellent framework for promoting the role and status of women in peace and security issues, especially in relation to preventive diplomacy and peacekeeping missions. It is critical that the United Nations direct a considerable amount of its collective energy to ensuring that the voices of women and children are represented in the development, human rights, and security spheres.

Historically, the United Nations has not shirked from this responsibility. UNESCO, UNICEF, the WHO and the UNHCR, to name just four, are specialized agencies with core missions of serving the most vulnerable. While there are many other national and regional organizations engaged in similar humanitarian activities, these specialized agencies, have, over the years, taken the lead in preparing research and policy documents and implementing programs aimed at securing the interests of women and children, the sick and dying, the displaced and marginalized. There is an urgent need for a reformed United Nations to recognize an elevated role for youth and women and the inclusion of minorities in all of its deliberations. It is imperative that there exist global institutions that give voice to those who are voiceless in decisions about their own future.

The fifth point, which flows from the fourth, is how much time and effort the world community should direct towards transforming the United Nations in order to ensure higher levels of humanitarian effectiveness as opposed to directing such energies towards national and regional initiatives with the same general objectives? This is a very legitimate question when one considers the huge amount of humanitarian and development work done by organizations such as the European Union and many national governments on a bilateral basis. There was a strong consensus at the meeting, however, that was reflected in a number of the chapters in this volume—despite all the excellent work being conducted at a regional level, there was still a profound need for the United Nations at a global level. In particular it is clear that if the United Nations did not exist it would have to be invented or reinvented.

Still left unanswered is the wider question of how much time and attention should be given to the promotion of regionalism and the enhancement of active civil society organizations in a variety of conflict and non-conflict zones. In particular, it seems vital to stimulate higher levels of non-military co-operation and expanded areas of mutual development and security interest.

There was substantial discussion of the role of the United Nations in relation to different regions, although there was considerable confusion and disagreement about how to define a region. Does one define region by geography, through the idea of communities of interest, by moral and religious persuasions, or through broader concepts of linguistic and epistemic communities? How do regions combine to become social and political systems?

Focusing on regional and global interdependence is a way of identifying which "spaces" individuals, states, markets, regional and global institutions operate within and where there are agreements to pursue higher levels of cooperation en route to integration.

The Charter provisions for regional organizations are very clear. Under Article 52, for example, there is a very explicit recognition of the role of regional organizations, in collaboration with the United Nations, to work together in the maintenance of international peace and security. In fact, this Article specifies that member states should make efforts to solve their disputes at regional levels before referring them to the Security Council. There are also provisions for the Security Council to delegate enforcement powers to regional organizations as well. Perhaps the regional organizations that have made most use of these diverse provisions are the European Union and OSCE in Europe. They provide important models for other regional organizations wishing to become more proactive in relation to conflict prevention, preventive diplomacy, crisis management, or post-conflict reconstruction.

One way the United Nations and affiliated organizations might begin assisting nation-states to move away from a militarized view of security is by encouraging civil society organizations and citizens to assume more direct responsibility for their own development and security. Movement in this direction would challenge many of the taken-for-granted assumptions about the role of states as the primary guarantor of security and perhaps stimulate a debate about ways in which this "central" taken-for-granted role of states might also be shared with citizens. In many of the world's most intractable conflicts it is the states themselves that are generating insecurity for their own citizens and for those of adjoining states. If the United Nations could focus more global attention on ways of empowering individual citizens, humanitarian groups, and regional organizations to assume higher levels of responsibility for systemic and individual security, it should be possible to think beyond the nation-state as the principle guarantor of individual security.

The sixth theme relates to the importance of understanding some of the bigger global dynamics at work in the world and what challenges these forces pose to an unreconstructed United Nations. Most global problems suggest a heightened rather than a diminishing role for the United Nations. The world is becoming much more closely interdependent in both positive and negative ways. We need to understand these dynamics if we are to generate transnational and multilateral institutions that will reinforce positive consequences while mitigating negative ones. In East and Southeast Asia, for example, most people will be living in mega-cities of over 25 million people by 2015. These cities will be larger in size than many current state members of the United Nations. How do global institutions ensure that the metropolitan interests of these vast, urban conglomerates are reflected in multilateral decision-making? What are the appropriate institutions for sharing wisdom and insight into ways of dealing with the challenges of globalization?

Similarly, the broader issues of climate change, youth population bulges, growing resource constraints, global pandemics, environmental degradation, water shortages, and political terror all need to be understood in ways that enable national, regional, and global decision-makers to generate positive responses and policy options.

None of these problems can be addressed satisfactorily at local or national levels alone. All require transnational diagnostics and multilateral solutions. The United Nations and a variety of regional organizations are the agencies best placed for dealing with these issues. It is important, therefore, that as many of these dynamics are understood rationally and scientifically so that they can be dealt with in a collaborative problem-solving fashion before they become lightning rods for polarization and division.

It is equally important in understanding transnational dynamics that attention is paid to positive trends as well. A reformed United Nations will focus on virtuous cycles as much as vicious ones so that solutions to problems from a variety of different levels can be captured and learned from. They will then become the basis for sophisticated option generation in relation to the problematic issues on the international agenda.

A seventh theme that needs to be addressed is related to reform of the United Nations regarding its political and administrative leadership. The conference took place before Ban Ki-moon won the top position and replaced Kofi Annan. It is still too soon to say exactly what sort of a leader

Ban Ki-moon will be, but it was considered vital that whoever occupies the position of secretary-general has his/her own distinctive vision for the organization, works out how much he/she wishes to be an activist secretary-general and has some clarity about how to mobilize political will behind different kinds of humanitarian and political interventions.

The eighth theme that ran through the conference discussions and a number of chapters has to do with processes of inclusion. Despite being staffed by some excellent professionals, the United Nations remains somewhat exclusive, inflexible, privileged, and elitist. Most participants felt that too many voices and perspectives were marginalized and excluded from UN institutions It is important, therefore, that the UN reform agenda generates 21st-century institutions which attract the best professionals from all around the world while being relatively permeable, flexible, and responsive to a wide variety of different and diverse perspectives. It was also considered vital to the effective functioning of the organization that there is a reiteration of the Hammarskjöld idea of an international civil service which owes primary allegiance to the world community rather than particular nation-states.

Ninth, there was considerable discussion about different concepts of development: development for whom, by whom and with what sorts of outcomes? It is fine to establish that "freedom from want" remains at the heart of all UN development initiatives, but what does this mean precisely for private and public sector actors? To what extent does development (seen primarily as growth) generate negative externalities and how might these be mitigated? The pursuit of the Millennium Development Goals was considered highly desirable both as a means of generating self propelling economic activity and as a means of addressing equity and fairness issues. The UN remains an important global actor in the development field but it has to ensure that the outcomes of its rights-based initiatives generate growth and justice.

Tenth, there was a strong sense that Cardoso's (2004) report, "We the Peoples: Civil Society," contained many useful suggestions for capturing the creative ideas and energies of a number of civil society organizations in relation to enhancing UN effectiveness. Perhaps the most critical relationships, however, are not those between the United Nations and civil society organizations directly, but those that have more to do with the complex relationships that exist between the United Nations, the forces of economic globalization, nation-states, civil society organizations, and the media. What is the role of the United Nations in relation to these particular institutional intersections? There was strong concern that the United

Nations needed to build on the Global Compact, the Cardoso report, and work in UNESCO on world information flows, if it wants to position itself more centrally in relation to all of these different sectors.

The eleventh theme had to do with new ways of conceptualizing sovereignty. It is crucial that a reformed United Nations does not rely on an outmoded concept of sovereignty that no longer reflects contemporary realities. Many state parties have a large and growing sovereignty gap in relation to their capacity to protect citizens, to deliver basic services, such as health and education to the whole population, and in terms of their own popular legitimacy. It might be more appropriate for the United Nations to think in terms of complex sovereignties where the taken-for-granted relationship between state and citizen is problematized. Many of the traditional assumptions about integrated unitary sovereign states do not reflect the realities in most UN member states. There are competing jurisdictions, autonomous and semi-autonomous regions, distinctive ethnic and cultural groups all posing challenges to the idea of a narrow unitary state. In recognition of this diversity it is important to become sensitized to new concepts of citizenship rights, obligations, and expectations. These questions are further complicated by new sets of relationships between the individual and the community. It is important that the United Nations is aware of ways in which these old relationships are being reconceptualized and challenged, especially in terms of the contractual commitment between state and security in relation to the trade off between security and loyalty. This question is particularly problematic in relation to the insistence of the United States that its own security threats are applicable to the rest of the "free" world. This logic suggests that in return for accepting the global leadership of the United States, its military muscle will be made available to friends and allies.

There is a need, however, for nation-states to generate their own threat assessments and devise their own national, regional, and global solutions to them. The United Nations can play a critical role here in responding to early warnings of impending security threat. It can and should deploy a range of diplomatic solutions to problems, but at some stage, if it wishes to launch military interventions in relation to its "responsibility to protect" citizens threatened by the action/inaction of their own states, it has to have some standing forces or an army of its own that is capable of mounting credible interventions.

The International Commission on Intervention and State Sovereignty [ICISS] (authors of the 2000 report The Responsibility to Protect) had its recommendations incorporated into the UN secretary-general's 2001

"Report on the Prevention of Armed Conflict." The central recommendations of all three reports were captured in the final report of the secretary-general to the United Nations in September 2005. In that report national sovereignty was reaffirmed as the fundamental building block of the international system, but it was, for the first time, significantly qualified.

The new norm (some argue it is essentially a reassertion of an old norm) is that national sovereignty does not rest primarily on the assertion of sovereign power but on the fulfillment of complex political and social responsibilities. The minimal responsibilities are the protection of citizens and the nation-state and a promise not to infringe the sovereignty of others. The more optimal responsibilities are the creation of social, economic, and political conditions within which all people might meet their basic human needs for identity, recognition, welfare and participation.

There is certainly a powerful injunction against any intentional or unintentional policies that do harm to citizens. While many of these ideas are imbedded in traditional democratic theory, their new significance is in relation to the articulation of constitutive norms for what might loosely be called an emergent "global" or "international community" with higher levels of responsibility and accountability.

In any event (despite the actions of the most powerful states in Iraq and in the global War on Terror), it is becoming more difficult for nation-states to justify egregious behavior with national or state interest arguments. The new norm is that the exercise of sovereignty does not confer any absolute rights on rulers and certainly provides no justification for abusing human rights or for generating harm to civilian populations in the pursuit of national or political interest. The crucial contribution of the ICISS is its argument that national sovereignty is based on a dual concept of responsibility. The first is a responsibility to respect the sovereign integrity of other nation-states and the second is the responsibility to protect its citizens. Having reconceptualized sovereignty as responsibility, the "responsibility to protect" advocates three specific responsibilities that are the benchmarks of good global citizenship (2001: xi). These responsibilities are:

a. The responsibility to prevent by addressing both the root causes and direct causes of internal conflict and other man-made crises that put populations at risk.

b. The responsibility to react by developing a capacity and willingness to respond to situations of compelling human need with appropriate measures, which may include coercive measures like sanctions, international prosecutions, and in extreme cases military intervention.

c.   The responsibility to rebuild by means of the provision of post-conflict assistance with recovery, reconstruction and reconciliation, while addressing the root causes of the harm that the intervention was designed to halt or avert.

If states abdicate these responsibilities they undermine their constitutional legitimacy. In particular, the Commission argued that where a population was suffering serious harm, as a result of internal war, insurgency, repression or state failure, and the state in question was unwilling or unable to halt or avert it, then the principle of non-intervention yields to the international responsibility to protect (2001: xii). As Ramesh Thakur (one of the report authors) put it recently:

> Reconceptualizing sovereignty as responsibility has a threefold significance. First, it implies that the state authorities are responsible for the functions of protecting the safety and lives of citizens and promotion of their welfare. Second, it suggests that the national political authorities are responsible to the citizens internally and to the international community through the United Nations. And third, it means that the agents of states are responsible for their actions, that is to say, they are accountable for their acts of commission and omission (qtd. *Yomiuri Shimbun* 12 April 2007).

Generating higher levels of political, military and judicial responsibility and accountability at a global level is a critically important way of creating macroconditions conducive to the promotion and maintenance of human rights and is a prerequisite for a deepening of respect for the international rule of law. While these norms are set in place in order to avoid genocidal violence, it can also be argued that they should also enhance the responsibilities of states in relation to ensuring freedom from fear and want. If states fail in these duties and begin moving from protector to persecutor then the ICISS and the United Nations suggest that a range of consequences should follow.

The first is that every effort should be made to prevent behavior likely to result in violence. These nonviolent, less intrusive preventive options need to be exhausted before any other kind of intervention is contemplated. Thus most effort should go to what the Carnegie Commission called long-term structural prevention. If these measures fail, then, secondly, the ICISS proposes a ladder of coercive responses aimed at enforcing compliance (ICISS 2000: xiii). These should only be contemplated when serious and irreparable harm to human beings is occurring or is likely to occur. These normally involve large-scale loss of life, a "failed state" and/or large-scale ethnic cleansing that involves killing, forced expulsion, acts of terror or rape.

While one can quibble about the scope of "responsibility to protect," since its focus is on gross violations of human rights, war crimes and genocide, there is no denying that it has legitimated a new norm that places a question mark over the idea of absolute sovereignty. The United Nations has certainly been operating on this assumption for the past decade or so.

There has been, for example, a very dramatic increase in UN Preventive Diplomacy, Conflict Resolution and Peacemaking activities. Over the past 16 years, for example, the United Nations has quadrupled its peacemaking activities and has managed to settle numerous national and transnational conflicts in the same time. There has been a doubling of peacekeeping operations, and a corresponding increase in post-conflict peacebuilding initiatives. Similarly, since the publication of Responsibility to Protect, in 2000, the Security Council has been more prepared to invoke economic sanctions and use force to ensure that state parties are in compliance with Security Council resolutions. All of this increased activity has resulted in the United Nations becoming a more active player in the prevention, management and resolution of violent conflict, and the United Nations has become much more actively involved in post-conflict reconstruction work as well. All of these new initiatives and the positive consequences that have flown from them have occurred within the existing UN institutional frameworks

Success has been achieved through a liberal, proactive and interventionist interpretation of different mandates and by the UN Secretariat harnessing national, regional and multilateral resources behind different initiatives.

Can the United Nations do better in all of these areas? It certainly can, but whether there is political will to vote the resources and to support changes that will make the United Nations a much more serious player in the international arena remains a moot point. Certainly, there is little enthusiasm for reform of the Security Council (its membership and modus operandi) and the General Assembly; neither of which truly represent what might be called a global community with common interests and purposes. This is one of the major challenges facing the United Nations as it seeks to reform itself. How does it speak for a post-sovereign borderless world when sovereignty remains so persistent? How can it articulate global interests when state parties wish to privilege the national interest? How can it advocate enlightened concepts of global citizenship when the globally integrated market (coupled to a narrow assertion of national sovereign rights) has diminished support for altruism, responsible governance, community-based strategies, and broader concepts of the public good?

The twelfth theme that came up through the meeting, and discussed in some of the chapters, was the necessity to ensure that western perspectives on global problems were accompanied by much more than lip service to the perspectives of Africa, Asia, Latin America and the Middle East. This is more than just a question of being epistemologically sensitive; it also has to do with ensuring higher levels of sensitivity to high context cultures and their particular approaches to relationships, time, space and decision-making. Good decision-making requires time and patience. It is vital that multilateral institutions take the time needed to design processes that are inclusive and consultative. Too often crisis management is the opposite of this kind of reflective decision-making. The United Nations needs to pay more attention to indigenous knowledge and non-Western religious and cultural traditions. This is not an optional extra. It is arguably an evolutionary imperative that the world's global institutions begin reflecting some of the world diversity in relation to decision-making. The most important point in relation to UN decision-making, therefore, is how we create social and political institutions (or adapt existing ones) where different concepts of democracy, liberty, order, justice, and social peace are debated and decided in ways that advance human progress rather than impede it or set it back.

The reform of the United Nations cannot be postponed. If the institution is to realize the promise of the Charter and its founders, it is vital that mechanisms be developed that advance higher levels of collaboration and cooperation, higher levels of genuine communication and dialogue and higher levels of confidence and trust. The large and growing numbers of civil society organizations that are doing so much practical, development, conflict transformation, and human rights work in collaboration with the United Nations cannot be expected, however, to substitute for the United Nations. There will always be a need for a strong, capable and legitimate United Nations to harness the resources of its member states, testify to the human interest rather than national interest and to develop a deeper capacity to keep the peace, provide emergency relief and long term development within a rights-based framework and in ways which will replace the culture of violence with a culture of peace. That is the promise and reality of UN reform to which this book is dedicated.

References

Annan, Kofi. 2005. *In Larger Freedom: Report of Secretary General to the United Nations*. New York: United Nations.

Boulding, Elise. 1999. *Building a Global Civic Culture*. New York: Columbia University Press.

Cardoso, Fernando Henrique. 2004. "We the Peoples: Civil Society." *The United Nations and Global Governance*. New York: UN Report.

Human Security Report. 2005. *War and Peace in the 21st Century*. New York: Oxford University Press.

International Commission on Intervention and State Sovereignty. 2000. *The Responsibility to Protect*. Canada International Development Research Centre.

Judt, Tony. "Is the UN Doomed?" *NY Review of Books*, February 15 (2007): 45-48.

Shawn, Eric. 2006. *The UN Exposed: How the United Nations Sabotages America's Security and Fails the World*. New York: Sentinel Press.

United Nations. *UN Charter*, 1945. http://www.un.org/aboutun/charter/ accessed May 2007.

United Nations Reform

Illusions of Reform: Needs, Desires, and Realities

Richard Falk

Metaphor and the Politics of Despair

Addressing the General Assembly, in 2003, on the urgent need for UN reform, then-secretary-general of the United Nations, Kofi Annan, resorted to a frequently used metaphorical trope: "Excellencies, we have come to a fork in the road. This may be a moment no less decisive than 1945 itself, when the United Nations was founded." He explains the rhetoric by saying "[n]ow we must decide whether it is possible to continue on the basis agreed upon or whether radical changes are needed." Further, Annan notes that he had earlier drawn attention "to the urgent need for the [Security] Council to regain the confidence of States, and of world public opinion—both by demonstrating its ability to deal effectively with the most difficult issues, and by becoming more broadly representative of the international community as a whole, as well as the geopolitical realities of today" (Annan 2003: 3).

To build support for the radical but necessary changes and to ensure that the right "road" is chosen at the "fork," Annan appointed two panels designed to shape an agenda for the General Assembly's reform summit scheduled for the fall of 2005, the 60th anniversary of the United Nations. Both appointed groups operated according to a realist calculus that tried to take account of what sorts of changes would be acceptable to a majority of the membership. The less significant of the two was the Panel of Eminent Persons on UN-Civil Society Relations, chaired by Fernando Henrique Cardoso, the former president of Brazil. Its mandate was narrowly framed to encourage proposals that would give civil society organizations somewhat better access and opportunities for participation, but within the existing pattern of the UN System. The recommendations of the Panel were rather technical and managerial in tone and, whether implemented or not, unlikely to alter the basic non-impact of global civil society on what are seen as more important UN undertakings (Falk 2005; The Cardoso Report 2004).

The more important initiative was the High-Level Panel on Threats, Challenges and Change that issued a widely discussed report entitled "A More Secure World: Our Shared Responsibility" (The United Nations 2004). In the transmittal letter to the secretary-general prefacing the report, the panel chair, Anand Panyarachun, observes that:

> [o]ur mandate from you precluded any in-depth examination of individual conflicts and we have respected your guidance. But the members of the Panel believe it would be remiss of them if they failed to point out that no amount of systemic changes to the way the United Nations handles both old and new threats to peace and security will enable it to discharge effectively its role under the Charter if efforts are not redoubled to resolve a number of long-standing disputes which continue to fester and to feed the new threats we now face. Foremost among these are the issues of Palestine, Kashmir and the Korean Peninsula (The United Nations 2004: xi).

This passage thinly disguises the double bind embedded in the mandate given to the Panel. It points to addressing threats to peace in the current global setting, but without discussing specific conflicts. As any inquirer knows, the only way to grasp the general is by attentiveness to the particular, and this is precisely what is precluded. Hidden here, in the bureaucratic jargon of the United Nations, is the decisive obstacle to the UN reform that is urgently needed if the organization is to realize the goals of its most ardent supporters and move in the direction encouraged by the UN Charter, especially its visionary Preamble.

Despite these restrictions, the Panel on Threats, Challenges and Change does face the realities of global conflict in the twenty-first century in ways worthy of discussion, especially on issues of peace and security. Three aspects of the Panel's approach are illustrative of its image of reform. Each is situated within a realist calculus of reformist feasibility, but each still lacks serious prospects for implementation because of a failure to take account of the minefield that makes taking the road to reform treacherous. The Panel suggests:

1) broadening the idea of security by taking account of increased support for the concept of "human security" and thus treating issues of disease, poverty, environmental degradation, and transnational organized crime as falling within the ambit of security (The United Nations 2004: 21-55);

2) that the new threats to world order associated either with transnational terrorism or crimes against humanity/genocide can be addressed within the existing Charter framework if the right of self-defense as set forth in Article 51 is "properly understood and applied" (The United Nations 2004: 3). The reformist element here is to insist that such an extended view of the use of force in self-de-

fense, including controversial justifications for preemption and intervention in internal affairs, requires *prior* UN Security Council authorization;

3) following the recommendation of the Canadian International Commission, an endorsement of "the emerging norm that there is a collective international responsibility to protect, exercisable by the Security Council authorizing military intervention as a last resort, in the event of genocide or other large-scale killing, ethnic cleansing or serious violation of international humanitarian law which sovereign Governments have proved powerless or unwilling to prevent" (The United Nations 2004: 66).

These proposals walk a series of tightropes. To begin, broadening security to include threats to human well-being, while being respectful of the overarching concern with threats to use force against a state mounted by state and non-state actors, is problematic. Also, it is difficult to acknowledge geopolitical pressures to engage in preemptive responses based on the rhetoric of the post-9/11, Bush approach to national security, while being sensitive to the wider allegations of unilateralism that have been directed at American foreign policy, especially in the wake of the Iraq War. The Panel's proposals also walk a third tightrope with the balancing act of responding to the importance of upholding human rights while being overtly deferential to the traditional prerogatives of sovereign states, expressed both by the norm of non-intervention and by a recognition that international action is only legitimate if states fail to address ongoing humanitarian catastrophes. Each of these moves seems entirely consistent with the Westphalian concept of world order based on the interplay of sovereign states, as modified by the development of international law, and as adapted to a changing global setting. The Panel's agenda, however, is subject to contradictory lines of criticism, both that the proposals are too extreme given the geopolitical climate and that they are also too modest given the Panel's intention to live up to Charter expectations as to collective security or to safeguard the world against the menace of unilateralism.

The United States, in particular, has made it abundantly clear that without regard to UN Charter constraints, it will determine on its own whether to rely on force to address international conflicts, given its insistence that threats must be dealt with by preventive and preemptive modes of warfare. As long as the veto is available to the five permanent members of the Security Council, any effort to impose *international* restraints on their behavior depends on their *voluntary* compliance. Further, it remains that the "responsibility to protect" is merely rhetorical without endowing the United Nations with independent capabilities or generating a political will on the part of leading states to provide necessary levels of support either in advance or in response to humanitarian emergencies. There is no evidence that such conditions will be met. The feeble response to the massive genocidal developments in Darfur in the face of the complicity of the Sudanese government is ample evidence that the political will is absent to support the Charter's responsibility to prevent. The reformist road advocated by the Panel seems blocked by geopolitical resistance.

The Panel's proposals purport to change policy without altering the constitutional status of the permanent members within the United Nations and without providing capabilities and institutional procedures to make their recommendations assume a meaningful *political* character. To be more specific, the only way that the Security Council could be empowered to implement the proposal in regards to extended claims of self-defense is to deny the availability of the veto to permanent members. However, this issue is not even mentioned, much less creatively addressed. Similarly, the only way that an interventionary mission to discharge the Charter's responsibility to protect could be credible would be through the establishment of a UN Emergency Peace Force that was independently trained, financed and recruited. Again, such an implementing procedure is not even discussed as a remote possibility. Finally, to make the proposed attention to human security more than rhetoric, the security agenda needs to be expanded to include these concerns on the agenda of the Security Council to the same degree as war and peace concerns. Such recognition would highlight the disparity of economic conditions in the world economy, creating pressures for a more equitable distribution of the benefits of economic globalization that arise from neoliberal policies. As such, there is no present prospect that the call for a comprehensive approach to security will yield behavioral results, except of a kind that would have been produced in any event, for instance, inter-governmental cooperation to control transnational organized crime.

For these reasons, the only responsible conclusion is that the report of the High-Level Panel failed from either a realist perspective of politics as the art of the possible or an idealist perspective as politics as the quest for the necessary and desirable. Its main proposals, although carefully formulated and sensitive to the global setting, only reinforced the mood of despair surrounding issues of global reform. In this sense, perhaps imprudently, the Panel accepted an assignment that seems an example of a "mission impossible." Returning to the fork in the road, there is no fork, only the old geopolitical pathway dominated by geopolitics and statism. Kofi Annan's use of this metaphor is an expression of false consciousness, especially as related to the combination of American unilateralism with respect to war-making and a general atmosphere of inaction in response to humanitarian crises. Prior to using the metaphor, the secretary-general calls attention to the dangerous precedent posed by "this argument" that "States are not obliged to wait until there is agreement in the Security Council. Instead, they reserve the right to act unilaterally, or in *ad hoc* coalitions." He adds that "[t]his logic represents a fundamental challenge to the principles on which, however, imperfectly, world peace and stability have rested for the last fifty-eight years" (Annan 2003). Annan admits that "it is not enough to denounce unilateralism, unless we also face up squarely to the concerns that make some states feel uniquely vulnerable, since it is those concerns that drive them to take unilateral action" (Annan 2003: 3). It is here that there is a failure of comprehension, and an insight into how such a mission impossible is launched. Of course, the whole discourse is beset by the taboo associated with mentioning particulars, that is, which state resorted to war for what apparent purpose.

It is obvious from the setting that Annan was talking about the US invasion of Iraq, but to suggest that this invasion was a response to an American post-9/11 sense of "vulnerability" is to ignore the overwhelming evidence that the Iraq War was initiated for reasons of grand strategy, and the anti-terrorist claims of an imminent threat were trumped up and quite irrelevant to the policy. This suggests that if the true pressures on the UN framework are not properly analyzed there is no way to fashion a relevant response. The High-Level Panel was completely responsive to the Secretary-General's mandate, providing momentary cosmetic relief, but also deflecting a more accurate understanding of the challenge being mounted by prevailing patterns of geopolitical behavior.

Decades before the Iraq War, the issue of Charter obsolescence had been widely discussed, perhaps most notably by Thomas Franck in "Who Killed Article 2(4)? Or: Changing Norms Governing the Use of Force by States" (1970). Many international law specialists have pointed to the practice of states that cannot be reconciled with Charter constraints on recourse to aggressive war as an instrument of policy, and have concluded that a strong reading of the prohibition on force is no longer *legally* justified (see Weisbrud 1997; Arendt and Beck 1993). Similarly, it has been argued that the failure of the Security Council to implement the mechanisms intended in Chapter VII to underpin collective security removes an essential element from the Charter approach of simultaneously prohibiting force and promising the victims of aggression the prospect of collective action in response. In recent years Michael Glennon has been tireless in his critique of what he regards as "legalism," even Platonism, contending that it interferes with a realization that the UN Charter system for restraining states was never truly implemented as a collective security mechanism, has not been respected by important states, and lacks constraining weight and authority (2006). Glennon goes further, extending a provisional vote of confidence to what he calls "*ad hoc* coalitions of the willing" that "provide an effective substitute ... *on specific occasions*" for the Security Council, referring to the Kosovo War launched in 1999 under NATO auspices as his justifying example (2006). He argues that it was correct to disregard the absence of Security Council authorization for a non-defensive use of force, and that the NATO authorization, although not based on international law, was sufficient (2006: 639; see the report of the Independent International Commission on Kosovo 2000 for a different approach). The Kosovo example is misleading as the coalition of the willing was responding to a credible humanitarian emergency of limited scope, and not embarking on a geopolitical adventure that rested neither on moral nor political imperatives. To move in Glennon's direction is to endorse the geopolitical management of world politics at a historical moment in which the dominant state enjoys diminishing legitimacy as a hegemonic actor and confronts deepening resentment arising from its policies (see Tucker & Hendrickson 2004; Falk 2007 or reference on relevance of legality to legitimacy). In this regard to legitimate the advocacy of global policy fashioned by coalitions of the willing by historical reference to the relative success of the Concert of Europe in keeping the peace during the nineteenth century is profoundly misleading and unresponsive to contemporary realities.

At the same time, the prohibition in the Charter is a key foundation for challenging the legality and legitimacy of state action by either moderate states or the forces of global civil society. To the extent that a post-Westphalian form of democratic and humane global governance is struggling to become a political project depends on the norms associated with the UN Charter and the Nuremberg tradition of imposing criminal accountability on leaders of states (for fuller exposition see Falk 2004; Falk, Gendzier and Lifton 2006).

To summarize, the metaphor as used by the secretary-general to encourage a process of UN reform was influential in guiding those entrusted with shaping an agenda of proposals and recommendations. But it was deeply misleading in the sense that it acted as if there existed an alternative to geopolitics that could be effectively developed by inter-governmental consensus. A far more appropriate metaphorical gesture of credible substance would have been the resignation of the secretary-general, precisely because there was no fork in *that* road! "Without a fork in the road I cannot continue to serve this worthy organization in good faith!" And elaborating by saying that "due to the recent circumstances highlighted by the Iraq War, the prevailing path has become untenable, a betrayal of the core principle of the Charter of the UN prohibiting aggressive war." If Kofi Annan had so used the metaphorical moment, two positive results could have been anticipated: first, a wider appreciation that much needed UN reforms of even minimal scope were presently unattainable; and secondly, a pointed recognition that the United Nations could not function as intended due to the obstructionist tactics of the main geopolitical actor, the United States. Such a posture would have given Annan a voice of his own as well as an audience *and legacy* in civil society that might well have regarded the occasion of this resignation as an opportune moment to launch a struggle for the soul of the United Nations. With a new secretary-general, Ban Ki-moon, there is seemingly a loss of the sort of reformist ambitions associated with Annan's leadership.

Whether the path presently being cleared by the more progressive forces in global civil society is more than a utopian gesture will not be known for decades, but it is the only path that makes the abolition of aggressive war, at least potentially, a "mission possible." Aligning with this struggle is the only emancipatory option available to those seeking a humane form of global governance (Badiou 2005). The metaphor of "a fork in the road" can thus be inverted so as to clarify the historical circumstance, acknowledging both the absence of choice from within a Westphalian framing of UN reform, and the possibility of choice achieved by way of a rupture with standardized organizational expectations associated with delivering the case for reform by relying on a rhetoric of urgency. This sense of urgency is immediately contradicted by patterns of performance that submit to the dual disciplines of bureaucratic inertia and geopolitical discipline. That the outcome of this dynamic, as evident in the two reports, whose recommendations were further diluted in the secretary-general's own later report, "In Larger Freedom" (United Nations 2005), has been pathetic from a reformist perspective should not come as a surprise. Nor should the bureaucratic celebration of the meager and marginal steps taken at the World Summit in 2005 come as any surprise, operating under the pretense that the Summit responded impressively, or even adequately, to the original urgent call for reform (The United Nations "Implementation of decisions from the 2005 World Summit Outcome for action by the Secretary-General" 2005). What manifests in the course of this cycle of delusion is a circular and mutually complicit demonstration of the exact opposite from what is officially explicated: namely, the *impossibility* of UN reform. Acknowledging this impossibility is the only way for it to be overcome. In that Kofi Annan simultaneously articulated the urgency of reform and provided the cover up of its failure, he played the villain's role in this geopolitical theater of the absurd. We are left with Glennon's overt dismissal of the United Nations, and avowal of the primacy of geopolitics, as a trustworthier rendering of the global setting in the early 21st century than is the false advertising associated with official UN efforts (Glennon 2006). In the end, better a cynical counsel of despair than an over-dosage of anti-depressants. This is better only because it prompts citizen resistance that is rooted in a clear recognition of the realities that exist, rather than perpetuating a pattern of escapist delusion.

Horizons and Metaphors of Hope

From its inception, the United Nations has represented an uneasy Faustian bargain between an idealist search for peace through law and the realist quest for stability through power. On the idealist side is the unconditional prohibition of force except in instances of self-defense strictly defined to require a prior armed attack, reinforced by collective security mechanisms that were intended to protect states that were victims of aggression. On the realist side, it is the grant of veto power to the five permanent members of the Security Council, further accentuated by the short-term dependence of the organization on financial contributions from member states, especially the leading ones, and by an overall relationship to the Charter that is premised on voluntary adherence, respectful of sovereign rights. Such normative incoherence is bound to generate disappointment, with idealists expecting too much and realists not expecting anything at all beyond discussion along with their fatalist submission to prevailing hegemonic patterns of world politics. The operative impact of this Faustian bargain has been evident in relation to the Iraq War, with idealists delighted that the Security Council refused to authorize the invasion in 2003, while realists bemoaned the irrelevance of the organization. Subsequent to the invasion, despite its flagrant violation of the most basis principle of the Charter, the United Nations acquiesced in the outcome, lent its support to normalizing the illegal occupation of the country, and refrained from criticizing the invasion and the many excesses of the occupation.

Through the years, off camera, the United Nations achieved many positive results, often beyond most reasonable expectations, and far beyond what its predecessor the League of Nations achieved, especially in such areas as human rights, environmental consciousness, health, care of children, education, and even in relation to peace and security whenever geopolitical actors happened to be united in approach. A testimony to this net contribution to human well-being is that no state has withdrawn from membership in the United Nations over the entire course of its history (the one partial exception is Indonesia, withdrawing for a year in 1965 to form a counter-organization of "new states," but returning after discovering an absence of receptivity to its efforts). Such an achievement and maintenance of universal membership is a great achievement that should not be overlooked, establishing on a voluntary basis the first ever truly global organization entrusted with the safeguarding of the planet.

Given this circumstance, it is not surprising that the UN reform process is so clogged. There are three sources of resistance to substantial reform, each quite formidable:

- the amendment process is constitutionally difficult, and is subject to the veto
- the entrenched advantages of some states, and the diverse priorities of different regions, make it difficult to achieve a consensus on specific steps (unless innocuous); and
- the leading states, especially the United States, are unwilling to cede control over vital dimension of global policy or to allow initiatives within the organization that express criticism of its global role or specific policies.

With these considerations in mind, it is hardly surprising that the United Nations has not been able to solve the most pressing demands for the kind of reform that would provide it with enhanced legitimacy in the 21st century:

- changing the membership of the Security Council to take account of shifts in influence since 1945;
- adapting the concept of self-defense to the current realities of international conflict without giving states the authority to wage discretionary wars;
- acknowledging the impact of the global human rights movement to the extent of creating capabilities and willingness to intervene in internal affairs in reaction to the threat or actuality of genocide or crimes against humanity;
- taking advantage of the end of the Cold War to embark upon a path of negotiated nuclear disarmament, to establish an emergency peace force to deal with humanitarian emergencies and natural disasters, to establish a global tax that will provide an independent revenue base, and to create a global parliament in recognition of the rise of civil society.

It is with this understanding of an agenda for UN reform that suggests a reliance on the metaphor of "horizons" as clarifying, acknowledging formidable difficulties of an authentic reform process without being demoralizing. A basic distinction needs to be drawn between horizons of feasibility and horizons of desire. Horizons of feasibility refer to those adaptations needed to make the organization effective and legitimate within its *existing* framework, that is, with an acceptance of the normative incoherence associated with the tension between the Charter as law and geopolitics as practice. In contrast, horizons of desire are based on overcoming this incoherence by minimizing the impact of geopolitics. This presupposes solving the challenge of global governance by *transforming* the United Nations in a manner that achieves primacy for the Charter's goals and principles. Such a possibility, currently an impossibility, would depend on a much more widely shared perception as to the dysfunctionality of war as an instrument useful for resolving conflict and creating security. A transformed United Nations in these ways would provide an institutional foundation for moral globalization. That is, for the realization of human rights comprehensively conceived to include economic, social, and cultural rights, as reinforced by a regime of global law that treated equals equally and was not beset by claims of exception and double standards in the application of general norms, as well as being receptive to an ethos of nonviolence.

As suggested in the discussion of "the fork in the road," it would be futile to consider such a transformative horizoning as relevant to the present or likely discourse on UN reform within the conventional arenas of statecraft, including the United Nations itself. Even the horizons of feasibility, other than moves to achieve managerial efficiencies and marginal adaptations, seem unpromising. It is possible, though, to imagine shifts in the political climate that could lead to adjustments in the UN Security Council to make it more representative or a successful initiative to establish some kind of emergency force that would give the United Nations more credibility with respect to interventions for humanitarian purposes. If we take account of the recent past, the most successful reform developments have resulted from "coalitions of the dedicated" that have been composed of likeminded governments and a movement of civil society actors. Both the anti-personnel landmines treaty and the International Criminal Court (ICC) came about despite the geopolitical resistance led by the United States, and illustrated the potential reformist capacity of a "new internationalism" that is neither a project of statist design nor of global civil society, but a collaboration that draws strength from this hybrid agency. Of course, it would be a mistake to attribute transformative potential to this new internationalism as it is unclear whether it can move beyond *formal* successes. The anti-personnel landmines treaty, while symbolically important, addressed a question of only trivial relevance to the priorities of geopolitical actors and the ICC has yet to demonstrate that it can make a robust contribution to the effort to make individuals who act on behalf of states criminally accountable.

The argument being made is based on an acknowledgement of the need for UN reform, while trying to rid the quest of false expectations and empty rhetoric. The metaphor of horizons establishes goals without regard to political obstacles, and then distinguishes between those goals that might be achieved by existing mechanisms of influence, horizons of feasibility, and those goals whose implementation is necessary (and desirable), but for which there cannot be currently envisioned a successful scenario. These latter goals of a transformative depth are thus situated over the horizon. Their pursuit can be understood either as a new political imaginary for world order in the manner depicted by Charles Taylor in *Modern Social Imaginaries* (2004), or as a waiting game for the inevitable breakdown of the Westphalian world order that might make a political project of a transformation of the United Nations. In this regard, it might be recalled that the League of Nations became a plausible, if flawed, project only after the devastation of World War I, and the United Nations was only conceivable in the wake of World War II. Each project was intended to "fix" fundamental deficiencies of world order by shifting the horizons of world order politics, and each effort moved beyond what seem previously attainable, yet each fell far short of horizons of desire and longer term necessities.

A Concluding Note

Returning once more to the metaphorical motif, this essay contends that there is no fork in either road, and that the metaphor of choice is profoundly misleading and distorting. Within the UN system, as now constituted, there is no reform choice, and no alternative to the persistence of a geopolitically dominated reality. Outside the United Nations, the commitment to UN reform by civil society actors is the only worthwhile path, although the realization of its vision cannot even be imagined at this point. Again, there is no choice to be made. Choosing the geopolitical road to the future is to close one's eyes to the near certainty of disaster. The only road that promises a sustainable and benevolent future for humanity now appears utopian, but given certain presently unforeseeable developments, could become politically viable.

Given this assessment, it follows that the fork in the road metaphor should be rejected. Instead, the reliance on the metaphor of horizons could be used in a dual mode: horizons of feasibility for reforms within existing structures, and horizons of desire for transformation that require radically modified structures. It is the further claim being made here that both horizons are part of an encompassing social imaginary that can be labeled as horizons of necessity.

The perspective is guided by ancient wisdom: "at the start, they laughed; later on, they began to listen, and a bit later, they cheered." At this point, given both our sense of imminent menace and our vision of a humane future, we need to summon the composure and stamina to withstand dismissive laughter for some years to come, but better laughter than sullen silence, or worse, complicity.

References

Annan, Kofi, The Secretary-General's Address to the General Assembly, Sept. 23, 2003.

Arendt, Anthony Clark and Robert J. Beck. 1993. *International Law and the Use of Force*. London: Routledge.

Badiou, Alain. 2005. *Metapolitics*. London: Verso.

Cardoso Report, The. *UN-Civil Society Relations: A Third World Network Analysis*, August 2004. http://www.un-ngls.org/08twn.pdf.

Falk, Richard. "Reforming the United Nations: Global Civil Society Perspectives and Initiatives." Glasius, Marlies, Mary Kaldor and Helmut Anheier (eds), *Global Civil Society* (2005/6). London: Sage Publications.

Falk, Richard. 2007. *The Costs of War: International Law, the United Nations, and World Order After Iraq*. New York: Routledge.

Falk, Richard. 2004. *The Declining World Order*. New York: Routledge.

Falk, Richard, Irene Gendzier and Robert Jay Lifton (eds). 2006. *Crimes of War: Iraq*. New York: Nation Books.

Franck, Thomas, "Who Killed Article 2(4)? Or: Changing Norms Governing the Use of Force by States." *American Journal of International Law* (1970) 64(809).

Glennon, Michael J., "Platonism, Adaptivism, and Illusion in UN Reform." *Chicago Journal of International Law* 6(2) (2006): 613-640.

Hendrickson, David C. and Robert W. Tucker. "The Sources of American Legitimacy." *Foreign Affairs* (Nov/Dec 2004): 18-32. New York: Council of Foreign Affairs.

Independent International Commission on Kosovo. 2000. *The Kosovo Report: Conflict, International Response, Lessons Learned*. Oxford: Oxford University Press.

Taylor, Charles. 2004. *Modern Social Imaginaries*. Durham: Duke University Press.

United Nations, *A More Secure World: Our Shared Responsibility*, report of the Secretary-General's High Level Panel on Threats, Challenges and Change, December 2004.

United Nations. 2005. "In Larger Freedom: Towards Development, Security and Human Rights for All." Report of the Secretary General.

United Nations, "Implementation of decisions from the 2005 World Summit Outcome for action by the Secretary-General," Report of the Secretary-General, 25 Oct 2005, A/60/430.New York: United Nations.

Weisbrud, A. Mark. 1997. *Use of Force: Practice of States since World War II*. University Park, PA: Penn State University Press.

Conceptual Foundations for a
New Internationalism

Ralph Pettman

The foundations for a new internationalism can only be found in the old internationalism. Short of a planetary catastrophe of some kind and the radical changes this would cause, we must start where we are, with the internationalism we have today. Even then, anticipating any future form of internationalism is a perilous task. Consider the internationalism we had at the inception of the United Nations, two generations ago. Those who built the United Nations looked out upon a world shattered by a major war, where the great European empires were collapsing and the United States and its allies were just beginning to engage with the Soviet Union and its allies in a sustained, albeit sublimated, struggle for global supremacy.

Internationalism was then about the global stand-off between these two powers, the self-determination of suzerain states in Asia and Africa, and the attempt to include these states in an international system bound by European diplomatic protocols and strategic expectations. Now we have a world where the Cold War is over, where the United States stands alone as a dominant power, where issues of global development, environment, and human security loom large, where states must share their system with diverse international organizations, transnational businesses, and global social movements, where the diplomatic protocols and strategic expectations are notably more cosmopolitan and environmentally self-aware, and where the United Nations stands in need of radical repair. What will we have two generations from now? Whatever it is, it is likely to be at least as different from the present state of international affairs as the present is from what prevailed after World War II.

Though world affairs are clearly in constant flux, there are patterns to these affairs nonetheless, and it is because of these patterns that we can talk about them as having conceptual foundations. World affairs may be

31

anarchic, in that there is not yet a global government, but world politics are not random. As a consequence they can be systematically described, explained, and prescribed for in policy terms. It is these patterns—the ones that underpin contemporary global politics, and provide us with more fundamental accounts of how they work—which I shall attempt to outline here.

We find these patterns even though we are thrown into a world already in train. We might like it to be otherwise, but we have to deal with this world as we find it. We might think we make world affairs, but we do not do so as we please. We do so in the particular political contexts we inherit from those who came before us. These people spent their lives behaving in ways that present themselves as the particular world affairs we encounter today. Out of these contexts emerge political structures that seemingly have a life of their own, and determine much of how we respond.

We also make these patterns. We act. Indeed, we must act if these structures and processes are to be perpetuated. We repeat the behavioral patterns that constitute them, thereby ensuring that this is what we find when we seek to know what current affairs happen to be. How we act is what makes for the conceptual foundations of these affairs.

This presents us with an immediate problem, since there is no one way to respond that exhausts the conceptual range of our political practices, and is able to fully specify their conceptual foundations. It is important to note that, in this regard, "internationalism" is not just the phenomenon that constitutes an interconnected world. It is also a label for one of the analytical languages used to describe and explain such phenomena, and to prescribe policy that might control these phenomena as they influence human purposes like survival, material well-being, and a sense of moral and sacral achievement.

Internationalism as a Way of Doing World Affairs

Let me be clear on this key point: internationalism is a way of doing world affairs and as such it is a notable feature of the way contemporary world affairs work. Indeed, the relations between states have become so diverse and dense by now that they have come to constitute their own level of analysis. They no longer represent the casual or intermittent relations between discernibly separate human groups that we deem sufficiently large to warrant calling "nations." They have come to represent a key aspect of the current global milieu and the system they create is one now populated by many other actors. These other actors are not sovereign, in the way that states are sovereign, in that they do not have armed forces and, at least in principle, a monopoly of the domestic means of force. Some though, like the private military service-providers, are armed forces and are used as police. These non-state actors include international governmental organizations, international non-governmental organizations, international corporations and international social movements. They are made up in practice of international diplomatic exchanges and alliances, military deployments, law-making initiatives, bureaucratic practices, trade and investment flows, production and distribution activities, the international dissemination of liberal norms (like those of human rights and democracy), the global dissemination of the very idea of nations, and the pursuit of causes like those that animate international social movements. They are also made up of the international movement of workers, tourists and refugees, international information and transport flows, the international spread of diseases and pollutants, and the international promotion of particular cultural values and spiritual faiths.

Internationalism as a Way of Thinking about World Affairs

At the same time, internationalism is one of the main doctrines or discourses used to account for all of the above. As such, it is that particular doctrine that highlights the politico-strategic as opposed to the politico-economic and the politico-social dimensions of world affairs, while articulating the assumption that human beings are not only rationalistic, but are essentially calculating. It envisages a tit-for-tat world of potential allies. As such it purports to do one better than the so-called realist account of world affairs, which is notably more pessimistic about human nature and sees a dog-eat-dog world of potential enemies as well-nigh inevitable. As such it also does one worse than the globalist account of world affairs, which is notably more optimistic about human nature and sees a hail-fellow-well-met world of potential friends as eminently possible instead. Internationalism (as an analytical language) is at odds as well with those who see the material nature of our nurturing environment as the essential source of international behavior, like the Marxists. It is at odds with those who see the mental nature of our nurturing environment as the essential source of international behavior, like the constructivists. And it is at odds with those who mix materialism and mentalism, like the meta-Marxists. Internationalism talks of an international system of states, or even an international society of states, with its own (international) laws, organizations, and diplomatic and strategic protocols (Walt 1998; Bull 1977).

When we talk of a "new internationalism," therefore, are we talking of new ways in which the international system as it currently exists might be constituted, or are we talking of new ways in which liberal internationalists might describe, explain and prescribe for this system, or are we talking about new ways in which other analytical languages might describe, explain and prescribe for this system? Or are we talking about all of the above, at one and the same time?

Doing Internationalism as Thinking about Internationalism

It is not possible to do world affairs without promoting an analytic discourse of some kind. For most Euro-Americans, this means doing world affairs in ways that are rationalist, in that they are in the process of globalizing a culture that prioritizes reason as an end in itself, *en masse*. This culture tends to be articulated in nation-statist, liberal-capitalist, socio-individualist terms, since making nation-states, owning the means of production, selling one's labor for a wage, and being an autonomous and self-determining individual, are promoted and protected by that culture as preferred ways to behave. There are nationalist/mercantilist and collectivist/socialist alternatives to the individualism that Euro-American rationalism promotes. There is also growing recognition of the shortcomings of rationalism itself, not only because it is cleft by class, race, and sex-role differences, but also because it is far from being as rationalistic as its promoters suppose. Rationalism remains the dominant cultural discourse, however, despite its eschewal by indigenous peoples, postmodernists, poststructuralists, psychoanalysts, romantics, phenomenologists, and sacralists.

There are many ways to think about doing internationalism anew. There are not as many ways as there are people on the planet, however. If there were, then there truly would be Babel. In practice, we clump into analytic camps, each one of which is characterized by the assumptions its members make about God, the primacy of reason, their place on the margins of the rationalist project, and the kind of human nature and nurturing practices that follow from the assumptions we make about how we behave in world affairs.

Realism, Mercantilism, and Nationalism

For example, as rationalists we are usually very interested in the politico-strategic (the diplomatic and military) dimension to world affairs.

We may also be relatively pessimistic about human nature. If so, then we are most likely to be what international relations analysts call realists (Morgenthau1972 [1948]; Carr 1991[1939]; Smith 1986; Guzzini 1998). This is a powerful case of concept-capture since it automatically depicts those who do not profess international relations realism as un-realists, that is, idealists. And who would want any sort of internationalism that is underpinned by the conceptual thinking of idealists, since there will always be those who are out to get us, and if we are not prepared for them, then more fool us? There will always be those, realists say, who will put their own interests above that of the commonweal, or our own, and we must be ready for them. Like jungle warriors, we must be constantly vigilant, eternally suspicious, and ready to fight to protect what we have and to get what we want.

What kind of internationalism does a conceptual doctrine like international relations realism portend? As we can infer from the brief sketch above, it is an internationalism constructed of shifting alliances and containment. It is one where state-makers come together with those they think will help them balance off common enemies. The same allies may be enemies at a later date, when national interests have changed. The realist form of internationalism is also one where we might agree to confer upon some overarching entity or group the power to keep order. Thus Thomas Hobbes describes us as needing the controlling presence of a Leviathan to keep us all "in awe" (Hobbes 1957 [1651]). The original frontispiece of Hobbes' 17th-century polemic depicts a crowned ruler with a raised sword in one hand and a symbol of his authority in the other. His body is made up of the masses he rules. Hobbes depicts this compelling authority as the only viable alternative to the conflicts that he sees as the only likely result of ungoverned living. His own idea pertains to domestic rule, though there is no reason why such a sovereign should not pertain to the international and provide an alternative to international anarchy. Indeed, many would look to the United States to perform this role today, particularly given the military arsenal at its command. Many Americans would already see themselves as the only power fit to loom large across the global landscape. As the conceptual foundation for a new kind of internationalism, then, realism anticipates endless conflict and competition unless we submit to a global autocracy or endless, shifting alliances that balance power. It sees no possibility for cooperation or collaboration, except as these expedite Leviathan-designating or power-balancing initiatives.

If we are pessimistic about our essential human nature, but interested in the politico-economic dimension to world affairs instead, then as rationalists we are most likely to be what international relations analysts call a mercantilist, an economic nationalist (List 1966[1885]; Weiss 1998). We will want to foster our own industries. We will want to prevent their appropriation by industrialists elsewhere so that their profits accrue to us, and our industries become strong enough to sustain competition at the international level without being destroyed. We will want to make sure that our property and our currency are not used by foreign speculators to augment the value of their assets, rather than our own. And we will want to prevent their goods displacing our goods, so that we do not end up consuming what they produce, adding to their productive power, at the expense of what we produce and our own productive power.

What kind of internationalism does a conceptual doctrine like mercantilism portend? Mercantilism makes for a world market characterized by economic self-protection, where highly competitive governments create productive cabals and international trading regimes are defensive, insular, and globally fragmentary. As the conceptual foundation for a new kind of internationalism, it serves us no better than realism does.

If, as rationalists, we are pessimistic about our essential human nature, but interested in the politico-social dimension to world affairs instead, then we are most likely to be what international relations analysts call nationalists (Anderson 1991; Smith 1995; Mayall 1990; Gellner 1983). We will want to reach back into our past to find reasons for celebrating our national identity in the present. If we are a state whose peoples have no such common ground, then we will want to start making such a ground by promoting the use of a common language, common norms, and a sense of shared destiny.

What kind of internationalism does a conceptual doctrine like nationalism portend? Again, it is no internationalism at all, since nationalism is a doctrine that creates disparate loyalties and diverse identities instead. It does not allow of the cohesion that internationalism requires. It creates international incoherence and disintegration.

There are enough examples in history of our capacity for international military violence, economic depredation, and civil intolerance, to suggest that any new internationalism we might want to construct on this basis would be radically compromised. Foreign policies of strategic defensiveness designed to foil imminent armed invasion and to operationalize the self-help that realism recommends, are widespread as a consequence. Foreign policies of tariff protection, designed to foil imminent economic exploitation, and to operationalize the self-protection that mercantilism recommends, are not compatible with internationalism either. Foreign policies of national assertiveness, designed to foil imminent rejection and to operationalize the self-identification that nationalism recommends, present likewise. There is certainly enough evidence that human nature is essentially bad to suggest that an ever-changing balance of power, a global version of Hobbes' Leviathan, high tariffs, or national solidarism, is all that we might fairly anticipate for the foreseeable future. Conceptual foundations like these make coercive internationalism, or the failure to sustain any internationalism other than the state-survivalist kind, the only "realistic" expectation.

Globalism, Socialism, Collectivism

However, there is also sufficient historical evidence of humankind's humanity at work in the world to warrant thinking we might be able to do better than the dog-eat-dog, Wild West version of internationalism (or lack thereof) that realism, mercantilism and nationalism provide. This does not mean ignoring our propensity as a species for inter-group violence, economic exploitation, or civic aggrandizement. It means not accepting these as the only bases on which to prescribe foreign policy. It is to see the part-truths they represent as not being the whole truth, or the only truth.

The most obvious alternative to the assumption that human nature is essentially bad is the assumption that human nature is essentially good. In politico-strategic terms, this much more optimistic assumption pre-disposes globalism, which as a doctrine argues that a world government is possible, and not just world government of the Hobbesian kind, where coercion creates compliance. It is world government of the persuasive or agenda-setting kind, where we comply because that is the world norm. In short, globalism provides the conceptual foundations for a new kind of internationalism that transcends all other internationalisms (Kant 1963[1795]; Hobson 1916; Heater 1996).

Some envisage global governance rather than global government (Yunker 2005). They envisage networks of international relationship becoming so dense that the concept of an anarchic world becomes re-dundant. They extrapolate, for example, from statistics to do with global population movement, and the vast planetary decanting of the world's people from the countryside into cities. They point at what is arguably the most significant social event of the last century, and at the sponta-neous inter-linking of the resultant cities through trade and exchange. They see in this inter-linking the makings of an ordered world affairs quite different from the state-centric one. They see it as the basis for a form of internationalism very different from the one that prevails today, albeit one just as possible and just as politically significant, namely, global governance.

Those who envisage global government tend to anticipate the advent of a kind of global Canada, where a central authority, less powerful than its component parts, acts as a global coordinator, in a confederal world of state-makers prepared to practice collaboration rather than competition. They envisage, for example, a future European Union coming together with an Asian, American and African equivalent to create a supra-regional authority that coordinates the common affairs of these four regional pillars. The proximal cause might be a cascade of functional practices, or economic incentives, or political decisions. The distal cause, however, would be the human capacity for a hail-fellow-well-met way of implementing over-arching rule of a more congenial kind that Leviathan represents.

The politico-economic articulation of human nature as essentially good is socialism (Stretton 2000). The internationalism that socialism anticipates is one able to ensure equality of outcome. It is one able to ensure that the largesse of the industrial revolution is distributed to all, rather than monopolized by the few. Internationalism of this sort seems extremely idealistic compared to mercantilism, say, but mercantilism, like realism and nationalism, is idealistic too. It is just that the ideals mercantilism promotes are different from the ones socialism promotes. Mercantilists are state- or nation-survivalists. Socialists are no less realistic than realists are like mercantilists and nationalists, merely more altruistic. The point here is that the human capacity for doing good is no less real than the human capacity to be bad, or at least, there is no scientific proposition to date that confirms the superior probity of pessimism rather than optimism in this regard. As a consequence, the optimistic articulation of the human propensity to do good is no less realistic as the conceptual foundation for a new internationalism than the pessimistic articulation of the human propensity to be bad.

The politico-social concomitant here is collectivism (Keck and Sikkink 1998). The internationalism that collectivists envisage is one where global social movements serve mostly the good of humankind, by making it possible for people to come together to promote shared values, regardless of the state they live in. While nationalism represents a nostalgic hearkening back to communalist sentiments of a pre-modernist kind, collectivism represents a forward-looking attempt to create human aggregates that promote common global causes. The result is a wide range of international actors of the non-state, non-governmental kind, and state border-crossing loyalties that make for a much more diverse international environment. As the conceptual foundation for a new kind of internationalism it presents much richer possibilities for individual action, whether this involves saving whales, banning landmines, or fighting trafficking in women, children, or indentured workers.

Liberal Internationalism, Liberalism, Individualism

A somewhat less obvious alternative to the assumption that human nature is essentially bad is the assumption that human nature is essentially calculating. In politico-strategic terms, this assumption predisposes what is called liberal internationalism, which describes and explains world affairs in terms of the international system of states (Richardson 1997; Doyle 1986; Keohane and Nye 1977).

This is one step beyond the pessimism of the realists, but one step short of the optimism of the globalists. It envisages, for example, the rule of international law, a creative role for international organizations and the rise of diverse regimes and arrangements that facilitate interstate relations of a tit-for-tat, win-win, co-contractual kind. As the conceptual foundation for a new internationalism it envisages more of the same, with a stronger world court, for example, where individuals are able to bring not only each other to justice, but also international actors like states, corporations and social movements. It also envisages a world where international regimes and organizations play a much larger part.

The politico-economic concomitant is liberalism *per se*, which is the opposite of mercantilism in that it seeks to reduce the role state borders play, particularly in relation to production, trade and investing practices. It seeks to augment the global freedom marketeers enjoy to make goods, distribute them, and seek out and place monetary investments (Smith 1892[1776]; Keynes 1926; Hayek 1991).

Liberalists see the opening rather than the closing or regulating of borders as providing much greater opportunities. As a doctrine it allows much greater scope for economic activity, and for drawing the world's peoples into a global web of production and exchange that makes possible a standard of living, and arguably a quality of life, that would not otherwise be the case. Liberalism is also seen to provide more opportunities than socialist planning does. The cost might be disparities in wealth and social inequalities, but the benefit, at least for liberalists, is the freedom to innovate, seek out and serve market niches that socialist planners would tend to overlook, as well as the ability to provide society's staples at a more competitive price.

As the conceptual foundation for a new kind of internationalism, liberalism envisages world markets that are much more emancipated than they are at the moment. Liberalists see the contemporary world market as too cribbed and confined still by the sort of state regulations that promote narrow national interests. The result inhibits the free play of comparative advantage, they say. Any new internationalism, therefore, is a liberalist one where free trade and investment, rather than state-centric economic suspicion, or the conscious attempt to determine what people need by centralized means, is the preferred global practice.

The politico-social concomitant is individualism (Taylor 1989; Fukuyama 1992). The internationalism that individualists anticipate is one that ensures global respect for human rights and human responsibilities, and the global realization of democracy. Human rights prioritize the individual. This creates a "duty to protect" that is at odds with state sovereignty, since it requires intervention on humanitarian grounds that sovereign autonomy actively precludes. The human rights doctrine provides the conceptual foundations for the kind of internationalism where individualism trumps statism. However, the persistence of state sovereignty as an internationalist norm means that a more individualistic kind of internationalism is not likely to prevail any time soon. It receives relatively widespread recognition, nonetheless, and is already making inroads into the sort of internationalism that state-centrics recommend.

As the conceptual foundation for a new kind of internationalism, individualists look to the globalization of democracy. They anticipate less international violence as a consequence, in line with the liberalist conclusion that democracies do not go to war with each other, though they may go to war with non-democracies. This conclusion remains open to question, since there is no analytic agreement as to what democracy is, or what constitutes war. Nonetheless individualists anticipate that the more democratic the world becomes, the more of a chance the world's people will have to hire and fire those who rule, and the less likely these rulers will be to come to blows. Most people most of the time are able to reckon the costs of large-scale conflict, liberalists argue. They are likely, therefore, to hire governments that do not incur these costs, or fire ones who do.

Liberalists also anticipate a world where more people felt personally emancipated, not just politically, but also economically, socially, culturally and sacrally. They envisage the global realization of the human rights regime, in short, with all the moral consequences that this would have.

Marxism, Neo-Marxism, and Constructivism

Some analysts do not see human beings as essentially anything. Instead, they see us as what we learn to be. For these analysts it is the essential nature of our nurturing practices that matter most, and in this regard, the main difference seems to be between those who highlight the materialist nature of our nurturing environment, the mentalist nature of our nurturing environment, or both.

The most conspicuous of those analysts who see the world in materialist terms are those rationalists who are Marxists, though one could put political geographers, as well as technological determinists of a non-Marxist kind, in this category too. Marxists do not subscribe to the division between politico-strategic, -economic and -social dimensions to world affairs, like those who make assumptions about our essential human nature do. Their analysis cuts across this division to highlight class-consciousness and class conflict. Marxists are often called political economists as a consequence, though this does not do justice to the wide-ranging character of what they have to say (Marx and Engels 1975[1848]; Wallerstein 1989).

Classical Marxists provide an account of historical change that, in simple terms, sees primitive communism giving way to slave-owning societies, and thence to feudalism, capitalism, proletariat-controlled socialism, and ultimately advanced communism. Currently the world is becoming capitalist. The class struggle that characterizes this particular mode of production, Marxists see as being one between owners and managers (the bourgeoisie), and those who sell their labor for a wage (the proletariat), and one where disparities in wealth and well-being will ultimately cause the latter to revolt. Once the proletariat takes over it will dismantle the state apparatus. Marx sees this socialism as the precursor to a time when the largesse of the industrial revolution is finally used to provide a material (and hence mentally) beneficial life for all, at which point people finally get the chance to realize their "species being." The driver of this world historical consequence is, in Marx's view, changes in the economic substructure. In the contemporary case, the most prominent superstructural consequence is capitalism, in that the world has to go capitalist before anything else can happen. As the conceptual foundation to a new internationalism, classical Marxists and liberalists have much in common. Both promote capitalist markets, modernist societies, and popular governments. In the liberalist case, however, this is because capitalism is the best of all possible worlds. In the Marxist case it is because capitalism is a historical stage that the planet's population must pass through before the best of all possible worlds becomes possible.

As the conceptual foundation for a new internationalism, Marxism anticipates a flood of cheap commodities, the consequent globalization of capitalist production and distribution, growing monopolization and working class emiseration, growing class conflict, and ultimately the revolutionary overthrow of capitalism itself. This is to be followed by a proletariat dictatorship strong enough to dismantle states and pave the way for advanced communism, history's last and most humane productive mode. More contemporary versions of classical Marxism note how expectations of global class structure are frustrated by the competing fact of state sovereignty and national difference, the embourgoisement of the world's workers, and the ability of the global ruling class to create compradors elites who serve its global interests at the expense of those who sell their labor for wages. These (essentially neo-Marxist) accounts of global dependency structures remain materialist in their inspiration, and as the conceptual foundation for any internationalism to come, they anticipate the perpetuation, and even the further consolidation, of a global hierarchy that has states arranged by core, semi-peripheral and peripheral status. This whole-system reading has owners and managers at the top, comprador elites in the middle, and the world's long-suffering masses underneath.

Meta-Marxists realize that capitalists read books, and having read what Marx says, go on to act to pre-empt his conclusions by crafting popular consciousness in ways that distort understanding of the plight of the world's workers, or prevent the formation of any such understanding at all. The objective, of course, is to prevent proletariat revolution, and to perpetuate global bourgeois rule. Meta-Marxists continue to acknowledge the significance of the material underpinnings to the global society, but they are acutely aware of the mentalist dimension to world affairs too, and the mental means used to obscure the extent, and even the existence, of the systematic exploitation of the world's workers. These means include the use of the global media to this effect, and of local school curricula. Both involve convincing those who would otherwise feel aggrieved that their situation is simply normal and natural and that it has no desirable alternative (Horkheimer 1972; Adorno 1973; Gramsci 1972; Cox 1987).

As the conceptual foundation for a new kind of internationalism, meta-Marxists highlight the continuing dissemination of what in their terms is false consciousness. They see the need to confront the bourgeois hegemony this represents. And they see the need for counter-hegemonic strategies, and for active opposition to a diffuse but well-orchestrated exercise in what they consider mental obfuscation.

Then there are the analysts who see ideas alone as the cause and condition for world affairs. They see the mentalist dimension to human nurturing as its essential dimension, that is, and the thought nature of world affairs as its key characteristic. To analysts like these we bring global practices and structures into being by thinking of them as thus and so, and acting as if they are thus and so. Our thinking is not neutral, since only those divine or insane have the objectivity that true neutrality requires. Our thinking always articulates norms and values. These determine in turn how and why we construct these particular world affairs, rather than any particular alternative to it.

This is the constructivist, or neo-Hegelian approach (Wendt 1999; Onuf 1989; Pettman 2000). It highlights the mentally self-fulfilling aspect to world affairs, and how we create what we think we find by thinking it into being. Constructivism does not specify what we think, or what the norms and values are that we articulate when we think. It does not envisage any particular kind of internationalism. It merely highlights how any kind of internationalism will be a mental one, rather than being caused by material imperatives, or some aspect of our essential human nature. As the conceptual foundation for any new kind of internationalism, it does not specify what kind of internationalism this might be, though it does point out how this will be a mental construction, and malleable in ways that material substructures are not.

Rationalism

Thinking of internationalism, and of new kinds of internationalism, takes place in Euro-American societies in the context of a culture that prioritizes reason as an end in itself, *en masse*. All persons that have the skills of mental abstraction and logical manipulation that the faculty of reason provides are rational. Not all persons who are rational are rationalists, however. To become a rationalist is to be taught to prioritize the use of reason, and to become the individuated kind of individual, mentally detached from its social context, who is able to sustain an objectifying outlook.

Rationalism is the dominant discourse of the day, not least because of its success in describing, explaining and predicting what goes on in the natural world in ways that make it much more amenable to human intervention. The technologies made possible by the scientific knowledge that rationalism provides vastly improve our human capacity to nourish, shelter, heal and entertain. Rationalism spreads because of its demonstrative worth in this regard.

Rationalism is a meta-discourse because it underpins all of the analytical languages mentioned above. So lively is the conversation these analytical languages provide that it is not often easy to see that every one of them is rationalist.

Rationalism incarcerates as well as emancipates. It makes possible clarity and a comprehensive mental outlook of an extremely powerful kind, but this comes at a cost. For example, rationalism requires us to be imprisoned in an individuated form of the self. It requires us to be detached from our communal context, and also our sacral context. It reduces our sense of reality to one able to fit the concept of time as linear, and the concept of space as Euclidean. It reduces the sense of the mind-body to a dichotomy between the body and the mind, and it reduces the mind to a dichotomy between reason and emotion. Rationalism enlightens, therefore, but it also blinds. It shows us the world in the light of the mind in an extremely powerful way, but it also requires an experiential kind of darkness to be drawn across our capacity to know the significance of the communal and the sacral, the temporal and the spatial, the mind-body nexus, and socially embedded forms of emotion and reason.

As the foundation for new kinds of internationalism, rationalism envisages a world of individuated individuals, who live and know that world in the way rationalism itself recommends. It envisages a world in its own image. It sees the entire planetary population practicing the objectifying mind-gaze that rationalism requires, and conversing among themselves in the analytical languages that articulate it. This is a very special kind of world. It is the Euro-American world, and as such, not one that all share, or want to share.

Rationalism is critiqued by rationalists themselves. It is in the nature of this way of thinking that pushed far enough, it will reveal its own shortcomings.

For example, hyper-rationalists want more of the same. This provides the foundation for a form of internationalism even more abstracted than the present form, that is, internationalism of the kind described by neorealists, game theorists, and those who see the world in terms of prisoners' dilemmas (Smith 2002).

Post-modernists turn reason back on itself to question (rationally) the point of prioritizing reason. They use reason, that is, to ask why such a priority should be placed upon reason (George 1994). This provides the foundation for a much more disparate form of internationalism, one less tolerant of the pursuit of the sort of grand cultural narratives that tell universal, absolute and eternal truth. This internationalism is much more amenable to difference and the co-existence of particular, relative and contingent truths, and one that creates thinking and speaking spaces for those whom rationalism makes marginal.

Post-structuralists highlight the use of language *per se*, and the assumptions built into language that predispose particular forms of the self, and particular analytic conclusions. They note the use of language to articulate anything, including our own identities, and the way in which language itself contains assumptions that predispose the conclusions we come to (Edkins 1999). As a foundation for new kinds of internationalism, post-structuralism highlights the growing significance of English, and therefore of the idiosyncrasies of English, such as the support it provides to those who prefer subject-object analysis, and those who disseminate dichotomies and dichotomised hierarchies.

Psychoanalysts talk of rationalism in the context of subconscious forces and forms of thought. They point out how rationalist thinking is subject to subconscious impulses that make rationalism much less rationalistic. (Freud 1971) As a foundation for new kinds of internationalism, psychoanalysis highlights the increasing influence on inter-state relations of the ubiquitous drive to sex, or power, or meaning.

Romantics retreat from rationalist abstraction to recover the emotive component to human experience. They point out the extent to which feelings are implicated in whatever we think (Bleiker 2001). As a meta-conceptual foundation for new kinds of internationalism it exalts our gut-feelings, and whatever alternatives gut-feeling might imagine.

Phenomenologism brackets-off rationalism in attempt to provide a more descriptive explanation of world affairs. It also uses reason, as manifest by the self re-embedded in its social context, to intuit the primal activities of the mind, and to describe how these intend what we think we know about world affairs. Phenomenologists point out the naiveté of a way of knowing (rationalism) they see as abstracted and objectifying. They promote richer descriptions of things-in-themselves, and the rational use of intuition to ascertain the fundamental thought forms of our own minds, and the way these intend the world affairs we think we know rather than those we attend to as rationalists (Odysseos 2002). As a foundation for new kinds of internationalism phenomenology exalts gut thinking, and whatever alternatives gut-thinking might imagine.

Feminism, Environmentalism, Indigenous-ism

Rationalists consign large numbers of people to the global margins that they do not deem to be sufficiently rationalistic. This includes most women, most environmentalists, most non-whites, and most indigenous peoples. Feminist, environmentalist and indigenous analysts respond by critiquing the patriarchal, eco-averse, racist and neo-imperialist character of this presumption. They do so either by articulating one or another of the analytical languages that rationalists themselves use, or by critiquing rationalism itself, using one or more of its meta-critiques. This provides the conceptual foundations for many new and different kinds of internationalism, that are less discriminatory with regard to sex roles, environmental awareness, and ethnic or indigenous identity. Feminists, for example, envisage a form of internationalism where sex role equality is the norm (Tickner 2001). Environmentalists envisage a form of internationalism where sustainable ecology is the norm (Dryzek 2005). Indigenous peoples may not opt in to rationalism at all, since the kind of self that rationalism requires is radically anti-communalist, and the opposite, therefore, of what they value (Tuhiwai Smith 1999). They either eschew it, or engage in it highly selectively, thereby providing the conceptual foundation for a new kind of internationalism that is radically non-rationalist.

Sacralism

Sacralists go even further to highlight the knowing that meditation, prayer and spiritual devotion make possible. As a foundation for new kinds of internationalism, this provides various, even more radical alternatives. If we consider some of the world's main religions, for example, and ask what they have to say about key aspects of world affairs, we begin to get some idea of just how radical and varied these alternatives might be (Pettman 2004). Consider, for example, the Taoist concept of strategics, where the restoration of harmony is the main principle, and reconciliation rather than retaliation (or retreat) the main political practice. Or consider the Buddhist concept of economics, where the liberal self is seen as illusory, "right livelihood" is a key principle, and happiness is seen in terms of spiritual awareness rather than consumer lust. Or consider Hindu constructivism. If Brahman really is Atman then we are faced with Constructivism with a capital "C," and the notion of constructivism as the thinking-into-being of world affairs begins to look very paltry indeed. Or consider pagan feminism. If the peace of Europe, six millennia ago, really was kept for a thousand years by a combination of sex role equality and the worship of earth goddesses rather than sky gods, then that may give us a key clue as to where we need to look if any new internationalism is to be peace-loving rather than continually torn by war.

Conclusion

The growing interconnections and interdependencies that character-ize the contemporary world can be described and prescribed in a range of ways. There is one international relations doctrine, called liberal internationalism that specifically highlights this phenomenon as it per-tains to the interstate system or society. This is only one way in which internationalism can be accounted for, however. There are others ways, and a comprehensive map of all of them is sketched above. Each has its own conceptual foundations, and each provides its own version of what a new kind of internationalism would look like. A systematic review of these versions is made above too.

What is the most likely version? Our answer to that question will depend on the particular sacral stance we take, how committed we are to the culture of rationalism (or to one or more of its auto-critiques), our place on rationalism's margins, and the assumptions we make, as rationalists, about human nature or nurturing practices.

Christians or Muslims anticipate a more Christian or Muslim kind of internationalism. Rationalists anticipate a grand narrative that delivers a progressively more rationalistic world. Rationalists critical of the ratio-nalist project anticipate one of a range of reflexive alternatives. Those marginalized by that project anticipate one of a range of international-isms where they are less marginalized. Rationalists who are pessimists anticipate endless competition and no new internationalism at all. Rationalists who are optimists anticipate international collaboration, up to and including global governmental collaboration. Rationalists who are calculative anticipate internationalism proliferating as far as our propensity for cooperation allows. Rationalists who are materialists anticipate new internationalisms arising that are commensurate with changes in production and technology. Rationalists who are mentalists anticipate norm entrepreneurs thinking up new internationalisms as they will. And rationalists who are both materialists and mentalists anticipate continuing iterations of global hegemony of the Gramscian or Frankfurt School kind, at least until the "lonely hour of the last instance" is at hand.

Where we stand in this regard really does determine what we conclude. There is no account that trumps all the others, unless we choose to have one of these accounts masquerade as the whole truth and nothing but the truth.

This is not to eschew the pursuit of Truth with a capital "T." It is to note that Truth is a grail in whose direction we grasp. It is to note that this grail does not dispense the wisdom we seek, including wisdom about the conceptual foundations of new forms of internationalism. Our only chance in this regard is to go beyond, rationalistically or sacrally, at which point we largely cease to make much sense.

References

Adorno, Theodor. 1973. *Negative Dialectics.* New York, NY: Seabury Press.

Anderson, Benedict. 1991. *Imagined Communities: Reflections on the Origin and Spread of Nationalism.* Rev. Ed. London: Verso.

Bull, Hedley. 1977. *The Anarchical Society: A Study of Order in World Politics.* London: Macmillan.

Bleiker, Roland. "The Aesthetic Turn in International Political Theory." *Millennium: Journal of International Studies* 30(3) (December 2001): 509-533.

Carr, E.H. 1991 (1939). *The Twenty Years' Crisis, 1919-1939: An Introduction to the Study of International Relations.* London: Macmillan.

Cox, Robert. 1987. *Production, Power and World Order: Social Forces in the Making of History.* New York, NY: Columbia University Press.

Doyle, Michael. "Liberalism and World Politics." *American Political Science Review* 80(4), 1986: 1151-69.

Dryzek, John. 2005. *The Politics of the Earth: Environmental Discourses.* Oxford: Oxford University Press.

Edkins, Jenny. 1999. *Poststructuralism and International Relations: Bringing the Political Back in.* Boulder, CO: Lynne Rienner.

Freud, Sigmund. 1971. *The Complete Introductory Lectures on Psychoanalysis.* London: Allen and Unwin.

Fukuyama, Francis. 1992. *The End of History and the Last Man.* London: Penguin.

Gellner, Ernst. 1983. *Nations and Nationalism.* Oxford: Blackwell

George, Jim. 1994. *Discourses of Global Politics: A Critical (Re)Introduction to International Relations.* Boulder, CO: Lynne Rienner Publishers.

Gramsci, Antonio. 1972. *Selections from the Prison Notebooks of Antonio Gramsci.* New York: International Publishers.

Guzzini, Stefano. 1998. *Realism in International Relations and International Political Economy.* London: Routledge.

Hayek, Friedrich. 1991. "The Fatal Conceit: The Errors of Socialism" in William Bartley's (ed.) *The Collected Works of F.A. Hayek.* Chicago: University of Chicago Press.

Heater, Derek. 1996. *World Citizenship and Government: Cosmopolitan Ideas in the History of Western Political Thought.* New York: St. Martin's Press.

Hobbes, Thomas. 1957 (1651). *Leviathan.* London: J.M. Dent.

Hobson, J.A. 1916. *Towards International Government.* London: George Allen and Unwin.

Horkheimer, Max. 1972. *Critical Theory: Selected Essays.* New York: Herder and Herder.

Kant, Immanuel. 1963 (1795). "Perpetual Peace" in Lewis Beck's (ed). *Kant on History.* Indianapolis: Bobs-Merrill.

Keck, Margaret and Kathryn Sikkink. 1998. *Activists Beyond Borders: Advocacy Networks in International Politics.* Ithaca, NY: Cornell University Press.

Keohane, Robert and Joseph Ney. 1977. *Power and Interdependence: World Politics in Transition* Boston, MA: Little, Brown and Company.

Keynes, John Maynard. 1926. *The End of Laissez-Faire.* London: Hogarth Press.

List, Friedrich. 1966 (trans. 1985). *The National System of Political Economy.* New York, NY: Augustus M. Kelley.

Marx, Karl and Friedrich Engels. 1975 (1848). *The Communist Manifesto.* Peking: Foreign Languages Press.

Mayall, James. 1990. *Nationalism and International Society.* Cambridge, MA: Cambridge University Press.

Morgenthau, Hans. 1972 (1948). *Politics among Nations: The Struggle for Power and Peace,* 5th ed. New York, NY: Alfred Knopf.

Odysseos, Louiza. "Radical Phenomenology, Ontology and International Political Theory." *Alternatives* 27(3) (Summer 2002): 373-405.

Onuf, Nicholas. 1989. *Worlds of Our Making: Rules and Rule in Social Theory and International Relations.* Columbia, SC: University of South Carolina Press.

Pettman, Ralph. 2004. *Reason. Culture. Religion. The Metaphysics of World Politics.* New York, NY: Palgrave.

Richardson, Jim. "Contending Liberalisms: Past and Present." *European Journal of International Relations* 3(1) 1997: 5-33.

Smith, Adam. 1892 (1776). *An Inquiry Into the Nature and Causes of the Wealth of Nations.* London: George Routledge and Sons.

Smith, Anthony. 1995. *Nations and Nationalism in a Global Era.* Cambridge, MA: Polity Press.

Smith, Michael. 1986. *Realist Thought from Weber to Kissinger.* Baton Rouge, LA: Louisiana State University Press.

Smith, Steve. "The US and the Discipline of International Relations: Hegemonic Country, Hegemonic Discipline." *International Studies Review* 4(2) (Summer 2002): 76-85.

Stretton, Hugh. 2000. *Economics: A New Introduction.* Sydney: UNSW Press.

Taylor, Charles. 1989. *Sources of the Self: The Making of Modern Identity.* Cambridge, MA: Cambridge University Press.

Tickner, J. Ann. 2001. *Gendering World Politics.* New York, NY: Columbia University Press.

Tuhiwai Smith, Linda. 1999. *Decolonizing Methodologies: Research and Indigenous Peoples.* London: Zed Books.

Wallerstein, Immanuel. 1989. *The Modern World-System.* New York: Academic Press.

Walt, Stephen. "International Relations: One World, Many Theories." *Foreign Policy* 110 (1998): 29-46.

Wendt, Alexander. 1999. *Social Theory of International Politics*. Cambridge, MA: Cambridge University Press.

Weiss, Linda. 1998. *The Myth of the Powerless State: Governing the Economy in a Global Era*. Cambridge, MA: Polity Press.

Yunker, James. 2005. *Rethinking World Government: A New Approach*. Lanham, MD: University Press of America.

Fulfilling the Mission: Empowering the United Nations to Live Up to the World's Expectations

Daisaku Ikeda

"The structure of world peace cannot be the work of one man, or one party, or one Nation... It must be a peace which rests on the cooperative effort of the whole world."[1]

These were the words with which US President Franklin D. Roosevelt—one of the parents of the United Nations, and the man who gave the organization its name—addressed the US Congress in March 1945. Roosevelt didn't live to see the birth of the international organization dedicated to his dream of world peace. He passed away in April 1945, just one month after speaking these words and a few weeks before the UN Conference on International Organization convened to draft the UN Charter.

At the San Francisco Conference, attended by representatives of fifty nations, there was a surging sense of joy and hope that the birth of this international organization would help humankind break the vicious cycles of war and tragedy and move the world toward peace and security. The conference was described as a landmark and a "milestone in the long march of man to a better future,"[2] indicative of the world's great hope and expectation in the birth of the United Nations.

The UN Charter was adopted after three months of intensive debate and discussions. It was the culmination of the vow "to save succeeding generations from the scourge of war, which twice in our lifetime has brought untold sorrow to mankind..."[3] These words, presented in the Preamble of the Charter, were not written merely as a reflection of the mistakes of the past, but they were informed by a sense of responsibility for the generations to come.

A Universal Forum

Thirteen years ago, I had occasion to visit the Opera House in San Francisco where the Charter was adopted. Reflecting on the dramatic moment in world history when the United Nations was born to serve as the parliament of humanity, I had a renewed sense of optimism for the significance of the mission with which the United Nations has been entrusted.

That mission, to prevent the world from experiencing the scourge of yet another world war, has since been constantly challenged. At times, it seemed that the organization could fail in accomplishing the most crucial task. This was certainly the case during the crises of the Cold War, when the world was split into rival blocs.

A variety of conflicts and tensions continue to plague the world, and the situation at the start of the 21st century is further aggravated with the emerging crisis of international terrorism. Furthermore, global issues such as poverty, hunger, environmental degradation, and refugee crises continue to pose fundamental threats to human security.

The difficult realities confronting the United Nations, 60 years after its birth, were expressed quite explicitly by UN Secretary-General Kofi Annan in his address to the 2005 World Summit: "deep divisions among Member States, and the underperformance of our collective institutions, were preventing us from coming together to meet the threats we face and seize the opportunities before us."[4]

Given that the United Nations is an intergovernmental organization whose constituent members are sovereign states, innovative reform ideas and efforts will inevitably face the impediments of conflicting national interests. This is the disempowering reality that has challenged the United Nations for many years. People's disappointment in the United Nations led to escalating criticism of the powerlessness of the international organization. In certain respects, the United Nations has failed to keep pace with the changing realities of our times, and there are certainly many major hurdles and criticisms that it has yet to overcome.

Nevertheless, as long as there are people in this world who suffer, who live under threats and crises, we absolutely cannot afford to dismiss the great value and mission of the United Nations. With a membership of 192 states, the United Nations is the most universal forum available; the United Nations alone is capable of promoting international cooperation and conferring legitimacy to such efforts and actions. Therefore, I believe that there is no other realistic solution than to provide effective support to the United Nations and work for its revitalization. We must start from the recognition that the United Nations has, for 60 years, provided humanitarian assistance to regions in need and acted as a forum for global dialogue where international consensus could be reached on issues of importance.

As I engage in dialogue with the world's political, cultural, and intellectual leaders, we often exchange thoughts on the future of the United Nations. If I were to distill and summarize their views, most of these leaders, while admitting the problems and challenges that the organization faces, subscribe to the view that the United Nations needs to be supported and empowered.

Many have pointed out that even if UN-centered initiatives are agreed on and ready to be implemented, there will always be national leaders who, wishing to protect national interest or position, distance themselves from commitment to specific action. In my conversations with former UN secretaries-general, Javier Perez de Cuellar and Boutros Boutros-Ghali, they have consistently pointed out the irony that while the world places the maximum expectations on the United Nations, it provides only minimal support.

The critical question, therefore, is how can this situation be resolved? First of all, we must constantly recall that a core purpose of the United Nations is to be the parliament of humanity, a venue where all voices can be heard and all perspectives represented. However seriously national interests clash and crises deepen, I believe that the answer lies in the commitment to a relentless process of dialogue, steadily creating the foundations for common efforts to resolve the challenges that face us.

Without dialogue, the world will continue to stumble through the confusion and darkness of division. Just as, in Greek mythology, Ariadne's thread made possible a safe exit from the Minotaur's labyrinth, dialogue can help us find our way out of the baffling maze of crises that surround us.

The continued process of dialogue fosters the ethos of coexistence and tolerance that our times demand. It is my firm belief that this will give birth to a "culture of peace," the advent of a critical transition in human history.

Today, the world faces mounting crises, including the deadlock in Iraq and the Middle East as a whole, the possible development of nuclear weapons capabilities by North Korea and Iran, the deteriorating state of affairs in Afghanistan and ongoing regional conflicts in Africa and elsewhere. But the complexity of these challenging problems is precisely the reason why it is crucial to patiently and persistently seek paths towards resolution by making maximum use of the channels for global dialogue that are both the United Nations' strong point and the wellsprings of soft power.

The advancing processes of globalization worldwide have been accompanied by deepening divisions and conflicts both within and between societies. We see around us a spreading of "culture of war" that justifies the use of war and violent means to realize desired ends.

It is absolutely vital that we dismantle this culture of war. We must use dialogue to advance resolutely toward the creation of a truly peaceful global society in which there is genuine respect for differences of position and outlook and where there is a shared reverence for human dignity.

I wish to urge again that the United Nations play a focal role in the grand project of constructing a civilization imbued with the spirit of dialogue.

Dag Hammarskjöld's Commitment to Dialogue

As we strive to envision the direction the United Nations should take in the twenty-first century, I believe there is much we can learn from the life and example of Dag Hammarskjöld, the second secretary-general of the organization. His achievements shine in the annals of UN history and his moral force and integrity, deemed as the "conscience of the UN," command wide respect to this day.

Dag Hammarskjöld was a statesman and economist born in Sweden just over a century ago. In the midst of the mounting tensions of the Cold War, Hammarskjöld took the lead in expanding the United Nations' responsibilities beyond a passive role of merely responding to crises, to a more proactive role in the promotion of peace in the world.

His talents were particularly visible through his efforts to resolve the Suez Crisis, as well as conflicts in Lebanon, Laos and elsewhere. His active pursuit of "quiet diplomacy," as he personally led missions to different regions in order to mediate conflicts, remains as his enduring legacy.

There were voices critical of this style of proactive diplomacy on the part of the United Nations and its secretary-general. The Soviet premier, Nikita Khrushchev, who demanded Hammarskjöld's resignation, denounced his actions. Hammarskjöld refused to succumb to this pressure and continued to promote UN leadership for the resolution of international crises.

Hammarskjöld expressed his unwavering resolve in his book *Markings*, published after his death:

> "The Uncarved Block"—remain at the Center, which is yours and that of all humanity. For those goals, which it gives to your life, do the utmost which, at each moment, is possible for you. Also, act without thinking of the consequences, or seeking anything for yourself.[5]

Driven by a sense of moral, even religious, mission, he continued to strive until the last moment of his life to empower the United Nations to achieve the world's expectations.

In September 1961, en route to a meeting with President Moise Tshombe of Katanga in an effort to resolve the Congo Crisis, Hammarskjöld's plane crashed in Northern Rhodesia (now Zambia), causing his death. He was 56. For his outstanding achievements, Hammarskjöld was posthumously awarded the Nobel Peace Prize for 1961. At the time of his death, Hammarskjöld was engaged not only in attempting to resolve the conflict in Congo, but in another important task. Hammarskjöld had profound respect for the "philosopher of dialogue," Martin Buber (1878-1965), and was planning to translate his classic work *I and Thou* into Swedish.

Their friendship began in 1952, a year before Hammarskjöld became secretary-general. As their exchanges and mutual respect deepened, a strong desire arose in Hammarskjöld to translate Buber's works. When he shared that wish with the philosopher, Buber suggested he translate *I and Thou*. This exchange took place just a few weeks before Hammarskjöld's fatal mission to Congo.

Upon this suggestion, Hammarskjöld contacted a publisher in Sweden and wrote a letter to Buber, telling him agreement had been obtained. As he left New York for Congo, he had with him the German-language edition of *I and Thou*, personally given to him by the author. He found time during his demanding schedule, in flight and during his short stay in Leopoldville (now Kinshasa), to work on the translation of Buber's book. Later, after the plane crash, the first twelve pages of the Secretary-General's manuscript translation were found among his personal effects.

Buber received Hammarskjöld's final letter just one hour after he heard the news of the plane crash on the radio. Buber deeply lamented the death of a man of passion and goodwill who had given everything, including his life, for his mission.

Hammarskjöld shared a deep conviction with Buber, which he fervently wished to convey through the translation of Buber's work. This was the firm belief that no matter how dire and challenging the situation may be, humans must engage in sincere dialogue with others; through genuine and sincere dialogue, it is always possible to bridge the gaps of distrust that divide the world. There is one well-known illustration of how Hammarskjöld put this conviction into practice. In 1955, in an attempt to secure the release of American prisoners of war captured during the Korean War, Hammarskjöld flew to China, then without a seat at the United Nations, and tried to meet with Premier Zhou Enlai.

People around him strongly advised him against the visit. Face-to-face with Zhou, without an official entourage and unable to use his own interpreter, Hammarskjöld stated the following during one of their private sessions:

> [I]t does not mean that I appeal to you or that I ask you for their release. It means that, inspired also by my faith in your wisdom and in your wish to promote peace, I have considered it my duty as forcefully as I can, and with deep conviction, to draw attention to the vital importance of their fate to the cause of peace... Their fate may well decide the direction in which we will all be moving in the near future: towards peace, or away from peace. [A]gainst all odds, [this case] has brought me around the world in order to put before you, in great frankness and trusting that we see eye-to-eye on the desperate need to avoid adding to existing frictions, my deep concern both as Secretary-General and as a man.[6]

I recall my own encounter with Premier Zhou Enlai in December 1974, a year before his death. Years earlier, in September 1968, at a time when there were no official diplomatic relations between China and Japan as no formal peace had been concluded between them, I had called for the normalization of relations and urged that China be represented in the United Nations. Zhou Enlai was aware of my efforts, and despite ill health, insisted on meeting with me at his hospital in Beijing. With intense passion, Premier Zhou shared his thoughts with me: "In this critical period in the history of the world, all nations must stand as equals and help each other." He expressed his strong desire for enduring friendship between China and Japan.

Based on this personal experience, I can easily imagine the kind of intent dialogue, the earnest soul-to-soul exchange that unfolded between Zhou and Hammarskjöld. The meeting created a bond of trust between the two men, which later led to the release of the eleven American airmen.

Whether it be intergovernmental relations or relations between the United Nations and member states, the most essential element is always encounter and dialogue between individual human beings. No matter how impossible a deadlock may seem, a breakthrough can always be found if we meet face-to-face and engage in genuine dialogue: I believe this was the conviction that motivated Hammarskjöld throughout his extensive travels as secretary-general, meeting with and mediating between the parties in conflict.

Hammarskjöld's passionate and relentless efforts to advance the peace process in the world embody the principles that should guide the United Nations in fulfilling its mission to build a new human civilization imbued with the spirit of dialogue. His legacy is one that must be passed on to the people of the twenty-first century.

Building Grassroots Support

Looking at the world today, the Middle East is just one of the regions where tensions remain high, and there is a strong need for the parties involved or affected by these tensions to communicate and engage in dialogue through the United Nations. This is critical to finding a break-through to persistent conflicts and bringing stability to the region.

After violent military clashes that continued for a month, a ceasefire in Lebanon was finally realized following a UN Security Council resolution calling for an immediate cessation of armed hostilities. But the underlying instability remains, as does the possibility that fighting may reignite at any time. These problems point to the urgent need to move proactively to the next step of rebuilding a stable and peaceful order in the region. It is my sincere hope that all parties will work through the United Nations to develop new channels for dialogue that will substantively further the peace process.

As I think about the profound mission the United Nations must embark on, I recall the words of Secretary-General Kofi Annan when he addressed the 2005 World Summit on September 14, 2005, attended by the leaders of 170 states: "We must find what President Franklin Roosevelt once called 'the courage to fulfill our responsibilities in an admittedly imperfect world.'"[7] The *raison d'être* of the United Nations, still entirely valid after 60 years, is encapsulated in this spirit of responsibility and courage.

It was the lifelong wish of my mentor, Josei Toda (1900-58), second president of the Soka Gakkai, to forge a global solidarity of ordinary citizens committed to support the United Nations. Along with the founding president of the Soka Gakkai, Tsunesaburo Makiguchi (1871-1944), Josei Toda was imprisoned for nearly two years during World War II because his uncompromising convictions, rooted in his religious faith, led him to a direct confrontation with Japan's militarist fascism. He was released from prison before the war ended, on July 3, 1945, just a few days after the San Francisco Conference adopted the UN Charter.

Toda's philosophy of peace was expressed in his call for the abolition of nuclear weapons and his ideal of "global nationalism," which in today's terms could be interpreted as a world citizenship that transcends all distinctions of nationality, ethnicity and ideology. Toda believed that the United Nations represented the distillation of wisdom of 20th-century humankind. He was convinced of the need to protect and develop this embodiment of the world's hopes into the next century. It was Toda's deepest desire to eliminate needless suffering from this planet by expanding the global solidarity of awakened and empowered individuals.

In my own family, four of my brothers were drafted into the war. My eldest brother died in battle. The grief experienced by my elderly parents was indescribably profound. Nothing is more cruel than war, nothing more miserable. This reality was engraved into my consciousness as a youth.

Soon after the war, I encountered Toda and determined that I would join my mentor in the lifelong struggle to break the unending cycles of war and violence, and to contribute to the realization of a world of peace. Immediately after my inauguration as the third president of the Soka Gakkai, as heir to my mentor's will, I took the first step in this effort when I traveled to the United States; this visit was motivated partly by my awareness that this was the country where the UN Headquarters, the focal point of efforts for global peace, was located.

I still recall with vivid clarity my first visit to the UN Headquarters in New York in October 1960. Dag Hammarskjöld was secretary-general and the 15th General Assembly was in session, along with the attendance of many of the world's leaders, including US President Dwight D. Eisenhower and Soviet Premier Nikita Khrushchev. As I observed the General Assembly and committee meetings, I was left with an indelible impression of the power and vibrancy emanating from the representatives of the newly independent African states participating in the discussions. At this General Assembly, seventeen nations, including Cameroon, Togo and Madagascar, were welcomed as member states of the United Nations. All of these new states, with the exception of Cyprus, were from the African continent.

It was deeply inspiring to witness the passion of the African representatives brimming with fresh energy, determined to contribute to the making of a better world through the United Nations. Every time I think about the important mission of the United Nations, I cannot help but reflect on this earlier experience.

Traveling to various different parts of the world, I have often sensed people's strong hopes and expectations for the United Nations. My efforts to engage in dialogue with political, intellectual and cultural leaders throughout the world stem from this desire to expand the network of likeminded people, thinking beyond national, ethnic and religious differences, committed to supporting the United Nations. While promoting dialogue among civilizations and among religions, I have at the same time felt the need to make concrete proposals for action. Every year since 1983, I have issued peace proposals in which I have set out ideas on ways to reinforce and revitalize the United Nations, stressing the importance of encouraging grassroots support.

Soka Gakkai International (SGI) has carried out a wide range of activities in support of the United Nations. As Cold War tensions mounted, we organized the exhibition "Nuclear Arms: Threat to Our World" in 1982, in support of the United Nations' World Disarmament Campaign. This exhibition, which opened at the UN Headquarters in New York, toured twenty-five cities in sixteen countries, including the Soviet Union and China and other nuclear weapons states. In total, some 1.2 million visitors viewed it.

After the end of the Cold War, the SGI organized the exhibition "War and Peace: From a Century of War to a Century of Hope" and updated the antinuclear exhibit, renaming it "Nuclear Arms: Threat to Humanity," in an effort to bring people together in their shared desire for peace and to generate a momentum toward realizing a world without war.

In the area of human rights education, the SGI organized the exhibition "Toward a Century of Humanity: An Overview of Human Rights in Today's World" in support of the UN Decade for Human Rights Education (1995-2004). With the end of the Decade, the SGI collaborated with other UN agencies and NGOs to promote the creation of a new international framework to follow up the work of the Decade. These efforts culminated in the formal adoption of the World Programme for Human Rights Education.

In the area of ecological integrity and sustainability, the SGI, together with other NGOs, proposed that the United Nations to call for a "Decade of Education for Sustainable Development." This was later adopted by the General Assembly, with the United Nations Educational, Scientific and Cultural Organization (UNESCO) designated as the lead agency to promote the Decade, beginning in 2005.

The SGI has long supported refugee relief activities through the United Nations High Commissioner for Refugees (UNHCR). In 1992, the SGI organized the Voice Aid campaign in response to the United Nations Transitional Authority in Cambodia's (UNTAC) request and donated 300,000 second-hand radios to support the smooth organization and administration of free and fair elections in Cambodia.

Buddhist Values and Philosophy

The SGI's grassroots network of ordinary citizens in support of the United Nations has now expanded to include 190 countries and territories. These efforts are compelled by Buddhist values and philosophy, which uphold the inviolable dignity of life. The core principles that guide the United Nations are cognate with the principles of Buddhist humanism: peace, equality and compassion. Motivated by these values, it is perhaps inevitable that SGI members feel compelled to support the United Nations.

In this context it is relevant to introduce the example of a contemporary of Shakyamuni—a woman by the name of Srimala appearing in the Buddhist canon. Her vow is recorded as follows: "If I see lonely people, people who have been jailed unjustly and have lost their freedom, people who are suffering from illness, disaster or poverty, I will not abandon them. I will bring them spiritual and material comfort."[8] Srimala lived true to her vow and devoted her life to help the suffering.

The teachings of the Buddhist reformer Nichiren (1222-82), which constitute the philosophical basis of the SGI's activities, are deeply imbued with the spirit of Mahayana Buddhism. Our efforts to support the United Nations as it strives to protect human dignity in our modern world are a natural consequence of putting into practice the Bodhisattva way represented by Srimala's compassionate vow and actions.

In recent years, the United Nations has focused its efforts on the promotion of human rights, human security, human development, culture of peace and dialogue among civilizations. These are all undertakings that strike a chord with the philosophy of peace expounded in Buddhism. The philosophical basis of our activities and thinking is elucidated in the treatise "On Establishing the Correct Teaching for the Peace of the Land," written by Nichiren in 1260 as he witnessed the sufferings of the ordinary people caught up in the incessant war and natural disasters that wracked 13th-century Japanese society. It is central in this treatise that instead of using either of the standard Chinese characters for "country," which have in their center elements that signify "sovereign" or "weapon," Nichiren uses a character with the element representing "ordinary people." For Nichiren, the heart of the nation is neither the authorities nor the territory, but the ordinary people who inhabit it. This same spirit animates the modern concept of human security where the foremost aim is to realize the peace and happiness of citizens.

Throughout this treatise, Nichiren critiqued the dominant philosophies of his times; he considered that their emphasis on introverted reflection encouraged an escapist attitude and made people feel incapable of effectively engaging in or transforming society. Instead, he promoted the belief that inherent in each individual is a robust power and potential and that each individual can become the protagonist and initiator of societal transformation. This belief shares much with the contemporary concept of empowerment that constitutes the core of human development.

Nichiren's treatise contains the following passage: "If you care anything about your personal security, you should first of all pray for order and tranquility throughout the four quarters of the land..."[9] This is a powerful call for the creation of a culture of peace, which is not limited to the security of the individual but seeks the security of the entire human race. The ultimate inspiration underlying the SGI's promotion of consciousness-raising at the grassroots level through exhibitions and seminars, as well as our support for UN activities for education in the fields of disarmament, human rights and the environment, is the desire to realize the security of the entire human race.

Furthermore, the treatise unfolds as a dialogue between two individuals, the host and the guest, who have completely differing perspectives and views but who are both pained by the tragic realities tormenting their society. The host tells the guest, "I have been brooding alone upon this matter, indignant in my heart, but now that you have come, we can lament together. Let us discuss the question at length."[10] An earnest dialogue takes place as the two exchanges their views on the causes of people's suffering, means to alleviate this suffering, and what can be done to this end. At the conclusion of the dialogue, the host and guest vow to unite their efforts and work together toward a common goal.

Dialogue has the power to inspire inner change in people and leads to positive action to transform society. This is the approach found in the wisdom of the Buddhist tradition since the days of Shakyamuni. In the SGI Charter adopted in 1995, this spirit is reflected thus: "SGI shall, based on the Buddhist spirit of tolerance, respect other religions, engage in dialogue and work together with them toward the resolution of fundamental issues concerning humanity."[11] Based on this spirit, the SGI has engaged in an open dialogue with people of diverse religious and cultural backgrounds, in the hope of expanding the solidarity of awakened individuals committed to seeking ways to resolve the challenges facing our planet.

The Soft Power Mission of the United Nations

As mentioned at the outset, I am convinced that the mission of the United Nations in the 21st century must be to defuse tensions and generate momentum toward peaceful coexistence through the power of dialogue. By centering its work on the processes of global dialogue it will best fulfill its function as a body for deliberation and action. In this way, it will lay the foundation for concerted action in such critical areas as human rights, human security and human development: the absolute prerequisites for the peace and happiness of the world's people.

In working toward these objectives, it is essential we remember that the core strength of the United Nations is its "soft power," the power of dialogue and international cooperation. This is true even in the field of global peace and security. While the UN Charter clearly recognizes the possibility of the exercise of "hard power," including military action, Chapter VI, on the pacific settlement of disputes, it details measures to be taken before the application of more coercive actions in Chapter VII. Precedence is thus firmly placed in Chapter VI, with the use of hard power reserved for crisis situations as a means of last resort.

The Spanish philosopher José Ortega y Gasset (1883-1955) defined civilization as "the attempt to reduce force to being the *ultima ratio* [last resort]."[12] When we think how the United Nations came into being as a reflection of the bitter lessons of two world wars, it is clear that this principle needs to be adamantly observed. I would like to reaffirm that the United Nations must continue to develop and enhance its soft power capacities. It should continue to focus on confidence-building and preventive measures and not be drawn into a reactive approach that attempts to solve problems through military force or other forms of hard power.

In the Eastern tradition, the 60th year marks the end of a cycle and the beginning of a new one. In that sense, I believe the United Nations' 60th anniversary, celebrated last year, provides a significant opportunity for the United Nations to renew its commitment to the noble mission with which it has been entrusted and make a new departure toward its fulfillment. Here, I would like to suggest one axial theme around which the United Nations could develop its future programs and actions; it is that of "humanitarian competition." The founding president of the Soka Gakkai, Tsunesaburo Makiguchi, in his 1903 work, "The Geography of Human Life," proposed the idea of humanitarian competition. Writing in an era when the forces of imperialism and colonialism were dominant throughout the world, Makiguchi criticized a state of affairs in which the crucial question of individual human happiness was being overshadowed by intense competition in the military, political, and economic spheres. Reviewing the evolution of competition through its military, political, and economic modes, he called for a transition from these predatory forms of competition to what he described as humanitarian competition—in which we strive, based on an ethos of coexistence, for the happiness of both ourselves and others. Makiguchi described the key elements of this transformation as follows:

> Traditionally, military or political power has been used to expand territory and bring more people under one's control. Economic power, which may assume a different appearance or form, has been employed to the same effect as that realized through the exercise of military or political power. Humanitarian competition consists in using the invisible power of moral suasion to influence people. In other words, in place of submission exacted by the exercise of authority, we seek to gain the heartfelt respect [and cooperation] of others.[13]

This process of supplanting the exercise of authority with the earning of heartfelt respect could be interpreted as the transition away from the competition of hard power, where societies seek to dominate each other through military and political strength or overwhelming economic might. Rather, each country should compete in the realm of soft power—vying to accrue trust and friendship by manifesting diplomatic and cultural strengths, through contributions in the field of international cooperation that deploy the full range of human resources, technology and experience. This, I believe, is the essence of Makiguchi's proposal.

If such humanitarian competition, a competition for extended influence based on soft power, firmly takes root, we will see the last of conventional zero-sum competition in which winners prevail through the victimization and suffering of losers. It will open a way for a win-win era where the dignity of everyone on the globe is honored, with each country competing constructively to make the greatest contribution to humanity.

Sadly, the world is still dominated by ruthless competition for advantage with no thought given to the price paid by others. Such modes of competition, played out on an ever-expanding global scale, have made for steadily growing gaps between the rich and the poor. Moreover, as threats to human dignity, the crisis of the global environment is emblematic and become borderless. We need to bear in mind that no individual state acting in isolation can mount a truly effective response. UN Secretary-General Kofi Annan expressed this reality succinctly when he stated:

> I believe that in the twenty-first century [different perceptions of what is a threat] should not be allowed to lead the world's governments to pursue very different priori-

ties or to work at cross-purposes… States working together can achieve things that
are beyond what even the most powerful state can accomplish by itself.[14]

It is therefore essential that the United Nations function to effectively
concentrate and coordinate the capacities of individual states and prevent
them from becoming diluted or dispersed. It could be said that the success
of efforts to develop the international organization into a body fully and
genuinely dedicated to the people of the world, depends on this process.
Each state naturally desires to take an honorable position as a respected
member of the international community. To tap this potential and chan-
nel competitive energies, not toward violence, but into humanitarian
objectives, I believe, lay the mission of the United Nations as the focal
center of humanitarian competition. This is the course it should take in
the 21st century.

To generate momentum in this direction and set benchmarks for firmly
establishing the ideal of humanitarian competition at the core of the
United Nations' activities, I would like to stress the importance of the
following three "shared" elements: a shared sense of purpose, a shared
sense of responsibility and shared fields of action. Based on this I would
like to set out what I view to be the United Nations' core challenges and
to suggest plans for reform.

Sharing Purpose

In terms of "a shared sense of purpose," I wish to propose the building
of a culture of peace dedicated to the dignity and happiness of all people
on the planet, based on the awareness that peace is much more than the
mere absence of conflict. In this respect, poverty, a daily affront to human dignity, is the foremost issue to be tackled. According to the United
Nations Development Programme (UNDP), in today's world, as many as
2.5 billion people subsist on less than two dollars per day.[15]

Noting that the targets of the Millennium Development Goals, including halving the proportion of people living in extreme poverty by 2015,
will not be achieved at the current rate as UNDP Administrator Kemal
Dervis warns:

> That would be a tragedy above all for the world's poor but rich countries would not
> be immune to the consequences of failure. In an interdependent world our shared
> prosperity and collective security depend critically on success in the war against
> poverty.[16]

In the shadow of a handful of countries that consume enormous
resources and boast affluent lifestyles, a vast portion of the world's in-

habitants are condemned to seemingly endless poverty, life in inhuman and degrading conditions that persist for generation after generation. It is an overriding humanitarian imperative to correct this gross distortion within the global community. This should not be an impossible task. The cost of eradicating poverty has been estimated to be about one percent of global income. If even a portion of the resources currently allocated to military spending could be directed towards poverty reduction, considerable progress could be made to alleviate the problem. I strongly urge each country to seriously reconsider its spending priorities and to actively support international cooperation for human development focused on the empowerment of all individuals afflicted with poverty, UNESCO's Education for All campaign in particular.

Together with poverty alleviation, disarmament, specifically nuclear disarmament, is vital if we are to put to rest the culture of war. If the ideal of humanitarian competition is to take root in the international community, we must firmly establish the awareness that no society can found its security and well-being upon the terror and misery of another; we must create a new set of global ethics.

The theory of nuclear deterrence, in seeking to ensure the security of one state by threatening others with overwhelming destructive power, is diametrically opposed to the global ethics the new era demands. The UN hosts an associated forum for multilateral talks on disarmament, the Geneva-based Conference on Disarmament. However, it is distressing that disagreement among parties has kept it virtually nonfunctional for almost ten years since its last achievement, the adoption of the Comprehensive Test Ban Treaty in 1996.

The stalemate persisted through last year, the sixtieth anniversary of the atomic bombing of Hiroshima and Nagasaki, whose symbolic significance could have been expected to provide impetus to disarmament efforts. The Nuclear Non-Proliferation Treaty (NPT) Review Conference in May closed without producing any concrete results. Then in September, the World Summit at the UN General Assembly issued an outcome document from which all mention of nuclear weapons had been deleted, to the great disappointment of all those who seek global peace.

It was against this backdrop that, in June 2006, the Weapons of Mass Destruction Commission, an independent group of international experts chaired by Hans Blix, the former chief UN arms inspector for Iraq submitted a proposal on nuclear disarmament and non-proliferation to Secretary-General Annan. This document calls for a World Summit to be held at the United Nations to address the issues of disarmament, non-proliferation and terrorist use of weapons of mass destruction. To break the present deadlock at the Conference on Disarmament in Geneva, it proposes that only a two-thirds majority, instead of unanimity, be required to place issues on the agenda. "All states possessing nuclear weapons," it also recommends, "should commence planning for security without nuclear weapons. They should start preparing for the outlawing of nuclear weapons..."[17]

These proposals are in line with the direction I have consistently asserted and it is thus very easy for me to support them. I earnestly hope that all states will take the Commission's carefully considered recommendations seriously and promptly launch diplomatic efforts to break the impasse that is impeding progress toward disarmament.

Ten years have passed since in 1996 the International Court of Justice issued an advisory opinion on the legality of nuclear weapons. In that opinion, the Court stated that "the threat or use of nuclear weapons would generally be contrary to international law," and "that there exists an obligation to pursue in good faith and bring to a conclusion negotiations leading to nuclear disarmament in all its aspects under strict and effective international control."[18] I think we should once again urge governments to recall the gravity of this opinion as we continue to build a committed international consensus for nuclear disarmament.

The report of the Blix Commission points, "Over the past decade, there has been a serious, and dangerous, loss of momentum and direction in disarmament and non-proliferation efforts." What is required is the political will for nuclear abolition. "And with that will, even the eventual elimination of nuclear weapons is not beyond the world's reach."[19] It is thus all the more important now that the people of the world raise their voices.

Toward this end, I would like to propose a UN decade of action by the world's people for nuclear abolition. With nuclear weapons proliferation continuing unabated, the first step in challenging the harsh reality must be to bring more people to the awareness that the nuclear threat is both relevant to their lives and something they can take action about. Such a decade of action, jointly promoted by the United Nations and NGOs, would be vital in promoting this awareness. I likewise support the early convening of a World Summit as called for by the Blix Commission or, alternatively, a Special Session of the UN General Assembly dedicated to intensive deliberation of disarmament issues. Such actions on the part of states would both reflect and support an emerging international consensus for disarmament.

The importance of working progressively toward the creation of a world without war through relentlessly pressing for nuclear disarmament and, ultimately, abolition was one of the points made by the late Sir Joseph Rotblat, emeritus president of the Pugwash conferences on Science and World Affairs, who passed away last year: I deeply agree.

If we are to bring down the curtain, once and for all, on an era lived under the threat of nuclear destruction, we must rethink the understanding of national interest that would justify nuclear weapons as a "necessary evil" essential for deterrence. Both the Russell-Einstein Manifesto (1955), co-signed by Dr. Rotblat, and my mentor Josei Toda's Declaration for the Abolition of Nuclear Weapons (1957) refuted the theory of deterrence and adamantly refused to acknowledge the use of nuclear arms under any circumstances.

As Toda strikingly phrased it, nuclear weapons threaten humanity's right to existence and are therefore an absolute evil; their abolition is humanity's common duty. The central goal of my proposal of "a decade of action by the world's people for nuclear abolition" would be to elevate Toda's statement into one of the central tenets of our time.

Here I have examined the challenges of poverty alleviation and disarmament from the perspective of a shared sense of purpose. There are, of course, many other issues that weigh heavily upon humankind. Among these is the global environmental crisis, the particular complexity of which lies in the fact that its resolution requires a fundamental reexamination of human civilization. My own sense of crisis has prompted me to call, in my annual peace proposals, for accelerated efforts to create an institutional framework that will bring together the wisdom of humankind toward the resolution of environmental challenges, including granting those issues greater centrality at the United Nations.

The issues of poverty, disarmament and the environment all demand the concerted efforts of international society based on a sense of belonging to humanity and a sense of responsibility toward the future. It is for these reasons that it is absolutely essential to establish a shared sense of purpose through the United Nations.

Sharing Responsibility

I next wish to focus on the need to foster a shared sense of responsibility, specifically by establishing frameworks that encourage the youthful members of the rising generations to actively engage in various deliberations at the United Nations and in its agencies' local activities.

In February of 2006, the Toda Institute for Global Peace and Policy Research, which I founded ten years ago, held an international conference in Los Angeles on the theme of reforming and strengthening the United Nations. I was particularly struck by the vision statement presented by UN Under-Secretary-General Anwarul K. Chowdhury, which included these words: "In future, the United Nations should be an organization that interacts more closely and substantially with the young people to benefit from their ideas and enthusiasm in shaping the future of the world."[20]

Gaining the understanding and unwavering support of as many of the world's citizens as possible is essential if the United Nations is to fully realize its potential. At the same time, the prerequisite for solving global problems is to supplant the prevailing mind-set, which places highest priority upon national interest, with a broad, shared sense of responsibility for the best interests of humankind and of the entire planet. Young people must be the protagonists in this endeavor.

I believe that the United Nations, having entered its 61st year, should make promoting young people's active engagement the central focus of its new departure. Archimedes is quoted as saying, "Give me a place to stand and with a lever I will move the whole world," and it is in this spirit that we must ensure that young people have a place to stand within the UN process.

It is said that about half of the countries emerging from conflict find themselves enmeshed in it again within five years. In societies that have experienced conflict and the tragedy of cycles of recurring violence, it is extremely difficult for members of the generation in power to disentangle themselves from the cycle of hatred and violence. Thus, it is important to focus on the next generation, who are less bound up in the past, and to find ways to enable youth to explore new ideas, avenues and approaches to establishing peace and shared prosperity.

The same formula applies to the challenges of poverty alleviation, disarmament and environmental degradation. Significant breakthroughs will only come about as the seeds of change planted in the hearts of the next generation through persistent, untiring efforts in the fields of education and awareness-raising come to fruition. My mentor's declaration against nuclear weapons, in entrusting the abolition of nuclear arms to young people, was based on just this kind of far-reaching future vision.

Along these lines, it would be worth considering holding a gathering of youth representatives from around the world every year prior to the annual UN General Assembly, giving world leaders an opportunity to listen to the views of the next generation. It would also be desirable to create means for students and young people to participate in local activities of UN agencies for a period of one or two years, positioning them to gain firsthand experience of the significance of the United Nations' activities the challenges it faces, the impact it has on people's lives—as well as engaging the youth to participate in the search for solutions.

About 5,000 people are currently dispatched to different parts of the world every year through the UN Volunteer (UNV) program. The average participant is 39 years old and is recruited principally from among experts with professional experience in specialized areas.[21] I believe it would be helpful to enhance these activities with an additional framework providing hands-on experience for students and young people in their twenties.

Another area worth examining is improving the system of UN internship programs. These should accept not only graduate students, but also undergraduates and young NGO staff members, providing them with the opportunity to support actual policy-making through preparing briefing papers for UN deliberations. Such a system would strengthen the framework by which young people can be involved in various aspects of the international organization. Graduates of Soka University of America are already active participants in the UN internship program.

Here I am reminded of a dialogue I conducted with the peace scholar Dr. Elise Boulding in which she maintained the importance of providing future generations with arenas where they can fully express their abilities, stressing that we need to create more opportunities for young people to grow into their role as global citizens. She told me she used to recommend the students in her international peace studies class to spend a semester working as interns at a local chapter of an international NGO and actively experiences its activities.

By implementing ideas such as these, I would hope that the structure of the United Nations as a whole could develop a sharper focus on youth, actively plan for greater participation of young people. In that sense, I would like to suggest that consideration be given to the creation of an agency dedicated to activities for the youth of the world or a department of youth within the UN administration.

Such efforts would parallel the growing calls among NGOs for the establishment of an agency dedicated to developing more effective and coordinated policies for empowering women, who are, after all, half the world's population. The UN must strive to promote the empowerment of young people and women living in difficult conditions in various parts of the world. If the United Nations can at the same time ensure the active participation of young people and women in its activities, reflecting an ever-greater diversity of opinions in the full range of its policy initiatives, this would go far toward bringing about a more promising era of humanity.

I would also like to call on the world's universities and institutions of higher learning to actively support the work of the United Nations as an integral part of their social mission. Some universities already have systems in place whereby researchers and research institutes provide academic support to various UN activities. While expanding this type of program, universities should take the initiative in actively offering classes on UN activities with the aim of becoming consistent centers for raising awareness among students and the general public. At the same time, I would like to emphasize the key importance of building a student-centered network to support the United Nations.

I have in the past proposed the creation of a global network of citizens to protect and support the United Nations. I believe that fostering a new generation of people of talent and capacity, people whose commitment is to the whole of humankind rather than the interest of a specific state or ethnicity, is the only way to provide the United Nations with the long-term support that it so seriously requires.

Students are the key to this. There are already NGOs dedicated to developing the network of UN support among students around the world. Further strengthening these, it should be possible to move toward a scenario in which individual students and universities connect with one another to form a web of networks supporting the United Nations, eventually permeating the entire globe. This is the future I envisage for renewed linkages between the United Nations, students and universities.

With respect to developing a shared sense of responsibility I would like to make one other proposal: To help resolve the United Nations' long-term challenge of securing stable sources of funding, a separate framework that is parallel to the contributions of member states might be initiated to solicit direct support from the world's citizens.

Securing a stable budget is essential if the United Nations is to fulfill its responsibilities to effectively respond to global issues. Delayed and overdue payment of assessed and pledged contributions undermines the United Nations' capacities. Financial restrictions often prevent it from engaging in urgent projects and important activities. To overcome these challenges, I would like to repeat my call that a people's fund for the United Nations be created to accept broad-based donations from civil society, making this an additional funding source to sustain the United Nations.

In point of fact, UNICEF's operating budget comes both from governmental contributions and private fundraising, with approximately one-third of funds coming from the private sector.[22] This is an example that demonstrates the potential for creating a new system whereby funds raised from individuals, organizations, and globally active transnational corporations are used to support UN activities, primarily in humanitarian areas.

Sharing Action

Finally, I would like to discuss the importance of "shared fields of action." To this end, I would like to propose the establishment of regional UN offices, whose role would be to further deepen relationships between member states and the United Nations, and coordinate various UN agencies' activities in each region.

It takes considerable time and effort to set UN activities in motion. In particular, when a society has fallen into crisis, the understanding and continuous support of the surrounding countries is essential.

Global issues are complex and inextricably intertwined in a way that makes separate, isolated efforts to resolve them unlikely to succeed. This is symbolized by the "PPE spiral," in which cycles of poverty, population growth and environmental degradation have set up a negative synergy. Global issues differ from area to area, demanding responses that are truly appropriate to the individual circumstances. In light of these factors, I am convinced that establishing coordinating UN centers in each region could enhance responsiveness to the exigencies of continuity, complexity and regionality. Such centers could be of great importance in the more comprehensive promotion of human rights, human security and human development through approaches focused on individual people's peace and happiness. Having said that, I do not think it is necessary to restructure existing agencies. The thrust of my proposal is to bring the United Nations and member states closer and to build a positive synergy among UN agencies in each region. This would enable them to establish shared fields of action and tackle regional issues in a more coordinated manner.

Specifically, existing bodies that might assume the functions of UN regional centers would include the five commissions under the Economic and Social Council (ECOSOC): the Economic and Social Commissions for Asia and the Pacific, for West Asia, for Africa, for Europe and for Latin America and the Caribbean.

Currently, as exemplified by the European Union and the African Union, regional integration and cooperation are progressing in different parts of the world. I believe there would be value in establishing UN regional centers that could act as a bridge between these organizations and the UN headquarters, as well as providing pivotal points to sustain UN-centered global governance.

I would like to emphasize, in addition to this plan, the need to strengthen partnership between the United Nations and civil society as the essential key to developing shared fields of action.

Civil society's participation in the United Nations dramatically increased through the series of UN conferences held in the 1990s. Partnerships of like-minded governments and NGOs brought about epoch-making achievements such as the conclusion of the Anti-Personnel Mines Convention and the adoption of the Rome Statute of the International Criminal Court.

The Panel of Eminent Persons on UN-Civil Society Relations was set up in 2003 and issued its report "We the Peoples: Civil Society, the United Nations and Global Governance" (the Cardoso Report) the following year. The work of the panel has been important in raising the awareness of civil society's role in supporting the work of the United Nations.

The Committee of Religious NGOs at the United Nations, whose president is currently the SGI's representative to the United Nations, together with UN organizations and agencies and governments, organized the Conference on Interfaith Cooperation for Peace in June 2005. That these three parties—civil society, governments and the United Nations—collaborated in this way, to hold an interfaith conference at the United Nations, was seen as a truly groundbreaking event.

For the United Nations' revitalization and to ensure that it fulfills the expectations of the world's peoples, it is indispensable that the United Nations, member states and NGOs and other representatives of civil society appreciate one another's unique qualities and roles, and deepen their partnership. I earnestly hope that the three parties will continue to sit at the same table to discuss the challenges facing humanity and develop creative new modalities of joint action in the spirit of dialogue and cooperation.

It is my sincere belief that these themes—a shared sense of purpose, a shared sense of responsibility, and shared fields of action—are key to the development of the United Nations of the 21st century.

The League of Nations was created as a response to World War I; the United Nations was born out of the determination never to repeat the horrors of World War II. As members of the human race, we must put into action our determination to save our planet from the repetition of this kind of tragedy. We must further strengthen the United Nations in order to enhance global governance for the sake of all the planet's inhabitants.

We are compelled to take the courageous first step toward this goal. To this end, it is essential to build momentum for reform from the bottom up, bringing together the voices of the people in support of the United Nations. We cannot afford to wait passively for top-down reform to emerge from intergovernmental deliberations. If we truly heed the warnings of the twentieth century, so plagued by tragedy, we can see that action and solidarity hold the keys to the 21st century. To the degree that people grasp this spirit and determine to forge widespread solidarity for change, we will be able to build a culture of peace throughout the world. This, I am convinced, is the central challenge facing humanity in the 21st century.

The protagonists in this endeavor are none other than individual human beings-citizens, and above all, young people.

The motivating vision of the SGI is a world of peace and mutual flourishing in humanity's new millennium. We will continue to join our efforts with those of goodwill and strive to enable the United Nations to fulfill the noble mission with which it has been entrusted.

Notes

1. Roosevelt 1945.
2. Lauren 1996, p. 161.
3. UN 1945.
4. Annan 2005a.
5. Hammarskjöld 1964, p. 159.
6. Qtd. in Urquhart 1972, p. 106.
7. Annan 2005a.
8. Cf. Wayman 1974, p. 65.
9. Nichiren 1999, p. 24.
10. Ibid., p. 7.
11. SGI 1995.
12. Ortega y Gasset 1932, p. 75.
13. Makiguchi 1996, p. 399.
14. Annan 2005b.
15. UNDP 2006, p. 8.
16. UNDP 2005.
17. WMDC 2006, p. 109.
18. ICJ 1996.
19. WMDC 2006, p. 17.
20. Chowdhury 2006.
21. UNV 2006.
22. UNICEF 2002.

References

Annan, Kofi. 2005a. "Address to the 2005 World Summit." http://www.un.org/webcast/summit2005/statements/sg.htm (accessed August 2, 2006).

————. 2005b. "'In Larger Freedom': Decision Time at the UN." Foreign Affairs, May/ June, 84 (3). http://www.foreignaffairs.org (accessed August 24, 2006).

Boulding, Elise, and Daisaku Ikeda. 2006. *Heiwanobunka no kagayaku seikihe* (Building a Century of a "Culture of Peace"). Tokyo: Ushio Shuppansha.

Chowdhury, Anwarul. 2006. "Vision Statement at the international conference on Transforming the United Nations: Human Development, Regional Conflicts, and Global Governance in a Post-Westphalian World" sponsored by Toda Institute for Global Peace and Policy Research, February 4-5, in Los Angeles, USA.

Hammarskjöld, Dag. 1964 (2003). *Markings*. Trans. by Leif Sjoberg and W. H. Auden. New York: Alfred A. Knopf.

ICJ (International Court of Justice). 1996. "Legality of the Use or Threat of Nuclear Weapons." http://www.icj-cij.org/icjwww/icases/iunan/iunanframe.htm (accessed August 24, 2006).

Lauren, Paul Gordon. 1996. *Power and Prejudice: The Politics and Diplomacy of Racial Discrimination*. Boulder, CO: Westview Press.

Makiguchi, Tsunesaburo. 1996. "Jinsei chirigaku" (The Geography of Human Life). *Makiguchi Tsunesaburo zenshu* (The Complete Works of Tsunesaburo Makiguchi) 2. Tokyo: Daisan Bunmeisha.

Nichiren. 1999. *The Writings of Nichiren Daishonin*. Trans. and ed. by The Gosho Translation Committee. Tokyo: Soka Gakkai.

Ortega y Gasset, José. 1932 (Reprinted 1993). *The Revolt of the Masses*. New York, NY: Norton.

Roosevelt, Franklin. 1945. "Address to Congress on the Yalta Conference." http://www.presidency.ucsb.edu (accessed August 25, 2006).

Rotblat, Joseph, and Daisaku Ikeda. 2006. *A Quest for Global Peace: Rotblat and Ikeda on War, Ethics and the Nuclear Threat*. London: IB Tauris.

SGI (Soka Gakkai International). 1995. "SGI Charter." http://www.sgi.org/english/SGI/ charter.htm (accessed August 23, 2006).

UN (United Nations). 1945. "Charter of the United Nations." http://www.un.org/aboutun/charter/index.html (accessed July 17, 2006).

————. 2004. "Strengthening of the United Nations System-Note by the Secretary-General." A/58/817. June 11, New York. http://www.un.org/reform/a_58_817.pdf (accessed August 4, 2006).

————. 2006. "Resolution 1701 (2006)." Resolution adopted by the Security Council. S/RES/1701. August 11. http://daccess-ods.un.org/TMP/186897.html (accessed August 23, 2006).

UNDP (United Nations Development Programme). 2005. "More Aid, Pro-Poor Trade Reform, and Long-Term Peace-Building Vital to Ending Extreme Poverty." http://hdr.undp.org/reports/global/2005/pdf/presskit/HDR05_PR1E.pdf (accessed August 24, 2006).

————. 2006. "2006 Annual Report." http://www.undp.org/publications/annualreport2006/english-report.pdf (accessed August 23, 2006).

UNICEF (United Nations Children's Fund). 2002. "2002 UNICEF Annual Report." http:// www.unicef.org/publications/files/pub_ar02_en.pdf (accessed August 4, 2006).

UNV (United Nations Volunteers). 2006. "UN Volunteers for Peace and Development." http://www.unvolunteers.org (accessed August 24, 2006).

Urquhart, Brian. 1972 (1994). *Hammarskjöld*. New York, NY: Norton.

Wayman, Alex, and Hideko Wayman. 1974. *The Lion's Roar of Queen Srimala: A Buddhist Scripture on the Tathagata-garbha Theory*. New York: Columbia University Press.

WMDC (Weapons of Mass Destruction Commission). 2006. "Weapons of Terror: Freeing the World of Nuclear, Biological, and Chemical Arms." http://www.wmdcommission.org/files/Weapons_of_terror.pdf (accessed August 4, 2006).

New UN Initiatives for the Protection of International Human Rights

Ved P. Nanda

At the first session of the newly-created United Nations Human Rights Council on June 19, 2006, the then-president of the General Assembly, Jan Eliasson, paid a special tribute to then-secretary-general Kofi Annan, for reinforcing "the vision of a United Nations founded on three pillars: development, peace and security, and respect for human rights, all mutually reinforcing."[1] He recalled the "decisive steps" taken by world leaders at the 2005 World Summit to strengthen the United Nations human rights machinery, which included "strengthening the Office of the High Commissioner for Human Rights, mainstreaming human rights throughout the UN system and creating a Human Rights Council."[2]

Historians will certainly marvel at such a rapid transformation of the idea of international human rights into a developed human rights system including mechanisms for enforcement and implementation at national regional and international levels, with the roots of the international human rights movement in the atrocities that humanity witnessed in the Second World War. The UN Charter embodied member states' obligations to "take joint and separate action" toward promoting "universal respect for, and observance of human rights and fundamental freedoms for all without distinction as to race, sex, language, or religion."[3] Also, in the Charter preamble, the peoples of the United Nations reaffirmed their "faith in fundamental human rights, in the dignity and worth of the human person, in the equal rights of men and women and of nations large and small."[4] However, protection of human rights was nowhere mentioned in the Charter.

Subsequently, in 1948 the UN General Assembly adopted the Universal Declaration[5] of Human Rights, which enumerated several civil, political, economic, social, and cultural rights. This was followed by the drafting and promulgation of the International Covenant on Civil and Political

Rights[6] and the International Covenant on Economic, Social and Cultural Rights.[7] Contrasted with the Declaration's nonbinding obligations, states ratifying the Covenants accepted legally binding obligations. Together, the Declaration and the Covenants are known as the International Bill of Rights.

These developments pertaining to human rights were in sharp contrast with the era preceding World War II when state sovereignty meant that a state could treat persons within its territory as it pleased. The only exception was for the alien, who had to be provided minimum standards of treatment so as to not offend the alien's government of nationality.

During the six decades since the establishment of the United Nations, international human rights law has come of age. On a wide range of human rights issues, a dynamic new body of norms, institutions, and procedures has transformed the subject, adding significantly to the corpus of international law. Regional human rights machinery, which exists in Europe, Latin America, and Africa, is often more effective than the United Nations in providing remedies. It should be noted that most of these changes have come about as a result of international, regional, and bilateral treaties. However, customary international law has also played an important role in promoting and protecting human rights.

Major UN initiatives for the promotion and protection of human rights have included the following:

1) the establishment of norms by international agreements and of treaty bodies to monitor implementation by member states of their treaty obligations;
2) the establishment of the UN Commission on Human Rights and its special procedures and now of the Human Rights Council, replacing the Commission and continuing with the mechanism created under the Commission;
3) the establishment of the Office of the High Commissioner for Human Rights, which in May 2005 submitted a strategic plan for the future of the Office, aimed at strengthening the Office so that it could "play its central role" in meeting the challenge of addressing today's threats to human rights posed by "poverty, discrimination, conflict, impunity, democratic deficits and institutional weaknesses [, which] will necessitate a heightened focus on implementation;"[8] and
4) the endorsement at the September 2005 World Summit of the "responsibility to protect" principle.

From among the various UN initiatives for the promotion and protection of human rights, two recent initiatives will be studied here: the establishment of the Human Rights Council by the General Assembly on March 15, 2006,[9] to replace the UN Commission on Human Rights, and 2) the endorsement of the "responsibility to protect" principle by Heads of State and Government who met at a World Summit at UN Headquarters in

New York from September 14 to 16, 2005.[10] The next sections will provide a historical context for this study. The following sections will review these initiatives. The final section, on appraisal and recommendations, will focus on the challenges of implementation and enforcement. The tragic events of Darfur, Sudan provide an apt case study that highlights the difficulty of translating the laudable principle of responsibility to protect into concrete action with a tangible outcome.

Historical Context

In 1946, the United Nations undertook the first major human rights initiative by creating an institutional structure, the UN Commission on Human Rights, but the Commission was not authorized to provide any redress to those who communicated to the United Nations that their human rights had been violated.[11] The Commission's 1947 decision that it had no power to take any action regarding any complaints concerning human rights was approved twelve years later in 1959 by the Economic and Social Council, the United Nations body to which the Commission reported.[12] However, since that time the Commission has undertaken "country mandates," investigating, examining, monitoring, advising, and publicly reporting on human rights situations in specific countries, and "thematic mandates" on major phenomena of violations of human rights anywhere in the world. The Commission has developed these special procedures and has appointed independent experts, special rapporteurs and representatives, and working groups on situations in specific countries, as well as on specific themes.

In 1947, the Commission established a Sub-Commission on Prevention of Discrimination and Protection of Minorities, whose name was changed in 1999 to Sub-Commission on the Promotion and Protection of Human Rights. The Sub-Commission, a body of independent, impartial experts, conducts studies on a range of issues related to discrimination and minorities and makes recommendations to the Commission.

To briefly recapitulate highlights of these developments, in 1967 the Economic and Social Council adopted Resolution 1235 authorizing the Commission and the Sub-Commission "to examine information relevant to gross violations of human rights and fundamental freedoms" and decided that the Commission "may, in appropriate cases ... make a thorough study of situations which reveal a consistent pattern of violations of human rights ... and report, with recommendations thereon, to the Economic and Social Council."[13]

Notwithstanding Resolution 1235's authorization to the Commission to examine relevant information pertaining to gross violations of human rights and to conduct studies regarding situations revealing a consistent pattern of violations of human rights, the Commission could not refer to the substance of the communications and complaints received because they remained confidential as required by the earlier Economic and Social Council mandate.[14] And there were no guidelines to consider or analyze those communications. To remedy this situation, the Economic and Social Council, pursuant to the Commission's recommendation, provided procedures for considering and analyzing communications relating to violations of human rights in Resolution 1503, adopted in 1970.[15]

A three-stage process was instituted under the human rights complaints mechanism created by Resolution 1503, the 1503 procedure, consisting of initial screening by a working group of the Sub-Commission, then by the Sub-Commission itself, and finally by the Commission. The confidential procedure authorizes submission of communications by individuals, groups, or nongovernmental organizations. Thus, the Commission would consider allegations of widespread patterns of gross violations of human rights in any country. The countries that are the subject of discussion are named under this procedure.

Along with the country procedures, thematic procedures were also instituted to address broader human rights issues ranging from disappearances, torture, arbitrary detention, and extrajudicial executions to the right to health, education, and the welfare of internally displaced persons and minorities, as mentioned earlier. The Commission's system of special procedures, aimed at the promotion and protection of human rights, includes independent experts, special rapporteurs, working groups, and special representatives of the secretary-general or the high commissioner for human rights, who seek and receive information and respond as appropriate. Various activities under special procedures include promoting human rights, responding to individual complaints, conducting studies, and advising on technical cooperation.

The range and scope of the mandates, mechanisms, and responsibilities under these procedures can be appreciated as one reviews the report of the Commission's concluding session[16] and the June 2006 Report of the newly-elected Human Rights Council (HRC) at the conclusion of its first session, as the Council decided to extend the mandates and the mandate-holders of all the Commission's special procedures.[17] These special procedures of the Commission and the Sub-Commission extended by the Council numbered more than fifty.

Regarding the second initiative studied here, the "responsibility to protect," unilateral or even collective "humanitarian intervention" has been controversial under international law.[18] Unilateral interventions by powerful states in the pre-UN era, purportedly undertaken on humanitarian grounds, were often simply pretexts for the intervening states to further their own interests. Hence, this new initiative was undertaken to ensure legitimacy of collective action under the auspices of the Security Council to protect human rights of individuals and groups suffering massive violations in failed states, states undergoing convulsions of civil wars, or states under tyrannical regimes.

The Human Rights Council

The 53-member UN Commission on Human Rights had come under severe criticism for many years as being ineffective and politicized. A task force of the American Bar Association's Section on International Law, on which I served, stated in August 2005 that "The standing of the Commission was severely compromised by the selection of Libya as chair, the re-election of Sudan as a member in the midst of the genocide in Darfur, and the shameful failure of the Commission last year to adopt a resolution clearly condemning that genocide."[19] The secretary-general's High-Level Panel on Threats, Challenges and Change reported in December 2004 that the Commission's capacity to perform its tasks had been "undermined by eroding credibility ... [as] in recent years States have sought membership of the Commission not to strengthen human rights but to protect themselves against criticism or to criticize others. The Commission cannot be credible if it is seen to be maintaining double standards in addressing human rights concerns."[20] Subsequently, the secretary-general in his March 2005 speech to the General Assembly noted that the Commission's "credibility deficit ... casts a shadow on the reputation of the United Nations system as a whole."[21]

In light of the Commission's obsession in singling out one country, Israel, for repeated condemnation,[22] while showing little concern and sensitivity to egregious abuses around the world, most observers applauded its replacement by the HRC. Louise Arbour, high commissioner for human rights, hailed the Council as

uniquely positioned to redress the shortcomings of the past. It is empowered to devise the means that will prevent abuses, protect the most vulnerable, and expose perpetrators. By presenting their candidates, as well as their pledges and commitments to promote and uphold human rights, Council members have already assumed solemn obligations in the eyes of all people.[23]

In his address to the Council, then-UN Secretary-General Kofi Annan said the establishment of the Council would be "remembered as a historic achievement," exhorting the Council members to bring about "a change in culture [to replace] the culture of confrontation and distrust, which pervaded the commission in its final years, [by] a culture of cooperation and commitment, inspired by mature leadership."[24] Earlier, on March 15, 2006, he had stated,

> The true test of the Council's credibility will be the use that member states make of it. If, in the weeks and months ahead, they act on the commitments they have given… I am confident that the Council will breathe new life in all our work for human rights, and thereby help to improve the lives of millions of people throughout the world.[25]

Then-president of the UN General Assembly, Jan Eliasson, in addressing the opening session of the Council, said, "We are entering a new chapter in the United Nations' work on human rights."[26] Human rights NGOs also welcomed the creation of the new Council.[27]

During the period leading to the establishment of the Council, many reform proposals addressed the Council's size, criteria for membership, composition, election process, status in the UN hierarchy, functions, and member responsibilities. Most suggestions were for a smaller body that would be nimble and elected directly by the General Assembly with a two-thirds majority of members present and voting, to ensure that abusers of human rights are not elected. The secretary-general's proposal, contained in his report of May 23, 2005, is worth noting:

> [The Council's] main task would be to evaluate the fulfillment by all States of all their human rights obligations. And, it should be equipped to give technical assistance to States and policy advice to States and United Nations bodies alike. Under such a system, every Member State could come up for review on a periodic basis. Any such rotation should not, however, impede the Council from dealing with any massive and gross violations that might occur. Indeed, the Council will have to be able to bring urgent crises to the attention of the world community.[28]

The ABA Task Force suggested that the Council should have equal status with the Economic and Social Council and the General Assembly, but as that would require amendment of the Charter, the Council be established as a subsidiary body of the General Assembly in the interim. It further recommended that the Council be converted to its enhanced status when Charter amendments are next presented to the membership.[29] Among the Task Force's other suggestions, one was that any member under Chapter VII action of the Security Council or under censure of the Human Rights Council should be prohibited from serving on the Council.[30] Another recommendation was for the Council to adopt a Code of

Conduct "committing the Member States to promote international protection of human rights—to cooperate with the investigative mechanisms of the Council ... and to appoint as heads of their delegations persons with substantial human rights expertise."[31] Finally, the Task Force made recommendations for the Council to enhance the participation of NGOs in the Council's work.[32] Among other recommendations, a major study undertaken pursuant to the US Congress' establishment of a bipartisan task force on the United Nations recommended that the US Government "support the creation of a Human Rights Council, ideally composed of democracies, to monitor and enforce human rights."[33]

The HRC, created as a subsidiary organ of the General Assembly under Resolution 60/251, mentioned earlier, is a body of 47 members divided among the five regional groups at the United Nations. There are thirteen from the African group, thirteen from the Asian group, six from the Eastern European group, eight from the Latin American and Caribbean group, and seven from the group of Western European and other states, elected by secret ballot by a majority vote in the General Assembly to serve for a period of three years.[34] Membership requires the "contribution of candidates to the promotion and protection of human rights and their voluntary pledges and commitments made thereto," and by a two-thirds majority of the members present and voting, the General Assembly "may suspend the rights of membership of a member of the Council that commits gross and systematic violations of human rights."[35] Under the resolution, elected members "shall uphold the highest standards in the promotion and protection of human rights, [and they] shall fully cooperate with the Council and be reviewed under the universal period review mechanism during their term of membership."[36] The Council is to submit an annual report to the General Assembly.[37]

These developments indeed show an improvement compared with the Commission's status, election procedures, and membership requirements. The Commission had been a subsidiary body of the Economic and Social Council and members were simply appointed by regional groups without any meaningful membership criteria. However, although the Council's size is reduced from 53 members on the Commission to 47 on the Council, this does not transform the body into a much smaller one, as many proposing reform had suggested. And despite the membership criteria enumerated in Resolution 60/251, Azerbaijan, China, Cuba, Pakistan, and Saudi Arabia, certainly no champions of human rights, were elected as members, although Iran failed to secure a seat. As UN Watch has assessed, 47 percent of the new Council's membership is non-democratic under Freedom House's standards.[38]

Resolution 60/251 specifies the Council's responsibilities to promote "universal respect for the protection of all human rights and fundamental freedoms for all, without distinction of any kind and in a fair and equal manner."[39] The Council's other functions include the following:

- to "address situations of violations of human rights, including gross and systematic violations, and make recommendations thereon"[40]
- to promote "human rights education and learning as well as advisory services, technical assistance, and capacity-building"[41]
- to serve "as a forum for dialogue on thematic issues on all human rights"[42]
- to make recommendations to the General Assembly "for the further development of international law in the field of human rights"[43]
- to promote "the full implementation of human rights obligations undertaken by states and [their] commitments related to the promotion and protection of human rights"[44]
- to undertake "a universal periodic review ... of the fulfillment by each State of its human rights obligations and commitments."[45]
- to contribute "through dialogue and cooperation, towards the prevention of human rights violations and respond promptly to human rights emergencies."[46]

The resolution states that the Council's work "shall be guided by the principles of universality, impartiality, objectivity and non-selectivity, constructive international dialogue and cooperation, with a view to enhancing the promotion and protection of all human rights."[47] Finally, it mandates elected members to "uphold the highest standards in the promotion and protection of human rights ... fully cooperate with the Council and be reviewed under the universal periodic review mechanism during their term of membership."[48]

Based upon the Council's first regular session of June 19-30, 2006, and its two special sessions, the first held on July 5 and 6, and the second on August 11, 2006, the record is mixed. On the positive side, the Council at its first regular session recommended to the General Assembly the adoption of two instruments: the draft International Convention for the Protection of All Persons from Enforced Disappearances[49] and the draft Declaration on the Rights of Indigenous Peoples.[50] Both of these instruments had been negotiated for several years by working groups established under the Human Rights Commission. The Council decided to continue three other working groups that the Commission had established; one negotiating an Optional Protocol to the International Covenant on Economic, Social and Cultural Rights to establish a complaints procedure,[51] one studying and making recommendations on the right to development,[52] and one studying existing treaty provisions on racism, to identify gaps and recommend improvements.[53] The Council also decided to extend "all mandates, mechanisms, functions and responsibilities of the Commission on Human Rights";[54] to establish a working group to review these mandates, mechanisms, functions and responsibilities,[55] and to establish a working group to "develop the modalities of the universal periodic review mechanism."[56]

All these Council decisions and resolutions were adopted by consensus but for the Declaration on the Rights of Indigenous Peoples, which passed by a vote of 30 in favor to two against and twelve abstentions. The Council also responded positively to NGO participation although NGO participants did not have sufficient speaking time.[57]

The Council's president made two statements at the first session. One was to welcome the entry into force of the Optional Protocol to the Convention Against Torture and Other Cruel, Inhuman or Degrading Treatment or Punishment as it received ratification by 20 states on June 22, 2006. He called upon states parties to give early consideration to signing and ratifying the Optional Protocol under which inspection of detention facilities will be required.[58] The second statement reaffirmed that "all acts of hostage-taking, wherever and by whoever committed, are a serious crime aimed at the destruction of human rights and are, under any circumstances, unjustifiable," and strongly condemned such actions anywhere in the world, calling for concerted efforts by the international community to bring an end to such abhorrent practices.[59]

On the negative front, notwithstanding the exhortations by the UN secretary-general and others, such as Jan Eliasson, who had called upon the Council to "strive to vindicate the expectations and hopes of all people whose welfare so urgently depends on this new body's decisions and action" from its very inception,[60] the Council took no decision and no action against any country but Israel. It censured Israel for its alleged violations in "Palestine and other occupied Arab territories" by a vote of 29 in favor, twelve against, and five abstentions. It requested the relevant special rapporteurs to report on the "Israeli human rights violations in occupied Palestine" to the next session of the Council and decided "to undertake substantive consideration of the human rights violations and implications of the Israeli occupation of Palestine and other occupied Arab territories at its next session and to incorporate this issue in following sessions."[61] Another resolution, on "incitement to racial and religious hatred," a reaction to the Danish newspaper cartoon controversy, was also adopted by a vote of 33 in favor to twelve against and one abstention.[62]

At its first special session the Human Rights Council expressed "deep" and "grave" concern at the alleged human rights violations against the Palestinian people by Israel in the occupied Palestine territory. It decided to dispatch "an urgent fact-finding mission" headed by its special rapporteur on the subject.[63]

At the second special session, on the human rights situation in Lebanon, the Council "[s]trongly condemn[ed] the grave Israeli violations of human rights and breaches of international humanitarian law in Lebanon and decided "to urgently establish and immediately dispatch a high-level commission of inquiry":

a)   to investigate the systematic targeting and killing of civilians by Israel and Lebanon;
b)   to examine the types of weapons used by Israel and their conformity with international law;
c)   to assess the extent and deadly impact of Israeli attacks on human life, property, critical infrastructure and the environment[.][64]

Subsequently, on August 7, the Sub-Commission condemned Israel in a statement for "massive denial and violation and denial of human rights in Lebanon," ignoring Hezbollah's role in attacking Israel and bombing Israeli cities, but also violating its own legal mandate, which forbids it from addressing country-specific situations under the UN Commission on Human Rights Resolution 2005/53.[65] Also, on August 3, the Committee on the Elimination of Racial Discrimination debated "the humanitarian crisis in Lebanon," notwithstanding the section being outside CERD's mandate.[66]

The Council's decisions and actions regarding Israel demonstrate that it is continuing to follow the one-sided approach, which was a hallmark of the Commission's activities and a major reason for its replacement. Major international human rights NGOs including Amnesty International, Human Rights Watch, and Human Rights First have uniformly condemned the Council's approach.[67] Furthermore, it is hard to explain the Council's indifference to the tragedy in Darfur, for although statements were made by some countries at the Council Meeting, it did not take any action on the subject.[68]

The Responsibility to Protect

The endorsement of the "responsibility to protect" doctrine at the World Summit of Heads of State and Government in September 2005 on the occasion of the United Nations' 60th anniversary is an important development moving away from the controversial concept of humanitarian intervention. Critics consider humanitarian intervention that is coercive intervention by military action against a state to protect people in that state suffering or risking massive violations of human rights, to be a prohibited intrusion on state sovereignty. They invoke the traditional concept of state sovereignty and especially cite Article 2(7) of the UN Charter, claiming immunity from intervention, as the article reads: "Nothing contained in the present Charter shall authorize the United Nations to intervene in matters which are essentially within the domestic jurisdiction of any state or shall require the Members to submit such matters to settlement under the present Charter."

In the contemporary state-centered international system, sovereignty and nonintervention are indeed seen as sacrosanct concepts under international law, the United Nations organization itself is based on the principle of the sovereign equality of its member states, and intervention could be perceived, especially in those states with colonial experiences, as undermining the sovereign authority of the state, by external forces.[69]

Notwithstanding a strict textual interpretation of the Article 2(7) mandate of nonintervention and Article 2(4)'s broad prohibition on the unilateral use of force in international relations,[70] humanitarian intervention has its proponents.[71] The rationale for the use of force was that if the UN Security Council is paralyzed and there is inaction on the part of regional organizations, an alternative must be found to protect people threatened with genocide, ethnic cleansing, or massive violations of human rights.

Secretary-General Kofi Annan's 2000 response to critics of humanitarian intervention is noteworthy, as he asks, "If humanitarian intervention is, indeed, an unacceptable assault on sovereignty, how should we respond to a Rwanda, to a Srebrenica—to gross and systematic violations of human rights that affect every precept of our common humanity?"[72] As early as a decade preceding the World Summit, Francis Deng, who served as the special representative of the secretary-general on internally displaced persons, had unequivocally stated in his studies that sovereignty entails responsibility—in Frontiers of Sovereignty (1995)[73] and Sovereignty as Responsibility: Conflict Management in Africa (1996).[74]

In his address to the General Assembly in 2003, Kofi Annan spoke about intervention, urging the Security Council members:

to engage in serious discussions of the best way to respond to threats of genocide or other comparable massive violations of human rights—an issue which I raised from this podium in 1999. Once again this year, our collective response to events of this type—in the Democratic Republic of the Congo, and in Liberia—has been hesitant and tardy.[75]

In light of the United Nations' inability to prevent and later stop the Rwandan tragedy, the international community searched for an effective response to situations when massive violations of human rights occur in a state and the state is unable or unwilling to protect the victims. This search led to several initiatives, including those by the Danish,[76] Dutch,[77] and Swedish[78] governments, US Department of State,[79] and the Council on Foreign Relations.[80] The most influential of these initiatives was a Canadian government study, resulting in a December 2001 report of the International Commission on Intervention and State Sovereignty, entitled "The Responsibility to Protect."[81]

The Canadian Commission had already completed its work on the report before the September 11, 2001, terrorist attack, but its co-chairs revisited the project on September 13 to refer to the tragedy in their foreword. There they stated that the report was in response to the challenge posed by the UN secretary-general in both 1999 and 2000 to the General Assembly, noted earlier.[82]

The co-chairs stated that the title of their report reflected its central theme, "the idea that sovereign states have a responsibility to protect their own citizens from avoidable catastrophe—from mass murder, rape, and starvation—but that when they are unwilling or unable to do so, that responsibility must be borne by the broader community of states."[83] In addressing the events of September 11, they stated that the report was not aimed at the kind of challenge posed by such attacks, but instead at providing "precise guidance for states faced with human protection claims in other states; it has not been framed to guide the policy of states when faced with attacks on their own nationals, or the nationals of other states residing within their borders."[84]

The Commission rejected the traditional language of the "right of humanitarian intervention" or the "right to intervene," finding such language unhelpful, and therefore shifted the debate to focus instead on "the responsibility to protect," suggesting that the "proposed change in terminology is also a change in perspective, reversing the perceptions inherent in the traditional language."[85] In clarifying the term, the Canadian Commission noted that it implies focusing on the point of view not of those who may be considering intervention but of those seeking or needing support.[86] Furthermore, it explained that—

[T]he responsibility to protect acknowledges that the primary responsibility in this regard rests with the state concerned, and that it is only if the state is unable or unwilling to fulfill this responsibility, or is itself the perpetrator, that it becomes the responsibility of the international community to act in its place, and that the responsibility to protect includes not just the responsibility to react but also the responsibility to prevent and the responsibility to rebuild.[87]

Before concluding that military intervention for human protection purposes is warranted as an extraordinary and exceptional measure, the Canadian Commission had undertaken consultations around the world and considered various legal, political, moral, and operational aspects of the subject. It determined that the threshold for such intervention is when:

> serious and irreparable harm [is] occurring to human beings, or imminently likely to occur, of the following kind: A. large-scale loss of life, actual or apprehended, with genocidal intent or not, which is the product either of deliberate state action, or state neglect or inability to act, or a failed state situation; or B. large-scale "ethnic cleansing," actual or apprehended, whether carried out by killing, forced expulsion, acts of terror or rape.[88]

The Commission enumerated four precautionary principles to guide the use of force when the above-mentioned "just cause" threshold had been reached: right intention, last resort, proportional means, and reasonable prospects of success—in halting or averting the suffering "with the consequences of action not likely to be worse than the consequences of inaction."[89]

The timing of the study was not auspicious. After the events of 9/11 in the United States, the world was preoccupied with seeking effective means to counter terrorism. One of the co-chairs of the Commission, Gareth Evans, who serves as president of International Crisis Group, said in an address at the University of New South Wales, Australia, that while the problems of humanitarian intervention were at the center of international policy debate throughout the 1990s, since 9/11 attention has rather comprehensively shifted to a range of other, and in some respects perhaps more glamorous, security problems: terrorism, Islamism, nuclear proliferation, stability in the Middle East post-Iraq and post-Hamas, and, related in turn to most of these, global energy security.[90]

Combined with the aftermath of 9/11, the invasion of Iraq was not helpful to the proponents of the responsibility to protect. For the invasion, justified in part on protecting Iraqis from Saddam Hussein's oppression, could be viewed as an illustration of how the concept could be misused or abused by powerful states.

The response by nongovernmental organizations was rather mixed. The World Federalist Movement's Institute for Global Policy, which initiated consultations about the Commission report to determine whether civil society would find the principles useful and to be supported for advocacy campaigns, reported that the NGOs consulted "showed little interest in advocating a doctrine aimed at justifying military interventions, particularly those that occur without Security Council or multilateral approval."[91] However, the crisis in the Darfur region of Sudan, which began making headlines in early 2003, focused the world's attention on the need to effectively respond to humanitarian crises and thus to the principles of the responsibility to protect.[92]

Following the secretary-general's September 2003 address to the General Assembly, he established a panel of eminent persons, a High-Level Panel on Threats, Challenges and Change, to examine the challenges to peace and security and the contribution of collective action to address such challenges. The panel gave its report in December 2004, concluding that state sovereignty "clearly carries with it the obligation of a State to protect the welfare of its own peoples and meet its obligations to the wider international community."[93] However, when a state is unable or unwilling to meet this responsibility, "the principles of collective security mean that some portion of those responsibilities should be taken up by the international community."[94]

The Panel acknowledged that Rwanda was the biggest failure,[95] as "[c]ollective security institutions have proved particularly poor at meeting the challenge posed by large-scale, gross human rights abuses and genocide."[96] The Panel specifically stated that the humanitarian disasters in Somalia, Bosnia, Rwanda, Kosovo, and Darfur "have concentrated attention not on the immunities of sovereign Governments but their responsibilities, both to their own people and to the wider international community."[97] Thus, the Panel noted that:

> There is a growing recognition that the issue is not the "right to intervene" of any State, but the "responsibility to protect" of every State when it comes to people suffering from avoidable catastrophe—mass murder and rape, ethnic cleansing by forcible expulsion and terror, and deliberate starvation and exposure to disease.[98]

After deliberating on the prior failures of collective security, the Panel determined:

> We endorse the emerging norm that there is a collective international responsibility to protect, exercisable by the Security Council, authorizing military intervention as a last resort, in the event of genocide and other large-scale killing, ethnic cleansing or serious violations of international humanitarian law which sovereign Governments have proved powerless or unwilling to prevent.[99]

Finally, the Panel addressed the criteria to determine the Security Council's legitimacy to authorize or endorse the use of military force. It enumerated five basic criteria: seriousness of the threat; proper purpose; last resort; proportional means; and balance of consequences (reasonable chance of success, and consequences of action not likely to be worse than the consequences of inaction).[100] The Panel called upon the Security Council and General Assembly to adopt declaratory resolutions embodying these guidelines.[101]

A June 2005 report by the US Institute of Peace, the outcome of a study undertaken by the Institute pursuant to the US Congressional action establishing a bipartisan taskforce on the United Nations, endorsed and called on "the UN Security Council and General Assembly to affirm a responsibility of every sovereign government to protect its own citizenry and those within its borders from genocide, mass killing, and massive and sustained human rights violations."[102] Among other recommendations, the Report called for the United States to provide leadership to the Security Council for it to take effective action on this issue. It also called on regional organizations and member states to act for humanitarian purposes when and if the Security Council is unable to take effective action in such situations.[103]

When the World Summit met in September 2005, the reports of all these initiatives were before the member states. The Summit endorsed the emerging norm that each individual state has the responsibility to protect its populations from genocide, war crimes, ethnic cleansing, and crimes against humanity, and it called upon the international community to assume responsibility to help to protect populations from these crimes and to support the United Nations in establishing an early warning capability.[104] It seems appropriate to note the exact language of the Summit outcome:

> Each individual State has the responsibility to protect its populations from genocide, war crimes, ethnic cleansing and crimes against humanity. This responsibility entails the prevention of such crimes... The international community should ... support the United Nations in establishing an early warning capability.[105]

Further it is said that:

> The international community, through the United Nations, also has the responsibility to use appropriate diplomatic, humanitarian and other peaceful means ... to help to protect populations from genocide, war crimes, ethnic cleansing and crimes against humanity. In this context, we are prepared to take collective action, in a timely and decisive manner, through the Security Council, ... on a case-by-case basis and in co-operation with relevant regional organizations as appropriate, should peaceful means be inadequate and national authorizes are manifestly failing to protect their populations from genocide, war crimes, ethnic cleansing and crimes against humanity.[106]

In conclusion:

> We fully support the mission of the Special Adviser of the Secretary-General on the prevention of Genocide.[107]

Subsequently, on April 20, 2006, the Security Council adopted Resolution 1674 on the protection of civilians in armed conflict,[108] in which it reaffirmed the "provisions of paragraphs 138 and 139 of the 2005 World Summit Outcome Document regarding the responsibility to protect populations from genocide, war crimes, ethnic cleansing and crimes against humanity."[109] In his statement at the Security Council open debate on the protection of civilians in armed conflict on June 28, 2006, then UN Under-Secretary-General Jan Egeland said:

> We as the UN, and you as the Security Council, now have the responsibility to protect as reaffirmed in Resolution 1674. There are too many times when we still do not come to the defense of civilian populations in need. When our response is weak, we appear to wash our hands of our humanitarian responsibilities to protect lives. The world is a safer place for most of us, but it is still a deathtrap for too many defenseless civilians, men, women and children.[110]

The endorsement by the World Summit of the "responsibility to protect" principle and its subsequent reaffirmation by the Security Council unambiguously put to rest the ongoing controversy regarding the nature and scope of a state's rights under the traditional doctrine of state sovereignty and the scope of the Article 2(7) prohibition on intervention in internal affairs.

However, the Security Council and the General Assembly have yet to enumerate guidelines for the use of force by the Security Council. And as the following discussion shows, the Security Council has shown little inclination to take effective action to halt the atrocities committed on the population of Darfur in western Sudan. Darfur, indeed, raises serious questions regarding the implementation and enforcement of the responsibility to protect principle.

Darfur, the African Union, and the United Nations

In his July 2006 report to the UN Security Council on Darfur, Kofi Annan provided a brief history of the conflict in the region:[111]

> When the current conflict erupted in February 2003, Darfur had already long experienced localized violence exacerbated by ethnic, economic and political dimensions and competition over increasingly scarce resources... The notorious Janjaweed, coupled with militia attacks and indiscriminate air bombardment, contributed to the razing and burning of villages, the rape of girls and women, the abduction of children, and the destruction of food and water resources. The result has been death, devastation and displacement in Darfur, with more than 200,000 civilian casualties, more than 2 million people displaced from their homes and condemned to misery, and millions more having their livelihoods destroyed.[112]

He added that the Darfur Crisis:

also threatens regional peace and security. The 1000 kilometer border between the Sudan and Chad has been repeatedly violated by armed groups and has ratcheted up tension between Khartoum and N'Djamena. The cross-border violence has also led to additional flows of refugees and internally displaced persons in both Chad and the Sudan, exacerbating the humanitarian crisis in the region.[113]

The African Union and its international partners, including the United Nations, had made several political efforts over the years to seek a solution to the crisis, which ultimately led to the signing of the Darfur Peace Agreement on May 5, 2006,[114] between the Sudanese government and the biggest Darfur rebel group. The African Union's political initiatives were also complemented by their deployment of 7,200 AU peacekeeping troops in Darfur.[115] In view of the signing of the Darfur Peace Agreement, the African Union Peace and Security Council decided on May 15, 2006, that "concrete steps should be taken to effect the transition from AMIS to a United Nations peacekeeping operation," a decision reaffirmed subsequently.[116]

The four elements of the agreement were power-sharing, wealth-sharing, comprehensive ceasefire and security arrangements, and the dialogue and consultation process under the African Union leadership aimed at promoting reconciliation and broader ownership of the Darfur peace process. Under power-sharing, the parties agreed to establish a federal system of government and to hold a referendum by July 2010 to determine the future status of Darfur, and to provide for the rebel movements' representation in the state legislatures, in the national civil service, armed forces, and the police.[117] As to wealth-sharing, a formula would be devised for transferring funding from Khartoum to the Darfur states and compensation would be provided for war victims.[118]

Concerning the security arrangements, the agreement was reached to strengthen the mechanisms for monitoring and verifying the existing ceasefire and to provide security for internally displaced persons. It was also agreed that the government would disarm the Janjaweed and armed militia.[119] Finally, under AU leadership, a Darfur-Darfur Dialogue and Consultation would be convened with the government, rebel movements, civil society organizations, tribal leaders, the United Nations, the European Union, and the League of Arab States participating on a preparatory committee.[120]

The secretary-general made specific recommendations regarding the UN peace support operation in Darfur,[121] based upon which the UN Security Council adopted Resolution 1706 on August 31, 2006, determining the mandate of the United Nations Mission in the Sudan (UNMIS).[122] The Security Council reaffirmed "its strong commitment to the sovereignty, unity, independence, and territorial integrity of the Sudan, which would be unaffected by transition to a UN operation in Darfur, and to the cause of peace."[123] It decided that:

> UNMIS shall be strengthened by up to 17,317 military personnel and by an appropriate civilian component including up to 3,300 civilian police personnel ... and expresse[d] its determination to keep UNMIS' strength and structure under regular review, taking into account the evolution of the situation on the ground.[124]

It gave a broad mandate to UNMIS in Darfur to support implementation of the peace agreement of May 5, 2006.[125] The Resolution specified several tasks, including assisting the parties "in promoting the rule of law, including an independent judiciary, and the protection of human rights of all people of the Sudan, [and ensuring] an adequate human rights and gender presence, capacity and expertise within UNMIS to carry out human rights promotion, civilian protection and monitoring activities that include particular attention to the needs of women and children."[126]

Earlier, the Security Council had adopted Resolution 1679 on May 16, 2006,[127] under which it determined that the situation in the Sudan continued to constitute a threat to international peace and security and hence, acting under Chapter VII of the UN Charter, it endorsed the decision of the African Union's 15-member Peace and Security Council taken on May 15, 2006, that, "in view of the signing of the Darfur Peace Agreement, concrete steps should be taken to effect the transition from AMIS [African Union Mission in the Sudan] to a United Nations operation."[128] However, the Council reaffirmed "its strong commitment to the sovereignty, unity, independence, and territorial integrity of the Sudan, which would be unaffected by transition to a United Nations operation, as well as of all States in the region, and to the cause of peace, security and reconciliation throughout the Sudan."[129]

As the AU peacekeepers were not only insufficient in number, but were also ill-equipped, under-funded, and without adequate resources to halt the violence in Darfur, need for transition to a UN operation was apparent. The Darfur issue received special international attention in September 2006, as the opening of the sixty-first session of the UN General Assembly provided an opportunity for world leaders to address it. On September 17, peace advocates around the world marked Darfur Day, demonstrating to demand action from their leaders to protect the civilian population in Darfur facing a severe humanitarian crisis.[130]

Addressing the UN General Assembly on September 19, 2006, United State President George W. Bush spoke to the people of Darfur:

> You have suffered unspeakable violence, and my nation has called these atrocities what they are—genocide… [W]e must strengthen the African Union force that has done good work, but is not strong enough to protect you. The Security Council has approved a resolution that would transform the African Union into a blue helmeted force that is larger and more robust. To increase its strength and effectiveness, NATO nations should provide logistics and other support. The regime in Khartoum is stopping the deployment of this force. If the Sudanese government does not approve this peacekeeping force quickly, the United Nations must act. Your lives and the credibility of the United Nations are at stake. So today I'm … naming a Presidential Special Envoy … to lead America's efforts to resolve the outstanding disputes and help bring peace to your land.[131]

On the same day, Secretary-General Kofi Annan reminded the Assembly of the solemn proclamation it had made at the highest level in 2005, stating the international community's responsibility to protect populations from genocide, war crimes, ethnic cleansing, and crimes against humanity.[132] And yet, he added, "[O]nce again, the biggest challenge comes from Africa—from Darfur, where the continued spectacle of men, women and children driven from their homes by murder, rape and the burning of their villages makes a mockery of our claim, as an international community, to shield people from the worst abuses."[133]

The flurry of activities at the United Nations included a statement by the UN special representative to Sudan, Jan Pronk that the Darfur Peace Accord "is nearly dead. It is in a coma. It ought to be under intensive care, but it isn't."[134] He added that with the Sudanese government again launching a major military offensive and several rebel factions vying for power, fighting had again intensified.[135] Responding to the Sudanese leaders' description of UN peacekeepers as a Western invasion force, he said, "We do not intend to re-colonize, nor are we laying the carpet for others to do so."[136]

On September 20, after a meeting at the United Nations, the African Union's Peace and Security Council declared that it would extend its peacekeeping force in Darfur for three months until the end of the year and that it would strengthen it while seeking to persuade the Sudanese government to accept a new UN force to replace it.[137] The president of Burkina Faso, Blaise Compaorè, whose country chaired the Council in September, said that the force would be strengthened "through contributions from Africa, logistical and material support from the United Nations, and a commitment by the Arab League to fund the operation." Responding to Sudanese President Omar Hassan al-Bashir's persistent opposition to the UN force, he said: "The UN must play a role when regional arrangements cannot contain a conflict," adding "We had the impression that in our discussions with the Sudanese they are willing to work with the United Nations."[138]

On September 22, US Secretary of State Condoleezza Rice, along with her Danish counterpart, Ber Stig Moller, convened a gathering of representatives from 25 states to maintain international pressure on Sudan. She renewed her call that Sudan halt its military offensive in Darfur and allow UN peacekeepers in the region to protect civilians there. In her words, "It is now time for the Sudanese government to accept the will of the UN. Time is running out. The violence in Darfur is not subsiding. It is getting worse."[139] A senior UN official said that for the Sudanese president to invite the United Nations into Darfur, "[t]he message has to come from the Arab League and the African Union."[140]

Appraisal and Recommendations

As mentioned earlier, the overall record of the Human Rights Council's first regular session and the two special sessions was mixed. No resolution was introduced on the Darfur situation, nor was there any resolution adopted on any specific country violation. It is recommended that at its future sessions, the Council should:

1) take its charge seriously and lend credibility to its work by depoliticization of its activities and by moving away from being selective in continuing to target Israel;
2) discuss specific country violations and take action against some of the violating states;
3) maintain and strengthen the current Special Procedures; and
4) establish a strong, universal, periodic review system. The agenda the Human Rights Council sets and the issues on which it focuses its attention will determine how legitimate and effective it becomes as a new institution contrasted with the discredited Human Rights Commission that it replaced.

As to the implementation of the responsibility to protect principle, it is essential that the Security Council and the General Assembly adopt resolutions enumerating guidelines for the use of force by the Security Council, as recommended by the High-Level Panel in its report in which it had enumerated five basic criteria of legitimacy: seriousness of threat; proper purpose; last resort; proportional means; and balance of consequences.[141] Should it be a matter of concern that the threshold suggested by the World Summit for taking collective action does not include massive and sustained violations of human rights? Perhaps the "crimes against humanity" and "ethnic cleansing" criteria would encompass such violations.

How these criteria are applied in particular situations will depend upon the Security Council's determination reached in a contextual setting. However, as Gareth Evans has noted, there remain the problems of civil and military capacity, including issues of training, command and control, logistic support, transportation and communications.[142] He has aptly stated that even though the principle of the responsibility to protect has been widely accepted:

[W]e certainly still cannot be confident that world will respond quickly, effectively and appropriately to new human rights catastrophes as they arise. Overcoming global indifference means addressing four big recurring problems: the problem of perception, getting the story out and its gravity understood; the problem of responsibility (confronting traditional taboos against international involvement in sovereign countries' internal affairs); the problem of capacity (having available the appropriate institutional machinery and resources); and, as always, the problem of political will (effectively mobilizing that capacity, in the face of competing priorities and preoccupations).[143]

The world community faces a formidable challenge to create the appropriate political will so that effective action can be taken for the protection of those suffering or threatened with massive violation of human rights. Darfur presents a compelling illustration of this challenge. The question is not whether what has happened in Darfur should or would be characterized as genocide, for there is clear evidence of gross and persistent violation of human rights and ethnic cleansing in that region. Thus there is no excuse for inaction; and yet, there has been no concerted international action against Sudan.

The reason for inaction is the lack of consensus among the major powers. That is why the Security Council has not acted and why the world community has not taken collective action to impose financial sanctions, enforced a no-fly zone over Darfur, or even warned Sudanese leaders that the International Criminal Court has jurisdiction to hold them personally accountable for crimes against humanity committed there.[144]

In conclusion, both the UN initiatives discussed here can and should be strengthened. The Human Rights Council can be transformed into an institution that effectively functions for the protection of human rights, thus meeting the expectations of those who replaced the Human Rights Commission with the Council so that it would serve as the conscience of humanity on human rights issues. Similarly, the principle of a collective responsibility to protect can be implemented and enforced, provided there is the appropriate political will to do so. Nonetheless, these are promising developments to be applauded.

Postscript

Following the Discussion on the Human Rights Council

A text on Darfur was adopted at the second session of the Human Rights Council, on November 28, 2006. Twenty-one voted in favor, with eleven opposed and ten abstentions.[145] A day earlier, however, the Council had adopted two resolutions—one on "Human rights in the occupied Syrian Golan," with 32 affirmative votes, one opposing, and fourteen abstentions,[146] and the other on "Israeli settlements in the occupied Palestine territory, including East Jerusalem, and in the occupied Syrian Golan," adopted by a vote of 45 in favor, one opposed, and one abstention.[147] While the two resolutions on Israel were highly critical of Israel's actions, expressing grave concern at the continuing Israeli activities in violation of international law, the decision on Darfur simply noted "with concern the seriousness of the human rights and humanitarian situation in Darfur," and called on "all parties to put an immediate end to the ongoing violations of human rights and international humanitarian law."[148] The Council even welcomed "the cooperation established by the Government of the Sudan with the Special Rapporteur on the situation of human rights in the Sudan,"[149] although it had been clearly evident for years that the Sudanese government had not been cooperating with the United Nations to stop the ongoing death and destruction perpetrated by the Janjaweed.

Subsequently, on December 13, 2006, the fourth special session of the Human Rights Council adopted a decision on Darfur without a vote:

> to dispatch a High-Level Mission to assess the human rights situation in Darfur and the needs of the Sudan in this regard, comprising five highly qualified persons, to be appointed by the President of the Human Rights Council following consultation with the members of the Council; as well as the Special Rapporteur on the situation of human rights in the Sudan.[150]

On January 26, 2007, the Council president announced the appointment of the five members of the mission serving in their personal capacity, led by Nobel Peace laureate Jody Williams and including Professor Bertrand Ramcharan, as well as the UN special rapporteur on the situation of human rights in the Sudan, Dr. Sima Samar.[151] But the Sudanese authorities refused to give a visa to Professor Ramcharan and the mission could not visit Darfur. But it produced its report based upon interviews with humanitarian agencies and Aftrican Union officials working in Darfur, and on visits to neighboring countries. It concluded that:

> [T]he situation of human rights in Darfur remains grave, and the corresponding needs profound. The situation is characterized by gross and systematic violations of human rights and grave breaches of international humanitarian law. War crimes and crimes against humanity continue across the region. The principal pattern is one of a violent counterinsurgency campaign waged by the government of Sudan in concert with Janjaweed/militia, and targeting mostly civilians. Rebel forces are also guilty of serious abuses of human rights and violations of humanitarian law... The Mission further concludes that the government of the Sudan has manifestly failed to protect the population of Darfur from large-scale international crimes, and has itself orchestrated and participated in these crimes. As such, the solemn obligation of the international community to exercise its responsibility to protect has become evident and urgent.[152]

The Mission made specific recommendations for the international community, the Human Rights Council, and the government of Sudan. These included for the Security Council to deploy a proposed UN/African Union peacekeeping/protection force. It also recommended that the Sudanese government cooperate fully in the deployment of the proposed hybrid peacekeeping force, to cease all support for the Janjaweed/militia forces, to hold accountable all perpetrators of human rights violations, and to cooperate with prosecutors at the International Criminal Court.[153]

At the fourth session of the Human Rights Council on March 30, 2007, the Council adopted without a vote a resolution where it expressed deep concern:

> [R]egarding the seriousness of the ongoing violations of human rights and international humanitarian law in Darfur, including armed attacks on the civilian population and humanitarian workers, widespread destruction of villages, and continued and widespread violence, in particular gender-based violence against women and girls, as well as the lack of accountability of perpetrators of such crimes.[154]

However, it did not adopt the High-Level Mission's report but simply took note of it,[155] although it decided to establish a working group of six individual experts on various areas of human rights with the secretary-general's special rapporteur of the situation of human rights in Sudan to serve as president and for the group to work with the African Union and the Sudanese government.[156] The group is to report at the Council's fifth session June 11-18, 2007.

One salutary development regarding the Council is the election of its membership in May 2007, when the UN General Assembly rejected Belarus, which has had a questionable human rights record and instead elected Bosnia.[157]

Although the Council continues to target Israel and its turning a deaf ear to the tragedy in Darfur for a considerable period of time was a matter of great concern, its recent decisions show promise.

Alluding to the End of the Section on Darfur

Between fall 2006 and spring 2007 several attempts were made by the United Nations, the United States, and other concerned states, even including China, to persuade the Sudanese government to consent to the deployment of a hybrid African Union-UN peacekeeping force, but to no avail. The administration in Khartoum often reneged on its promises to allow the UN peacekeepers in Darfur to protect the civilians and establish a ceasefire. The International Criminal Court issued warrants against a government official and a Janjaweed officer, charging them with crimes against humanity.[158] The United States further strengthened its sanctions regime against Sudan,[159] but the Security Council took no action on sanctions.

The International Court of Justice on February 26, 2007, issued a decision in the Case Concerning the Application of the Convention on the Prevention and Punishment of the Crime of Genocide (Bosnia and Herzegovina v. Serbia and Montenegro),[160] ruled that the 1995 massacre of 8,000 Bosnia Muslim men and boys in Srebrenica was an act of genocide. This was the first time ever that a state was tried for genocide before the World Court and has broad implications for the government of Sudan with respect to the Darfur tragedy:

With this decision, the court has strengthened international law and established an important precedent: a state that is in a position because of its influence and authority to prevent genocide must act to stop it. Under the broad implications of this rationale, for example, Sudan is responsible to halt the genocide in the Darfur region, where, with its backing, the Arab janjaweed militia has burned villages, committed mass rapes, killed nearly 400,000 people, and forced 2-2.5 million to flee as internally displaced or as refugees into Chad.[161]

Notes

1.   Statement by Jan Eliasson at the First Session of the Human Rights Council, Geneva, 19 June 2006, available at www.ohchr.org/english/bodies/hrcouncil/docs/jan_eliasson.pdf [hereafter Eliasson Statement].
2.   Ibid.
3.   UN Charter, arts. 55(c), 56.
4.   UN Charter, Preamble.

5. Universal Declaration of Human Rights, G.A. Res. 217A, U.N. GAOR, 3rd Sess., Pt. 1, Resolutions, at 71, U.N. Doc. A/810 (1948).
6. International Covenant on Civil and Political Rights, 16 Dec. 1966, *entered into force* 23 Mar. 1976, 993 U.N.T.S. 171, reprinted in 6 I.L.M. 368 (1967).
7. International Covenant on Economic, Social and Cultural Rights, 16 Dec. 1966, *entered into force* 3 Jan. 1976, 993 U.N.T.S. 3, reprinted in 6 I.L.M. 360 (1967).
8. Report of the Secretary-General, *In Larger Freedom: Towards Development, Security and Human Rights for All*, U.N. Doc. A/59/2005 Annex, at 2, May 26, 2005 [hereinafter In Larger Freedom].
9. The Human Rights Council was created by G.A. Res. 60/251, U.N. Doc. A/RES/60/251 (Mar. 15, 2006).
10. G.A. Res. 60/1, paras. 138-39, U.N. Doc. A/RES/60/1 (Oct. 24, 2005).
11. The UN Economic and Social Council established the Commission on Human Rights under article 68 of the UN Charter, which empowered ECOSOC to set up a commission "for the promotion of human rights."
12. *Communications Concerning Human Rights*, ECOSOC Res. 728F (XXVIII), 28 U.N. ESCOR Supp. (No. 1) at 19, U.N. Doc. E/3290 (1959).
13. ECOSOC Res. 1235 (XLII), 42 U.N. ESCOR Supp. (No. 1) at 17, U.N. Doc. E/4393 (1967).
14. Supra note 12.
15. ECOSOC resolution 1503 (XLVIII) of 27 May 1970 (cf. II.1).
16. Commission on Human Rights, Report of the Sixty-Second Session (13-27 Mar. 2006), ESCOR Supp. (No. 3), Res. 2006/1, Annex, at 1-4, U.N. Doc. E/2006/23, E/CN.4/2006/122 (2006).
17. U.N. Doc. A/HRC/1/L.6, Annex, Jun. 29, 2006.
18. See e.g., V.S. Mani, *Humanitarian Intervention Today*, 313 Recueil des Cours 13-323 (2005); F. Teson, *Humanitarian Intervention: An Inquiry into Law and Morality* (2d ed. 1996); Ved Nanda, *Tragedies in Northern Iraq, Liberia, Yugoslavia, and Haiti—Revisiting the Validity of Humanitarian Intervention under International Law*—Pt. I, 20 Denv. J. Int'l L. & Pol'y 305 (1992); Ved Nanda, et al., *Tragedies in Somalia, Yugoslavia, Haiti, Rwanda and Liberia—Revisiting the Validity of Humanitarian Intervention under International Law*—Pt. II, 26 Denv. J. Int'l L. & Pol'y 827 (1998); Thomas G. Weiss, "The Sunset of Humanitarian Intervention? The Responsibility to Protect in a Unipolar Era," 35 *Security Dialogue* 135 (2004).
19. *Replacing the Commission on Human Rights with a Human Rights Council*, 2005 A.B.A. Sec. Int'l L. Rep. 8, App. 1, sec. 1 [hereafter ABA Report]. Other examples of those elected to the Commission in recent years included Cuba, Saudi Arabia, and Zimbabwe.
20. U.N. General Assembly, Note by the Secretary-General: *A More Secure World, Our Shared Responsibility—Report of the High-Level Panel on Threats, Challenges and Change*, U.N. Doc. A/59/565, paras. 282-83, Dec. 2, 2004 [hereafter High-Level Panel Report].
21. In Larger Freedom, supra note 8, para.182.
22. As UN Watch has noted, over a 40-year period at the Commission, 30 percent of the resolutions condemning human rights violations by specific states were against Israel and that percentage had risen to half in the few years preceding the Commission's replacement by the Council. In 2005, the Commission adopted four resolutions against Israel and the combined total of resolutions against all other states in the world was also four, one each against Belarus, Cuba, Myanmar, and North Korea. *UN Watch, Reform or Regression: An Assessment of the New UN Human Rights Council*, Sept 6, 2006, at 6 n.3, available at http://www.unwatch.

org/site/apps/nl/content2.asp?c=bdKKISNqEmG&b=1330819&ct=2922277 [hereafter UN Watch].

23.   Address by Louise Arbour, UN High Commissioner for Human Rights on the Occasion of the First Session of the Human Rights Council, Geneva, 19 June 2006, *available at* http://www.ohchr.org/english/bodies/hrcouncil/docs/HC.pdf.

24.   Secretary-General's Address to the Human Rights Council on 19 June 2006, *available at* www.un.org/apps/sg/printsgstats.asp?nIbid=2090.

25.   Secretary-General's Statement on the Human Rights Council, Antananarivo, Madagascar, 15 Mar. 2006, available at www.un.org/apps/sg/sgstats.asp?nIbid=1951.

26.   Eliasson Statement, supra note 1.

27.   See, e.g., Human Rights Watch, *New Rights Council Offers Hope for Victims*, Press Release, Mar. 15, 2006; Amnesty International, *UN Human Rights Council: A Victory for Human Rights Protection*, Press Release, Mar. 15, 2006, cited in UN Watch, supra note 22, at 8 n.12.

28.   From the Secretary-General's address to the Commission on Human Rights, Apr. 7, 2005, quoted in *In Larger Freedom*, supra note 8, para. 6.

29.   ABA Report, supra note 19, at 9.

30.   Ibid. at 13-14.

31.   Ibid. at 15.

32.   Ibid. sec. VI, at 21.

33.   US Institute of Peace, *American Interests and UN Reform (Report of the Task Force on the United Nations)*, Jun. 2005, at 34-35.

34.   Resolution 60/251, supra note 9, para. 7.

35.   Ibid., para. 8.

36.   Ibid. at para. 9.

37.   Ibid. at 5(j).

38.   Human Rights Watch, supra note 22, at 10.

39.   Supra note 9, para.2.

40.   Ibid. para. 3.

41.   Ibid. para. 5(a).

42.   Ibid. para. 5(b).

43.   Ibid. para. 5(c).

44.   Ibid. para. 5(d).

45.   Ibid. para. 5(e).

46.   Ibid. para. 5(f).

47.   Ibid. para. 4.

48.   Ibid. para. 9.

49.   Human Rights Council, *Report to the General Assembly on the First Session of the Human Rights Council*, Res. 2006/1—International Convention for the Protection of All Persons from Enforced Disappearances (adopted June 29, 2006), U.N. Doc. A/HRC/1/L.10, at 31, June 30, 2006. For the Convention text see ibid., Annex, at 32.

50.   Human Rights Council, *Report to the General Assembly on the First Session of the Human Rights Council*, Res. 2006/2—Working Group of the Commission on Human Rights to Elaborate a Draft Declaration in Accordance with Paragraph 5 of the General Assembly Resolution 49/214 of 23 Dec. 1994 (adopted June 29, 2006), U.N. Doc. A/HRC/1/L.10, at 56. For the text of the Declaration, see ibid., Annex, at 58.

51.   Human Rights Council, *Report to the General Assembly on the First Session of the Human Rights Council*, Res. 2006/3—Open-ended Working Group on an Optional Protocol to the International Covenant on Economic, Social and Cultural Rights (adopted June 29, 2006), U.N. Doc. A/HRC/1/L.10, at 73, 30 June 2006.

52.   Human Rights Council, *Report to the General Assembly on the First Session of the Human Rights Council*, Res. 2006/4—The Right to Development (adopted June 30, 2006), U.N. Doc. A/HRC/1/L/10/Add.1, at 9, 5 July 2006.

53.   Human Rights Council, *Report to the General Assembly on the First Session of the Human Rights Council*, Res. 2006/5—The Intergovernmental Working Group on the Effective Implementation of the Durban Declaration and Programme of Action (adopted June 30, 2006), U.N. Doc. A/HRC/1/Res./5, at 11, 5.

54.   Ibid. at 10, 2006/102.

55.   Ibid. at 19, 2006/104.

56.   Ibid. at 18, 2006/103.

57.   UN Watch, supra note 22, at 24-26.

58.   Human Rights Council, *Report to the General Assembly on the First Session o f the Human Rights Council*, 2006/PRST.1—The Entry into Force of the Optional Protocol to the Convention Against Torture and Other Cruel, Inhuman or Degrading Treatment or Punishment, U.N. Doc. A/HRC/1/L.10/Add.1, at 23, 5 July 2006. The Optional Protocol came into force during the session.

59.   Human Rights Council*, Report to the General Assembly on the first Session of the Human Rights Council*, 2006/PRST.2—Hostage-taking, U.N. Doc. A/HRC/1/ L.10/Add.1, at 24, 5 July 2006.

60.   Eliasson, supra note 1.

61.   Human Rights Council, *Report to the General Assembly on the First Session o f the Human Rights Council*, 2006/106—Human Rights Situation in Palestine and Other Occupied Arab Territories (adopted June 30, 2006, by a vote of 29-12, with 5 abstentions), U.N. Doc. A/HRC/1/L.10/Add.1, at 22, 5 July 2006.

62.   Human Rights Council, *Report to the General Assembly on the First Session o f the Human Rights Council*, 2006/107—Incitement to Racial and Religious Hatred and the Promotion of Tolerance (adopted June 30, 2006, by a vote of 33-12, with 1 abstention), U.N. Doc. A/HRC/1/L.10/Add.1, at 23, 5 July 2006.

63.   Human Rights Council, *Report on the First Special Session of the Human Rights Council*, S-1/Res.1—Human Rights Situation in the Occupied Palestinian Territory (adopted July 6, 2006 by a vote of 29-11 with five abstentions), U.N. Doc. A/HRC/S-1/3, 18 July 2006.

64.   Human Rights Council, *Report on the Special Session*, Res. S-2/1—The Grave Situation of Human Rights in Lebanon Caused by Israeli Military Operations (adopted Aug. 11, 2006 by a vote of 27 to 11 with eight abstentions), A/HRC/S-2/L.1, 9 Aug. 2006.

65.   See UN Watch's assessment in UN Watch, supra note 22, at 20.

66.   See Ibid. at 21.

67.   See Ibid. at 19.

68.   See Ibid. at 21-22.

69.   UN Charter, art 2, para1.

70.   Art. 2(4) reads: "All Members shall refrain in their international relations from the threat or use of force against the territorial integrity or political independence of any state, or in any other manner inconsistent with the Purposes of the United Nations."

71.   In addition to the authorities cited in note 18.

72.   See Richard B. Lillich, *Forcible Self-Help to Protect Human Rights*, 53 Iowa L. Rev. 325 (1967); Steve G. Simon, *The Contemporary Legality of Unilateral Humanitarian Intervention*, 24 Cal. W. Int'l L.J. 117 (1993); Byron F. Burmester, *On Humanitarian Intervention: The New World Order and Wars to Preserve Human Rights*, 1994 Utah L. Rev. 269 (1994); James A.R. Nafziger, *Humanitarian Intervention in a Community of Power*, 22 Denv. J. Int'l L. & Pol'y 219 (1994);

Ruth E. Gordon, *Intervention by the United Nations: Iraq, Somalia, and Haiti*, 31 Tex. Int'l L.J. 43 (1996); Richard B. Lillich, *The Role of the U.N. Security Council in Protecting Human Rights in Crisis Situations: U.N. Humanitarian Intervention in the Post Cold War Era*, 3 Tul. J. Int'l & Comp. L. 1 (1995); and Fernando R. Tison, Collective Humanitarian Intervention, 17 Mich. J. Int'l L. 323 (1996). Quoted in Report of the International Commission on Intervention and State Sovereignty, *The Responsibility to Protect* vii (Dec. 2001) [hereinafter International Commission Report].

73.   Francis M. Deng, *Frontiers of Sovereignty*, 8 Leyden J. Int'l L. 249 (1995).

74.   Francis M. Deng, et al., *Sovereignty as Responsibility: Conflict Management in Africa* (1996).

75.   Secretary-General's Address to the General Assembly, Sept. 23, 2003, available at www.un.org/apps/sg/printsgstats.asp?nIbid=517.See also Kofi A. Annan, The Question of Intervention (UN 1999).

76.   Danish Institute of International Affairs, *Humanitarian Intervention: Legal and Political Aspects* (1999).

77.   Advisory Council on International Affairs and Advisory Committee on Issues of Public International Law, Humanitarian Intervention (2000).

78.   Independent International Commission on Kosovo, *Kosovo Report: Conflict, International Response, Lessons Learned* (2000).

79.   US Dept. of State, Inter-*Agency Review of US Government Civilian Humanitarian and Transition Programs* (2000).

80.   *Humanitarian Intervention: Crafting a Workable Doctrine* (Council on Foreign Relations: Alton Frye ed., 2000).

81.   International Commission Report, supra note 70.

82.   Supra note 72.

83.   Ibid. at viii.

84.   Ibid.

85.   Ibid. at xvii; §§ 2.28-2.29.

86.   Ibid. at xvii; §2.29.

87.   Ibid.

88.   Ibid. at xii.

89.   Ibid.

90.   Gareth Evans, *Crimes Against Humanity: Overcoming Global Indifference* (2006 Grandel Oration for B'nai B'rith Anti-Defamation Commission), Apr. 30, 2006, available at www.crisisgroup.org/home/index. cfm?Ibid=4087&1=1 [hereafter Gareth Evans].

91.   William R. Pace & Nicole Deller, *Preventing Future Genocides: An International Responsibility to Protect*, 36 World Order No. 4, at 15, 22 and n. 18 (2005).

92.   See, e.g., Ibid. at 22 n. 19.

93.   High-Level Panel Report, supra note 20, para 29.

94.   Ibid.

95.   Ibid., para. 87.

96.   Ibid., para. 36.

97.   Ibid., para. 201.

98.   Ibid., emphasis in original.

99.   Ibid., para. 203.

100.   Ibid., para. 207.

101.   Ibid., para. 208.

102.   US Institute of Peace, *American Interests and UN Reform* (Report of the Task Force on the United Nations), June 2005, at 28.

103.   Ibid. at 30-31.

104. G.A. Res. 60/1, para. 138, supra note 10.
105. Ibid.
106. Ibid., para. 139.
107. Ibid., para. 140.
108. UN Doc. S/RES/1674 (Apr. 28, 2006).
109. Ibid., para. 4.
110. Statement of Under-Secretary-General, Jan Egeland at the open meeting of the Security Council on the Protection of Civilians in Armed Conflict, 28 June 2006, available at www.ochaonline.un.org/DocView.asp?DocIbid=4693..
111. U.N. Security Council, *Report of the Secretary-General on Darfur*, U.N. Doc. S/2006/591 (28 July 2006) [hereafter 28 July 2006 Report on Darfur].
112. Ibid., para. 4. By using scientific sampling techniques and data from camps for displaced people, John Hagan and Alberto Palloni have estimated that 255,000 people in Darfur have died. John Hagan & Alberto Palloni, *Death in Darfur*, 313 Science 1578 (Sept. 15, 2006).
113. 28 July 2006 Report on Darfur, supra note 111, para. 4.
114. See Ibid. paras. 22-34 for the agreement. See generally Ved Nanda, "Darfur Accord Must Succeed," *Denver Post*, May 9, 2006, at B7.
115. 28 July 2006 Report on Darfur, supra note 111, para. 8.
116. Ibid., para. 11.
117. Ibid., para. 23.
118. Ibid., paras. 24-25.
119. Ibid., paras. 26-27.
120. Ibid., para. 28.
121. Ibid., paras. 61-144; U.N. Doc. S/2006/591/Add.1 (28 Aug. 2006).
122. U.N. Doc. A/RES/1706 (Aug. 31, 2006).
123. Ibid., preamble.
124. Ibid., para. 3.
125. Ibid., paras. 8-9.
126. Ibid., para. 8(k), (l).
127. U.N. Doc. S/RES/1679 (16 May 2006).
128. Ibid., para. 3.
129. Ibid., preamble. See also S.C. Res. 1556 of July 30, 2004, where similar language was used by the Council to reaffirm its commitment to the sovereignty, unity, territorial integrity, and independence of Sudan. U.N. Doc. S/RES/1556 (30 July 2004).
130. See, e.g., "Demonstrations Around the World Draw Attention to Darfur Crisis," *NY Times*, Sept. 18, 2006, at 18A, col. 1; Steve Bloomfield, "World Marches to Save Darfur," *Independent* (London), Sept. 18, 2006, at 24; and David Ronnie & Graeme Wilson, "Sudan Must End Violence or Pay Price, Warns Blair," *Daily Telegraph* (London), Sept. 18, 2006, at 19.
131. President Bush Addresses United Nations General Assembly, *available at* www.whitehouse.gov/news/releases/2006/09/print/20060919-4.
132. Kofi Annan, *Struggle to Confront Three Global Challenges—Development, Security, Human Rights*, UN Doc. SG/SM/10643; GA/10501, available at www.un./org/News/Press/cdocs/2006/sgsm10643.doc.
133. Ibid.
134. Colum Lynch & Glenn Kessler, "Bush to Name Envoy for Darfur; Natsios Will Lead US Efforts to Quell the Violence in Sudan," *Washington Post*, Sept. 19, 2006, at A16.
135. Ibid.
136. Ibid.

137. See Warren Hoge, "African Union Peacekeepers' Stay in Darfur is Extended as Accord on U.N. Force is Awaited," *NY Times*, Sept. 21, 2006, at A14, col. 1.
138. Ibid.
139. Colum Lynch, "Rice, Others Press Sudan to Open Darfur to U.N. Force," *Washington Post*, Sept. 23, 2006, at A13.
140. Ibid.
141. High-Level Panel Report, supra note 20, para. 207.
142. Gareth Evans, *The Responsibility to Protect: Unfinished Business*, G8 Summit 2006: Issues and Instruments (The Official Summit Publication), 15-17 July 2006, available at http://www.crisisgroup.org/home/index.cfm?Ibid=4269&l=1.
143. Gareth Evans, supra note 90.
144. See generally John McCain & Bob Dole, "Rescue Darfur Now," *NY Times*, Sept. 15, 2006, at A9 (full-page advertisement reprinted from the Washington Post, Sept.10, 2006, calling on the international community to impose sanctions on Sudan.
145. U.N. Doc. A/HRC/2/L.11/Add.1, November 28, 2006, Decision 2/115. Darfur.
146. Ibid. Res. 2/3. Human rights in the occupied Syrian Golan.
147. Ibid. Res. 2/4. Israeli settlements in the occupied Palestinian territory, including East Jerusalem, and in the occupied Syrian Golan.
148. Ibid. Res. 2/115, at para. 2.
149. Ibid. at para. 5.
150. U.N. Doc. A/HRC/S-4/SR.4, January 23, 2007, Decision S-4/101.
151. U.N. Human Rights Council, 4th session, Report of the High-Level Mission on the situation of human rights in Darfur pursuant to Human Rights Council decision S-4/101, U.N. Doc. A/HRC/4/80, March 9, 2007, para. 2.
152. Ibid. at para. 76 (italics in original).
153. Ibid. at para. 77.
154. U.N. Doc. A/HRC/4/L.11/Add.1, Res. 4/8, para. 3. Follow-up to decision S/4/101 of 13 December 2006 adopted by the Human Rights Council at its fourth special session entitled "Situation of Human Rights in Darfur," March 30, 2007.
155. Ibid. at para. 2.
156. Ibid. at paras. 6-7.
157. U.N. General Assembly, Human Rights Council Election (17 May 2007), available at http://www.un.org/ga/61/elect/hrc/.
158. International Criminal Court, ICC-01/04-01/06 Case The Prosecutor v. Ahmad Muhammad Harun ("Ahmad Harun") and Ali Muhammad Ali Abd-Al-Rahman ("Ali Kushayb"), Situation in Darfur, Sudan, available at http://www.icc-cpi.int/cases/Darfur.html.
159. The targets of the heightened sanctions "include five petrochemical companies and the country's national telecommunications operator, Sudatel," a sugar producer, and an automobile company. They also name two senior officials—Ahmad Haroun, the minister for humanitarian affairs, and Awad ibn Auf, the country's director of military intelligence—and Khalil Ibrahim, leader of the rebel group "Justice and Equality Movement." Oil May Provide a Way for Sudan to Escape the Full Pain of the New US Sanctions, *NY Times*, May 30, 2007, at C3.
160. International Court of Justice, *Case Concerning the Application of the Convention on the Prevention and Punishment of the Crime of Genocide* (Bosnia and Herzegovina v. Serbia and Montenegro), 2007, 26 February, General List No. 91.
161. Ved Nanda, "Bosnia Ruling a Victory for International Law," *Denver Post*, Feb. 28, 2007.

The United Nations' Role in the Management and Equitable Distribution of Global Natural Resources

Sovaida Ma'ani Ewing[1]

Introduction

In a world where the well-being of people and the development of economies so keenly depend on having certain critical resources like oil, gas, nuclear energy and water, it no longer makes sense for those nations that happen to control a particular resource that everyone needs, to decide alone how the resource is managed and distributed. It certainly seems unfair that the rest of the world should be at the mercy of those nations as they dictate terms often based on short-term self-interest and fluctuating expediency. It also makes no sense to allow a major cause of boundary disputes and conflicts in general to continue when removing it would make the world a more peaceful place. In the interests of peace and security, proponents of United Nations reform should support the establishment of a supra-national authority under the auspices of the United Nations, responsible for controlling, regulating and ensuring equal access to these critical resources. Although such a proposal is likely to face stiff resistance from nations and private concerns that currently control such resources, our leaders need to recognize that the application of several core principles—including the oneness of peoples and nations, justice, equity and fair treatment of all peoples, the curtailment of excessive national sovereignty, and international cooperation and unity of action—all dictate that critical resources be subject to control, regulation and equitable distribution by a supra-national authority. Centralizing control of the world's critical resources in the hands of one authority will also require our leaders to create a proper system of oversight, transparency, and accountability to forestall possible corruption within the system.

When the leading nations of Europe sought to rebuild their devastated continent after World War II without recreating the age-old competition between France and Germany for coal and steel resources, they took the bold and imaginative step of pooling their several resources in one European Coal and Steel Community (ECSC). That leap of faith by historically bitter enemies has proven, so far, to be more successful than most commentators at the time ever dreamed, having led the way first to the European Common Market for nearly all economic sectors and on to the European Union and its stronger joint institutions and common policies on many fronts, including international relations and social policy. The ECSC serves as a model for how countries now can address comparable issues for managing energy resource to avoid strife and improve the lives of their citizens.

The purpose of this chapter is to propose some initial, practical steps toward the global management by the United Nations of critical natural resources. Part I delineates the broad contours of an umbrella supra-national authority composed of four arms to manage different types of global natural resources. Part II proposes the creation of a High Authority for Oil and Gas based on the experience of the European Coal and Steel Community as a first step towards the creation of the umbrella supra-national authority. Part II (A) discusses the problems caused by the current system of oil and gas production and distribution. Part II (B) examines the European Coal and Steel Community as Jean Monnet originally envisioned it and as it evolved in practice as a possible model for solving our present-day problems with oil and gas production and distribution. Building on the lessons of the ECSC, Part II (C) proposes that countries create an international High Authority for oil and gas modeled on the original European Coal and Steel High Authority proposed by Jean Monnet. This institution should be charged with systematically gauging the needs for oil and gas around the world and for ensuring that production keeps up with those needs, all with a view to ensuring that all nations have equal access to these critical resources and that they are supplied on equal terms. Moreover, the High Authority should see to it that uniform standards for the protection of the environment, labor and human rights are applied, and that commercial honesty and the rule of law are upheld.

I. Creation of a Supra-National Critical Resources Authority

This chapter provides both a long-term vision for the centralized control and equitable distribution of the world's critical resources as well as a proposal for the first step to be taken now in the direction of that vision. Although the ultimate goal proposed is the creation of a global supra-national authority that will regulate all the world's critical resources, including oil, gas, nuclear energy, water and certain key minerals, the nations of the world may not be ready to make the leap required to tackle the regulation of all these resources simultaneously. A more practical approach may dictate breaking the journey towards the long-term goal into a series of smaller steps beginning with the establishment of a supra-national authority for oil and gas alone. This section (I) will describe the long-term vision and the next section (II) will suggest how the nations can begin by establishing a supra-national authority for oil and gas.

Eventually, it is recommended that a supra-national authority for the management, regulation and equitable distribution of global natural resources be created in the form of an umbrella authority with four separate arms, each responsible for a different category of resource. The first arm would have control over major natural energy resources such as oil and gas, which are crucial to human existence and development today. An extensive discussion of how this arm might successfully be created now will follow in section II below.

The second arm would manage all the key resources that can be used to create nuclear energy and weapons, such as uranium and plutonium, together with the facilities for processing them and all nuclear reactors. It would also be responsible for distributing nuclear fuel in an equitable manner and would act as a reserve fuel bank to guarantee the supply of fissile material to civilian nuclear users. Another important function would be to impose and enforce international standards regarding the tracking and disposal of nuclear waste and spent fuel. Stronger tracking is needed to avoid situations like that reported in 2005, in which nuclear energy authorities lost track of spent fuel from three nuclear plants in the United States—Vermont, Connecticut and California—said to be missing.[2] Tracking such waste is critical to ensure that it does not fall into the hands of dangerous state or non-state actors.

The third arm would monitor the supplies and need for clean water worldwide and be responsible for ensuring that all the peoples of the world have fair access to clean water supplies, especially in view of the prediction that by the year 2015, 1.8 billion people will lack access to water.

The fourth arm would regulate and monitor the mining and extraction of certain other priceless resources to be agreed upon by the international community. In creating the relevant list of resources, world leaders should draw on the information provided and conclusions made in the reports of several expert panels appointed by the Security Council in recent years demonstrating the nexus between certain conflicts such as the ones in Liberia, the Democratic Republic of Congo, Angola, and Sierra Leone and the exploitation of natural resources.[3] Based on these reports and other studies conducted by non-governmental organizations working in this area[4], the list ought to include diamonds, gold, coltan, cobalt and timber, because the desire to control such resources has been shown to trigger conflicts. Their illicit mining and trade by warring factions has funded and sustained civil wars within many countries and has proven to be one of the biggest drivers of conflict and violence in the developing world.

One of the crucial responsibilities of the high authority's fourth arm would be to craft and enforce rules governing natural resource extraction. The rules would be designed to ensure that covered resources do not fund rebel groups or insurgents, for example, by requiring transparency and accountability of financial transactions related to the mining or extraction activities. Initial attempts to ensure this kind of transparency and accountability have already been made but need to be further refined and tightened.[5] Another responsibility would be to consider the environmental damage caused by improper mining and extraction and attempt to arrive at solutions to mitigate such damage. For example, in the area of metal and gold mining, the prevalent use of cyanide solution to separate gold from rock is making some mines almost like nuclear waste dumps that must be tended in perpetuity.[6]

Although this chapter envisions that the supra-national authority to control, regulate and distribute critical resources will ultimately be composed of four arms, it nevertheless proposes that the authority be built one piece at a time, beginning with the creation of a High Authority for Oil and Gas. The latter can then be used as a model to structure other branches of a supra-national umbrella authority that deal with the remaining critical resources mentioned earlier namely, water, nuclear energy and certain precious minerals.

II. First Step: Creating a High Authority for Oil and Gas

Oil and natural gas form two sources of energy that have become integral parts of industrial lives today. These resources are necessary for economies to prosper, for supplying electricity and for industrial output and transportation.[7] Nations must be able to produce or have access to enough affordable fuel and electricity to keep their economies running. Increasing demand for electricity in the United States and Europe outpaces the supplies of power and natural gas. In emerging economies such as Brazil, India, and China, energy demand is likely to double by 2020. Yet roughly 2.4 billion people in developing countries have almost no access to electricity or liquid fuels and rely on wood, straw or manure for their energy needs. They endure lives that breed resentment, despair, and conflict.[8] While demand for oil and natural gas is increasing, production increasingly lags behind, driving a race for energy-hungry nations to ensure their energy security by obtaining and preferably locking in access to energy supplies. In the frenzy to keep the oil and gas flowing at all costs, little attention is given to other long-term goals, like preventing climate change, developing alternate sources of energy, and ensuring that developing countries have adequate access to energy.

A. Problems with the Present System

The current system of oil and gas production and distribution has spawned a wide range of problems all of which corrode the social, moral and economic fabric of the community of nations and ultimately undermine its peace and security.

1. Expediency and Turning a Blind Eye to Destructive Behavior. Unequal access to oil and gas and uneven distribution of hydrocarbon resources cause severe economic and social problems. Nations that depend on access to oil and gas for their economic development and whose needs are increasing at a fast pace, such as China and India, increasingly worry that these needs may not be met. Similarly, nations that have relied on oil and gas to develop their economies and who wish to maintain their standards of living, such as the United States and the nations of Europe, are equally keen to assure access to oil and gas. Seeking to secure adequate supplies, such nations have often been willing to turn a blind eye to the deplorable behaviors of energy-rich countries.

Taking the example of China, her rapid growth has fueled her need for oil. In 2003 alone her oil imports rose by 33 percent making her the world's second largest importer of oil after the United States, surpassing even Japan, which depends entirely on imported oil.[9] Although China is naturally endowed with large deposits of coal, rapid economic development and environmental and health concerns have prompted it to look for cleaner burning sources of energy such as oil and gas. Consequently,

China, like other energy-hungry countries, has sometimes been willing to do whatever is expedient to ensure an adequate supply of energy. Occasionally this has meant that it has even been willing to ignore bad behavior, such as the violation of human rights by energy-rich countries, in return for access to their oil and gas reserves. For instance, China, Malaysia, and India have obtained rights to drill for oil in the Sudan, most of which apparently is bought by China.[10] At the same time, however, China has been reluctant to join the majority of other nations in imposing sanctions on the Sudan for the widely documented human rights atrocities occurring in Sudan's Darfur region and which many regard as genocide.[11]

Similarly, both India and China are aggressively courting Iran as a supplier of natural gas and oil, despite the multinational crisis surrounding Iran's nuclear program and its ongoing human rights violations. India and Iran are negotiating to create a strategic oil pipeline between the two countries, while Beijing closed a $70 billion deal with Iran for liquefied natural gas and crude oil in the fall of 2004.[12] In addition, China has been content to continue supplying arms to Iran.[13]

2. *Culture of Impunity—Political Pressure, Bribery, Blackmail, and Intimidation.* Another problem is that countries naturally endowed with an abundance of oil and natural gas have sometimes misused their natural wealth to exert political pressure or as a means to bribe, blackmail, and intimidate other countries that depend upon these resources. Such misuses lead to a culture of impunity on the part of oil and gas-rich nations that elicits, in response, a culture of expediency on the part of dependent countries. The risk to the international community of such behavior has reached an all-time high, because the global crude oil market is pumping at nearly full capacity, making the actions of even the smallest producers important and giving them undue power to threaten global energy security.[14]

A recent example of such misuses involves Russia. In early 2006 Russia followed through on its threat to cut off supply of natural gas to the Ukraine if the Ukraine did not agree to a large price increase demanded by the state monopoly Gazprom. Although Gazprom may merely have been trying to increase revenues, some observers believe that Russia acted to punish the Ukraine for distancing itself from Kremlin control and leaning towards the European Union and NATO.[15] The cutoff lasted three days and prompted concerns about supplies to European countries west of the Ukraine, which are supplied Russian gas by pipelines transiting the Ukraine. At the end of 2006, Russia similarly threatened another country between it and Europe, Belarus, asking it to pay more than double the price for natural gas that it had been paying.[16] Belarusian natural gas supplies were disrupted for a short while. Soon after a deal was struck in which Belarus agreed to increases in the price of natural gas, Russia halted the supplies of crude oil running by pipeline through Belarus to Western Europe. This shut down affected supplies destined for Germany, Poland and the Ukraine and rekindled concerns in Europe about the reliability of energy supplies from Russia.[17] Observers have argued that Russia's energy tactics have made it "impervious to the criticism that once might have modified its behavior" causing those who might have once criticized it to "largely acquiesce to the new behavior."[18]

Other countries have more explicitly threatened to cut off energy supplies unless other countries changed their policies. Iran's president reportedly responded to suggestions in 2005 that its nuclear program be referred to the UN Security Council as a threat to international peace by threatening, "If Iran's case is sent to the Security Council, we will respond by many ways, for example by holding back on oil sales."[19] Similarly, in early 2006, Venezuela's oil minister stated that it might steer oil exports away from the United States, which obtains more than 10 percent of its oil imports from Venezuela.[20]

3. Border, Interstate and Intrastate Conflicts. Experience demonstrates that the drive for control over natural resources, including oil and gas, is one of the leading causes of border conflicts, civil conflicts within one country, and inter-state conflicts. Examples of such inter-state and border conflicts abound: It was Japan's need to secure oil supplies that drove it to its fateful attack on Pearl Harbor in December 1941, and the desire to control Middle East oil was a factor that led Russia to invade Afghanistan in 1979. A similar drive prompted Saddam Hussein to invade and annex Kuwait in 1990.[21] Nigeria and Cameroon fought over the potentially oil-rich Bakassi peninsula in the Gulf of Guinea for more than a decade, until a UN-brokered deal finally induced Nigeria to withdraw troops in 2006.[22]

Africa seems particularly plagued by its uneven distribution of energy resources. Research by Oxford economist Paul Collier suggests that in any given five-year period, the chance of civil war in Africa ranges from less than 1 percent in countries without resource wealth to almost 25 percent in those with such wealth.[23] Thus in Nigeria, the sub-Saharan African country with the largest proven oil reserves, disputes over oil have been causing bloodshed for years.[24] In the Niger Delta region of the country, militant groups frequently clash with each other and with the federal government over oil revenue resulting in the indiscriminate kill-ing and displacement of tens of thousands of villagers and the disruption of oil production—sometimes to the extent of 800,000 barrels a day.[25] In Sudan, oil has been a prime cause of a prolonged civil war between the government-controlled North and the oil-rich South, while the $1 million per day of oil-export revenues have funded purchases of arms needed to fight that civil war and used in the Darfur region, which is known to have major yet untapped oil reserves.[26]

Conflict initiated by the desire for oil is by no means confined to Af-rica. In the Pakistani province of Balochistan, the national government is currently trying to exploit oil, gas and copper reserves in the face of armed opposition from local Balochi tribes. Beneath the East China Sea lies the 700 square kilometer Chunxiao/Shirakaba oil and gas field, within maritime territory to which both China and Japan claim rights.[27] In the Caucasus, the development of Azerbaijan's oil sector has made possible a huge spike in defense spending which is likely to make the Nagorno-Karabakh dispute with Armenia more difficult to resolve according to the International Crisis Group.[28] Disputes over natural resources also fuel conflicts in Burma and Indonesia's Papua province.[29]

Once a resource-related conflict has started, revenues from the exploi-tation of natural resources fund the parties to the conflict. Yet, because of the prospect of large revenues that the resources bring to the victor, the parties are reluctant to give up the fight. A prime example was the conflict between the UNITA rebels and the Angolan government. Although the parties found ready support from the United States and the Soviet Union during early years of the Angolan War, the conflict continued long after the end of the Cold War, as diamonds sustained the rebels and oil funded the government.[30]

4. Corruption and Poverty. As one observer has noted, "There is a close connection between the exploitation of natural resources and the prevalence of corrupt and oppressive regimes."[31] Controlling large and steady flows of money provides dictators with the incentive to stay in power to benefit themselves. It also provides them with the means to do so while ignoring the basic desires and needs of their people. In addition, studies have shown time and again that countries rich in oil tend to suffer from dictatorial or unrepresentative government.[32]

For example, in Angola, although oil is reported to account for an estimated 90 percent of the country's revenues, two-thirds of Angolans have no access to safe drinking water, and the country is one of the world's poorest. Of the $3-5 billion annual state budget, $1 billion is reported to go missing every year. Although economists say the government has more money than it can spend, a combination of corruption, incompetence, and the aftereffects of the Angolan civil war seem to have conspired to paralyze the government and render it unable to address even basic issues of clean water and sewers that would prevent such epidemics.[33]

Another example can be found in Chad where oil was discovered in the 1960s. Thanks partly to World Bank financing, oil finally began to flow through a Chad-Cameroon pipeline in 2003. Hoping to avoid the resource curse, the World Bank insisted on an independent oversight committee to funnel a large portion of the oil revenues to education and economic development and toward a fund for future generations of Chadians. Soon after the oil began to flow, however, the Chadian government suddenly announced that it would put more money in its general budget, bypassing the oversight panel, and would increase its spending on security. A US government interagency review conducted in the first six months of the project indicated that of the $25 million signing bonus awarded to the government 60 percent had already been spent "outside of established budget procedures," that "Chadian governance was weakening, civil conflict and risk of famine were increasing and parliamentary elections appear to have been postponed."[34]

Corruption is by no means limited to Africa. In Latin America, for example, Ecuador, although rich in oil, ranks as one of the most corrupt countries.[35] In Kazakhstan, despite the billions of dollars in oil revenue, one-third of the population lives on less than $1 a day while the autocratic president directly administers the oil fund and has recently engineered a constitutional amendment to enable him to continue ruling for the rest of his life.[36]

5. Slowdown in Economic Growth. Even without corruption, over-reliance on revenues from extraction of natural resources can paradoxically slow a nation's economic growth. The phenomenon is known as "Dutch Disease" for the economic collapse suffered by The Netherlands in the 1950s and early 1960s after the discovery of oil off the Dutch shore.[37] When North Sea oil started to flow from Norwegian territories, the Norwegian economy similarly began to show symptoms of this disease, but reversed it by taking oil revenues out of the mainstream economy and putting it into a trust fund for the future. Such a reversal is difficult and requires great discipline, sound governance, and transparency.

6. Lack of Transparent Information Regarding Supply and Demand. According to the Saudi Arabian oil minister, Ali Al-Naimi, speaking in 2005, one of the biggest problems the petroleum industry faces is "[t]he absence of accurate and clear information … especially in vital subjects such as supply, demand, production and stockpiles."[38] Although ministers from energy-hungry consumer countries met with some of the world's large producers in November 2005 to inaugurate a new International Energy Forum and unveil a database of information provided by the world's main oil producing and consuming countries designed to meet this problem, information submitted on a voluntary basis by some nations is insufficient. There needs to be a central body that has the authority to collect information from all the nations of the world on a regular basis and to use this information to regulate the oil and gas market.

7. Environmental Pollution and Damage. The lack of common standards for the extraction of resources like oil and gas often leads to massive environmental pollution and damage. For example, in the Niger Delta the local community has long complained that oil spilled from deteriorating old pipelines has destroyed fishing in the area.[39] Environmental destruction of the pristine beaches in the Cabinda area of Angola as well as the destruction of the fishing industry there are also ongoing problems.[40] Huge reserves of oil and gas have been discovered in the Amazon, which Brazil needs to keep its economy going. To this end, the first of a series of pipelines was being built there in early 2007. This extraction of oil and gas from the Amazon has prompted environmentalists to caution Brazil to consider the resulting environmental damage, including deforestation.[41]

8. High Prices and Volatility. Steep rises in the price of oil coupled with volatility in prices is another problem caused by the uneven access to oil and gas. Since 1998 there has been a surge in oil prices from a historical low of about $9.50 a barrel to $50 a barrel. The cause was a combination of tight supply, rising demand, financial speculation and a lack of spare production capacity. Violence caused by terrorism or sabotage also has contributed to the high price of oil, as demonstrated by the 2.6 percent increase in oil prices that occurred on February 20, 2006, after a series of violent attacks in the Niger Delta shut down roughly a fifth of Nigeria's oil production.[42] In addition, experts claim that chronic underinvestment in the oil industry for at least two decades, resulting in a shortage of infrastructure crucial to oil and gas production and distribution, such as oil rigs, refinery capacity, tankers and petroleum engineers, has led to tight supply and unstable prices.[43] The International Energy Agency, the industrialized world's energy-market watchdog, has forecast that world oil demand will rise 37 percent by 2030, to 115 million barrels a day from about 85 million today. But the oil-producing nations with the greatest pumping potential either will not or cannot tap their resources sufficiently to meet those projections.[44]

The problem with volatility in the price of oil and gas is that it leads to economic instability, and surges in oil prices hurt global economic growth. Experts say that high oil prices hurt not only the consumers, but also oil firms and producers as well.[45] Volatility is also problematic because it exacerbates the tendency of countries that need to import large quantities of oil to do whatever it takes to lock in access to oil reserves.

That the current system for the production, regulation and distribution of oil and gas is seriously flawed, unfair, and fraught with dangers is evident. It is no longer conducive to the present-day needs of the international community and needs to be replaced by an equitable, rule-based, international system that ensures equal access to oil and gas for all.

B. The European Coal and Steel Community as a Model for Solving the Problem

The European Coal and Steel Community was created in the early 1950's to tackle similar problems to the ones discussed in Part I but involving coal and steel instead of oil and gas. The idea of pooling natural resources under the management control of a supra-national High Authority was a groundbreaking and innovative idea for its time. It proved very successful in resolving some of the key problems it was created to solve, especially ensuring the end of conflict between the historical enemies, Germany and France. Alas, it was not as successful as it could have been in resolving some other problems because the negotiators of the Treaty setting it up deviated from the original plan for its creation proposed by Jean Monnet in some key respects. The purpose of this part of the chapter is to examine the strengths and weaknesses of the ECSC both as it was originally conceived by Jean Monnet and as it was in fact crafted to determine its value as a model for the establishment of an international supranational institution for the management and regulation of oil and gas.

1. What to Do about Germany? After the Second World War, Europe was both economically and militarily in ruins. Western European nations bent all their energies towards economic reconstruction, for which they needed large quantities of coal and steel. Steel was necessary for a variety of purposes: to build railways, buildings, machinery, ships and vehicles. Although the demand for steel was high, there was a shortage of raw materials necessary to produce it, especially the coal to fire steel furnaces. Germany had always been naturally blessed with an abundance of coal, but it had also started two World Wars on the basis of its powerful coal and steel industries. The question was what to do about German coal and steel?

The victorious powers initially planned to dismember Germany's coal and steel industries and to cap German steel production. Such a regime would assure access to German coal for production of steel outside Germany and to German markets for the sale of steel products, albeit at the expense of retarding Germany's own revitalization. However, Britain and the United States soon changed their minds, concluding that Europe's best interest actually dictated that Germany play a part in its economic rehabilitation. For this, Germany needed to remain unified and her economy to be revived.[46]

In addition, the new threat on the horizon was perceived to come from communism and the USSR. The US considered Germany the perfect buffer to protect the rest of Western Europe from the threat of Soviet expansion. But to serve this purpose Germany needed to be strong and firmly within the non-Soviet camp.

With its coal and steel industries intact, by 1949, Germany was making a spectacular economic recovery. France, meanwhile, desperately needed access to Germany's coal and steel on favorable terms for its own recovery and was eager to control Germany's heavy industry to prevent the rebuilding of a German war machine that could be used against France yet again.

2. Jean Monnet's Plan. A brilliant new plan was devised. Its mastermind was Jean Monnet, planning commissioner for France, charged with modernizing his country. The plan represented a total shift in French policy, away from confrontation and control of Germany towards deep cooperation with France's historical nemesis. Recognizing the central importance of coal and steel to the economic and military power of European nations and to its peace, Monnet proposed placing the coal and steel production of France, Germany and any other European country that wished to participate under the management of a jointly-agreed High Authority. A customs union and common market for these products would also be created, within which the High Authority was to ensure the supply of coal on equal terms to participating nations.[47] Monnet was able to win the approval of the French foreign minister, Robert Schuman, who announced the plan in a now-famous radio broadcast on the afternoon of May 9, 1950. In 1951 the Treaty of Paris was signed establishing the European Coal and Steel Community among the six nations of Belgium, the Netherlands, Luxembourg, Italy, France and Germany.

Monnet's plan was not the first time the nations of Europe had attempted to craft solutions to the problem of access to European raw materials. The 1920s and 1930s had witnessed several such attempts. A Supreme Economic Council was established in early 1919 with the aim of ensuring an adequate supply of raw materials for the areas devastated by the First World War. This was followed in August 1919 by the creation of a European Coal Commission to coordinate coal production and distribution in Europe. Later in the 1920s the International Steel Cartel was created, followed by the short-lived Franco-German Commercial Treaty of 1927. All of these attempts involved traditional inter-governmental agencies. They all failed largely because the institutions created were not given adequate power and authority to enforce and regulate the agreed-upon policies. Rather, these were left in the hands of the individual nations.[48]

Monnet recognized that the nations of Europe were not yet ready to cede sovereignty in large policy areas. European federalists had been calling for the creation of a United States of Europe for some time. After the First World War, many intellectuals and then-French Prime Minister Aristide Briand had called for the creation of a federation of European nations. In the 1930s, Winston Churchill joined with many others to support such ideas, until the Great Depression, the rise of fascism, and the outbreak of the Second World War ended any hopes for such cooperation. Soon after the end of the Second World War, Churchill again took up the call describing the "quivering mass of tormented, hungry, careworn and bewildered human beings" in war-torn Europe "who wait in the ruins of their cities and homes and scan the dark horizons for the approach of some new form of tyranny or terror," and calling again for the construction of a United States of Europe.[49] Yet, these calls remained unheeded.

Monnet calculated that the only hope for success in integrating Europe lay in creating a supra-national institution that was limited in its sphere of operation.[50] Eventually, he hoped that success in integrating a narrow sector of the economy would encourage the Europeans to integrate their economies in ever-expanding areas, creating links in the chain of European integration that would evolve by degrees. It turned out that Monnet was right. A group of six nations were willing to cede control over a small measure of their sovereignty, because they perceived that they had certain common interests and believed that together they could achieve more than they could alone.[51] Thus was established the ECSC which became the foundation of the future development of the European Economic Community and the European Union.

Prior to the creation of the ECSC, its six member nations had attempted to craft the markets to maximize their individual advantage. As
it became clear that even their national reconstruction plans similarly
relied on increasing steel production and the economic revival of West
Germany, which was the main source of machines and machine tools
as well as a large consumer of food and steel, they opted to pool their
coal and steel resources for their collective advantage. In doing so, they
were motivated by a combination of economic necessity, enlightened
self-interest and a dose of idealism.

3. Goals of the ECSC. As envisioned by Monnet and articulated in
Schuman's declaration, the ECSC was intended to create a solid and
united Europe in which the standard of living would rise and prices for
coal and steel products would drop.[52] The ECSC would aim to expand,
modernize and improve the quality of production, ensure that the common
market was regularly supplied with coal and steel at consistent prices and
terms to consumers in all member countries, and serve as a joint buyer
and seller for the community. It would steer investment, develop exports
to other countries, and both equalize and better the conditions of labor in
these industries.[53] Schuman recognized that because the member states
would be starting from very different production conditions, they would
need a transitional period during which measures would be implemented
to allow the Treaty to progressively come into force.

4. Innovative Features of the ECSC. As originally envisioned by
Monnet the ECSC included several radical new ideas. First, participating countries would forego sovereignty in a limited but well-defined
field. Commenting on the Schuman proposals, Monnet said that they
were "revolutionary or ... nothing." "The indispensable first principle
of these proposals," he explained was "the abnegation of sovereignty in
a limited but decisive field" and that a plan without such a principle as
its basis could make no useful contribution towards solving the major
problems plaguing Europe. He added that cooperation between nations
was insufficient to solve the problem and that what was required was "a
fusion of the interests of the European peoples and not merely another
effort to maintain the equilibrium of those interests..."[54]

Second, Monnet was determined that the High Authority be a strong,
independent and autonomous body. He wanted to avoid the pitfall of the
traditional intergovernmental organizations, which generally required
the subordination of the executive to representatives of member states.
Therefore he proposed that the member states transfer their powers over
coal and steel production to the supra-national High Authority, which was

to assume full executive power over the coal and steel sectors of the six member states. The High Authority was to be composed of well-qualified and independent persons to be appointed by joint agreement between the governments. Its members, president and auditor of accounts were all to be appointed jointly. It was critical to him that these persons possess not only technical capacity but a concern for the general interest.[55] He was adamant that it was possible to find a small number of persons of "real stature" who were "capable of rising above particular or national interests in order to work for the accomplishment of common objectives..."[56] At the conference organized to negotiate the establishment of the ECSC, Monnet set the tone by saying: "We are here to undertake a common task—not to negotiate for our own national advantage but to seek it to the advantage of all. Only if we eliminate from our debates any particularist feelings shall we reach a solution."[57]

Monnet got his wish; the requirement of independence was incorporated in the Treaty of Paris, which provided that the members of the High Authority were to be completely independent in the performance of their duties and that they were neither to seek nor accept instructions from any governments or any other body. The Treaty even said that they were to "refrain from any action incompatible with the supra-national character of their duties."[58] To bolster the High Authority's independence further, its operations were to be financed through the imposition of levies on the production of coal and steel and by borrowing so that it would not have to rely on national contributions, which had theretofore been the usual way to finance intergovernmental organizations and which would give governments an undue influence over its work.[59]

Third, the creation of the ECSC was animated by a principle of equality among member states. Therefore the High Authority was to operate as a college with decisions made by a majority vote where there was a quorum greater than one-half of the membership. There was to be no requirement of unanimity nor any right of veto, as both of these were considered shortcomings associated with the traditional intergovernmental organizations that Monnet was trying to break away from.

Fourth, Monnet was determined to create an integrated supra-national organization that offered the prospect of permanent compliance by governments. Europe's past experience with intergovernmental agencies had demonstrated that it was not enough to rely on the good faith of national governments to ensure compliance.[60] It was for this reason that another salient feature of the ECSC was the direct effect of its decisions upon and within the member states, as well as its power to exercise direct control within their territories. The High Authority's decisions were binding on all the member states and directly enforceable within their territories. It also had the right to fine or penalize enterprises, which violated the provisions of the Treaty. In addition, it had the power in certain instances to suspend payment of sums it owed to a delinquent member state and to adopt measures or authorize other members to adopt measures to correct the effects of noncompliance.[61] This kind of supra-national power was novel and created quite a stir among the six nations that had signed the Treaty of Paris establishing the ECSC. During the national debates leading to the ratification of the Treaty of Paris, some parliamentarians in Belgium were shocked at the idea that institutions set up by the Treaty would have legislative, judicial and executive power over Belgian citizens and Belgian property. And yet the parliaments overcame their reservations and threw in their lot to create the ECSC.

   5. *The Compromises Made to Monnet's Plan.* Nonetheless, Monnet's plan, as reflected in his proposed draft Treaty of June 1950, was never really given the chance it deserved because it was not implemented in its totality. Some of its key features were significantly modified as a result of compromises made in the negotiations leading to the Treaty of Paris, which established the ECSC. These compromises reflected a reluctance to give the High Authority the power it needed, thereby weakening its efficacy and that of the ECSC as a whole.

   The most significant compromises involved the creation of two in-stitutions that were not envisioned by Monnet, namely the Council of Ministers and the Common Assembly, along with the requirement that the Council provide its assent to certain decisions of the High Authority. This requirement interfered with the work of the High Authority and was especially apparent in the rare circumstance when the High Authority was allowed under the Treaty to intervene directly in the area of production, namely in times of crisis. Unfortunately, the Treaty required the High Authority to obtain the assent of the Council before it could intervene to establish a system of production quotas, or to allocate coal and steel resources and establish consumption priorities when the community faced a serious shortage of products.

   This weakening of the High Authority ultimately became the cause of its undoing. In May 1959 during a coal crisis, the Council twice refused to give its assent. Reflecting on this crisis, the High Authority stated in its Eighth General Report "its profound and unanimous conviction that it could not possibly fulfill its responsibilities if the only means at its disposal were that of persuasion, and if the operation of the Community were based on the principle of unanimity."[62]

C. Proposal to Create a Global Supra-National Oil and Gas High Authority

In his famous declaration of 1950 announcing the proposal for creating the ECSC, Robert Schuman said: "World peace cannot be safeguarded without the making of creative efforts proportionate to the dangers which threaten it."[63] These words still hold true today. Oil and natural gas have become the dominant sources of energy and are as important to the economic development and prosperity of the nations of the world as coal and steel were to the rebuilding of Europe in 1950.[64] To address the problems resulting from unequal access to the critical resources of oil and gas discussed in Part I, the world community should establish a supra-national High Authority for oil and gas under the auspices of the United Nations along the lines originally recommended by Monnet for the ECSC. Europe's experience with a significantly watered down version of Monnet's plan has demonstrated the necessity of applying Monnet's model in its totality to avoid the pitfalls created by the modifications that were subsequently made to it. Europe's subsequent experience in successfully creating a European Community followed by the European Union has allowed it to learn other crucial lessons as well about ceding power to supra-national organizations. The world community has watched these developments and observed the benefits to be reaped from such a supra-national approach.

The High Authority for oil and gas should be a supra-national organization rather than a purely intergovernmental one, to which the nations of the world should cede a measure of their sovereignty in a limited sphere of operation, namely the production and regulation of oil and gas. The international community faces a litany of problems discussed in Part II (A) because of the excessively nationalistic approach to the production and distribution of oil and gas. It should convince nations that it is both necessary for their continued economic development as well as in their self-interest to forego some limited control of their sovereignty. This is a sphere of activity in which they must recognize that the advantage of the part can best be attained by assuring the advantage of the whole. Achieving a higher standard of living for all, ensuring a regular supply of oil and gas based on accurate and clear information relating to supply, demand, production and stockpiles, and providing access to it on equal terms for all can only be an incentive to commit to a supra-national system. Creating a system that ensures equal access to oil and gas will vastly reduce civil wars, border conflicts and international conflicts driven by the desire to control these resources. As Chancellor Adenauer commented about the Saar region over which France and Germany had fought many wars and which had changed hands between them many times, since the creation of the ECSC's High Authority would mean that the Saar's production would be going to the general Franco-German pool, the question of whether the territory was French or German had lost much of its importance.[65] Moreover, equalizing and enhancing labor conditions for all involved in the oil and gas industry worldwide as well as setting international standards to minimize the damage to the environment from oil and gas production should serve as further incentives.

The High Authority should initially be given the full power to exercise management control over the production of oil and gas worldwide. Over time, as the institution establishes its credibility and efficacy, the nations of the world may be willing to grant it further power by transferring to it the public ownership of oil and gas production facilities around the world. Based on the experience of the ECSC, it is to be expected that there will be strong forces of opposition to the idea of such a supra-national High Authority, particularly from industrial interests. In the face of such opposition we should remember two things: First is the reaction of the French high commissioner for Germany to concerns expressed by a committee of industrialists: "[the concerns] prove[d] only that the industrialists have little imagination and that they have great difficulty understanding a system which deviates from what they have been accustomed to since childhood…"[66] The second is that the opposition of the industrialists in several of the ECSC member countries, especially France, Belgium and Germany, soon dissipated after the system was up and running.

The members of the High Authority should number nineteen. These members can initially be appointed by joint agreement between the governments of the world. Eventually, however, it would be best to move from appointment to election. There should be a two-step process for elections: the parliaments of the world should first each elect one qualified member to represent their nation. Then all the members so elected should elect nineteen from among their number to run the High Authority. In this way, the people of the world will have more confidence in an institution, which they believe has been elected democratically. Regardless of whether the members are appointed or elected; they should possess both technical expertise in their field and be known for their concern for the general interest rather than their own national interest. Moreover, they should not be influenced by or take instructions from any government or private interests. In order to further ensure the independence of this organization, its operating fund should come from levies on the production of oil and gas worldwide rather than from national contributions.

The High Authority should be given the power to set the policies and rules for regulating the production of oil and gas, ensuring that there is ample supply for all nations, ensuring modernization and the lowering of prices as much as is possible, ensuring access to oil and gas on equal terms to all the nations of the world, monitoring supply and demand, steering investment as necessary, and taking measures to intervene in times of shortage to establish fair quotas for all. In addition, it should take steps to equalize and better the labor conditions in the oil and gas industry world wide as well as create and enforce international standards for ensuring the protection of the environment to the extent possible during such production.

The High Authority should be empowered to take decisions by a simple majority in most cases, with the possibility of a two-thirds requirement in rare circumstances on condition that there is a quorum of at least one half of the membership. Most importantly, it should never be hamstrung by a requirement of unanimity or the power of veto. Nor should its ability to exercise power be hindered by requirements of obtaining the assent of any other institution.

The policies and rules set by the High Authority in managing and regulating the world's production of oil and gas should be binding on all the nations of the world. Moreover, the High Authority should be given the power to enforce these policies and rules through the application of fines or sanctions. Such sanctions should be enforceable within the territory of the member states using the state's own legal and enforcement apparatus. However, decisions of the High Authority should be appealable to an ad hoc court of arbitration, as envisioned by Monnet. This court should be made a permanent specialized chamber of the International Court of Justice, which over time would develop the expertise and a body of precedent to consider and pass judgments in cases involving oil and gas. For any given case, the members should, as far as possible, be chosen from nationals of states not parties to the particular case. The judgments of this ad hoc court should be executory within the territory of the member states under the same conditions as the imposition of penalties by the High Authority.

The High Authority should be assisted by the creation of a Consultative Committee akin to the one created by the ECSC Treaty based on the idea recommended by Monnet. This Consultative Assembly would act as an advisory body to the High Authority. It would be composed of representatives of the various sectors involved in the production of oil and gas, especially producers, industry workers, and consumers. The Committee would be available for consultation with the High Authority, providing it with important information and input. However, its opinions would not be binding and all decisions would be left solely to the High Authority.

Finally, as with the establishment of the ECSC, there will probably need to be a period of transition to allow production facilities that are starting from different points of strength to implement transitional measures to bring themselves in alignment with each other.

III. Conclusion

The current inequitable and uneven system of access to critical global natural resources including oil and gas must give way to a new system that ensures equal access to all members of the international community of nations. To this end, this chapter has proposed that state leaders begin by creating a supra-national High Authority for the management and regulation of oil and gas under the auspices of the United Nations. It is hoped that once this organization has been established and successfully operated, it will pave the way for the creation of similar equitable and rule-based institutions for the management and regulation of other critical resources, including nuclear energy, water and certain precious minerals. In crafting such institutions the international community can draw on both the model of the ECSC as envisioned by Monnet and other models that it has experimented with over the years. The end result should be a more peaceful, secure and prosperous world for all.

Notes

1.   Copyright 2007 by Sovaida Ma'ani Ewing, author of *Collective Security Within Reach*, published by George Ronald publication in October 2007.
2.   Vedantam, Shankar. "Nuclear Plants Not Keeping Track of Waste." *Washington Post*, April 12, 2005.
3.   Final report of the Panel of Experts on the Illegal Exploitation of Natural Resources and Other Forms of Wealth in the Democratic Republic of the Congo, S/2003/1027 and subsequent Press Release by Security Council entitled "Security Council Condemns Continuing Exploitation of Natural Resources in Democratic Republic of Congo", SC/7925, November 19, 2003; Report of the Panel of Experts Appointed Pursuant to Security Council Resolution 1306 (2000) in relation to Sierra Leone, S/2000/1195, December 20, 2000; Report of the Panel of Experts pursuant to Security Council Resolution 1343 (2001) concerning Liberia, S/2001/1015, Oc-

tober 26, 2001; Report of the Panel of Experts on Violations of Security council Sanctions Against UNITA pursuant to Security Council Resolution 1237 (1999) of May 7, 1999, S/2000/203 of March 10, 2000.

4.   These NGOs include Global Policy Forum, Global Witness, World Vision, Human Rights Watch, International Peace Academy, Save the Children Alliance and the International Crisis Group.

5.   Examples include the Kimberley Process designed to stem the flow of "conflict diamonds," the Extractive Industries Transparency Initiative (EITI) for oil, gas and minerals, and the EU's Forest Law Enforcement, Governance and Trade initiative (FLEGT) for identifying and tracking legal timber. See Grono, Nick, Vice President of the International Crisis Group. "Addressing the links between conflicts and natural resources." Speech at the Conference on Security, Development and Forest Conflict, Brussels, 9 February 2006.

6.   Perlez, Jane and Johnson, Kirk. "Behind Gold's Glitter: Torn Lands and Pointed Questions." *New York Times*, October 24, 2005.

7.   Whitesides, George M. and Crabtree, George W. "Sustainability and Energy: Don't Forget Long-Term Fundamental Research in Energy." *Science*, February 9, 2007:797.

8.   See, Robert, Paul. "The Undeclared Oil War." *Washington Post*, June 28, 2004; and Falksohn, Rudiger. "A Nuclear Power Renaissance." *Der Spiegel*, January 16, 2007.

9.   Wolfe, Adam. "China's Demand for Energy is Reshaping Power Structures Around the World." Power and Interest News Report, February 25, 2004.

10.   "Glittering Towers In a War Zone." Economist, December 7, 2006.

11.   Ibid.

12.   Follath, Eric. "Natural Resources are Fuelling A New Cold War." *Der Spiegel*, August 18, 2006; and "China, Iran sign biggest oil & gas deal," October 31, 2004 found at http://www.chinadaily.com.

13.   Yeomans, Matthew. "Crude Politics—The US, China and the race for oil security." *The Atlantic Monthly*, April 2005: 49.

14.   "Once Marginal, But Now Kings of the Oil World." *The New York Times*, April 23, 2006 at http://www.nytimes.com.

15.   Myers, Steven Lee. "Memo from Moscow: Belarus Learns that Days of Wine and Roses are Over." *The New York Times*, January 12, 2007 at http://www.nytimes.com.

16.   Kramer, Andrew E. "Gazprom threatens to cut off gas if Belarus rejects higher price." *The New York Times*, December 27, 2006 at http://www.nytimes.com.

17.   Myers, Steven Lee Myers. "Belarus and Russia Spar Over Crude Oil Cut Off." *The New York Times*, January 9, 2007 at http://www.nytimes.com.

18.   Myers, Steven Lee. "Memo From Moscow: Putin's Assertive Diplomacy is Seldom Challenged." *The New York Times*, December 27, 2006 at http://www.nytimes.com.

19.   "Iran Hints of Reduction of Oil Sales over Nuclear Dispute," Reuters, reported in *The New York Times*, October 2, 2005 at http://www.nytimes.com.

20.   Forero, Juan. "Venezuela Cautions US It May Curtail Oil Exports." *The New York Times*, February 27, 2006 at http://www.nytimes.com.

21.   Yeomans, "Crude Politics" supra note 13.

22.   "Nigeria to Yield Oil Territory to Cameroon." Agence France-Presse reported in *The New York Times*, June 13, 2006.

23.   Grono, Nick. "Natural Resources and Conflict." Speech given at the EIS Symposium on Sustainable Development and Security, European Parliament, Brussels, 31 May 2006, found at http://www.icg.org.

24.   "Africa's Oil Comes with Big Downside." Associated Press report in *The New York Times*, August 28, 2005.
25.   International Crisis Group Report, "Fuelling the Niger Delta Crisis," *Africa Report*, No. 118, September 28, 2006 found at http://www.icg.org; and "Fight for oil wealth fuels violence." *Human Rights Watch*, February 7, 2005, found at http://www.globalpolicy.org.
26.   Dunkel, G. "What Imperialists Don't Say: Oil is Behind Struggle in Darfur." *Workers World*, April 27, 2006 found at http://www.globalpolicy.org; and Morse, David. "War of the Future: Oil Drives the Genocide in Darfur." TomDispatch, August 18, 2005, found at http://www.globalpolicy.org.
27.   Tanter, Richard. "Gas Dispute Deepens Neighborly Tensions." Nautilus Institute at RMIT, Summer 2004/5 found at http://www.nautilus.org.
28.   International Crisis Group at http://www.icg.org.
29.   Grono, "Natural Resources and Conflict," supra note 23.
30.   Grono, Nick. "Addressing the links between conflicts and natural resources." Talk given at Conference on Security, Development and Forest Conflict, Brussels, February 9, 2006, reported at http://www.icg.org.
31.   Soros, George. "Transparent Corruption." DebtChannel, February 2003, found at http://www.globalpolicy.org.
32.   Palley, Thomas I. "Lifting the Natural Resource Curse." Foreign Service Journal, December 2003, found at http://www.globalpolicy.org.
33.   LaFraniere, Sharon LaFraniere. "In Oil-Rich Angola, Cholera Preys Upon Poorest." New York Times, June 16, 2006, found at http://www.nytimes.com; and "Fuelling Poverty: Oil, War and Corruption," a report produced by Christian Aid, 2003.
34.   Polgreen, Lydia. "World Bank Reaches Pact with Chad over Use of Oil Profits." *The New York Times*, July 15, 2006, found at http://www.nytimes.com.; and Daphne Wysham, "World Bank OK with Blood for Oil." TomPaine, January 5, 2007, found at http://www.globalpolicy.org.
35.   Palley, "Lifting the Natural Resource Curse," supra note 32.
36.   Christian Aid Report, "Fuelling Poverty," supra note 33.
37.   Sachs and Warner reported in Christian Aid Report, "Fuelling Poverty," 4-6, supra note 33.
38.   "Global Oil Producers Discuss Supply," Reuters reported in *The New York Times*, November 19, 2005, found at http://www.nytimes.com.
39.   International Crisis Group Report, "Fuelling the Niger Delta Crisis," supra note 25.
40.   Christian Aid Report, "Fuelling Poverty," supra note 33.
41.   Rohter, Larry. "Vast Pipelines in Amazon Face Challenges Over Protecting Rights and Rivers." *The New York Times*, January 21, 2007, at http://www.nytimes.com.
42.   Mouawad, Jad. "Oil Prices Leap after Attacks in Nigeria." *The New York Times*, February 20, 2006, at http://www.nytimes.com.
43.   "Oil in troubled waters." *Economist*, April 28, 2005.
44.   Bahree, Bhushan and Cummins, Chip. "In Oil's New Era, Power Shifts to Countries with reserves." *The Wall Street Journal*, June 14 2006: A1.
45.   "The real trouble with oil." *Economist*, April 28, 2005.
46.   Stirk, Peter M.R. and Weigall, David. *The Origins and Development of European Integration: A Reader and Commentary*. London and New York: Pinter, 1999, page 11; and Dedman, Martin J. The Origins and Development of the European Union 1945-95 London: Routledge, 1996, p. 58.
47.   Dedman, The Origins and Development of the European Union 61.
48.   Dedman, The Origins and Development of the European Union 33; and Goorma-

ghtigh, John. "European Coal and Steel Community." *International Conciliation*, 1997 v. 30. Buffalo, New York: William S. Hein & Co., Inc., p. 348.

49.   Churchill, Winston. Speech given in Zurich, 19 September 1946, found at http://www.ena.lu/mce.cfm.

50.   Fontaine, Pascal. A New Idea for Europe: The Schuman Declaration 1950-2000. Luxembourg: European Commission, 2000, p. 12.

51.   Goormaghtigh. "European Coal and Steel Community," 348 supra note 48.

52.   Fontaine, A New Idea for Europe 13 supra note 50; and Goormaghtigh, "European Coal and Steel Community," 347 supra note 48.

53.   Goormaghtigh, "European Coal and Steel Community," 350 supra note 48; and Fontaine, A New Idea for Europe 19-20 supra note 50; and Gillingham, John. Coal, Steel, and The Rebirth of Europe, 1945-1955. England: Cambridge University Press, 1991, page 232.

54.   Fontaine, A New Idea for Europe 17 supra note 50.

55.   Memo prepared by Jean Monnet for David Bruce, American Ambassador to France to send to the US State Department, found at Stirk and Weigall, The Origins and Development of European Integration 64.

56.   Letter from Jean Monnet to Edwin Plowden, Chief Planning Officer at the UK Treasury, date May 25, 1950 found in Stirk and Weigall, The Origins and Development of European Integration 77 supra note 46.

57.   Monnet, Jean. Memoirs. London: William Collins and Son Ltd, 1976, page 323 quoted at Fontaine, A New Idea for Europe 15 supra note 50.

58.   Article 9 of the Treaty of Paris, 1951 quoted in Stirk and Weigall, The Origins and Development of European Integration 87-79 supra note 46.

59.   Fontaine, A New Idea for Europe 19 supra note 50; and Goormaghtigh, "European Coal and Steel Community" 365 supra note 48.

60.   Dedman, The Origins and Development of the European Union 63 supra note 46.

61.   Article 88 of the Treaty of Paris, 1951, quoted in Goormaghtigh, "European Coal and Steel Community" 364 supra note 48.

62.   Stirk and Weigall, The Origins and Development of European Integration 71-72 supra note 46.

63.   Robert Schuman's famous Declaration of May 9, 1950 quoted in Fontaine, Pascal. Europe A Fresh Start: The Schuman Declaration 1950-90. Luxembourg: European Commission, 1990, pages 44-46.

64.   Bahree and Cummins, "In Oil's New Era", supra note 44.

65.   Goormaghtigh, "European Coal and Steel Community" 352 supra note 48.

66.   Stirk and Weigall, The Origins and Development of European Integration 85 supra note 46.

Improving Early Warning, Analysis, and Response Regarding Armed Conflicts

Hayward R. Alker

The Present Situation

"Early Warning and Early Response" and "early warning and analysis discourse has recently been recognized as important for the prevention of armed civil, transnational or inter-state conflicts. Major governments and well-resourced NGOs may have fairly effective warning practices but the more difficult issue is responding with early and effective preventive actions (Carnegie Commission on Preventing Violent Conflict, 1997: 43-47; Alker et al. 2001; Carment and Schnabel, 2003: Ch 9 & 10; High-level Panel on Threats, Challenges and Change, 2004: p. 37; Kofi Anan, 2006: paragraph 86-97). In 2002, David Hamburg argued that "prevention is pervasive in discussions of war and peace" (Hamburg 2004: 277). Hamburg was then president of the Carnegie Corporation of New York, responsible for funding much work in the 1990s on early warning and early response. The Carnegie Commission further argued in 2004 that "a preventive approach would have saved the international community almost $130 billion" over the estimated actual cost of "about $200 billion [spent] on the seven major interventions of the 1990s, in Bosnia and Herzegovina, Somalia, Rwanda, Haiti, the Persian Gulf, Cambodia, and El Salvador, exclusive of Kosovo and East Timor"1(ibid.). Increasing the United Nations' effectiveness in conflict prevention or mitigation after "the high-profile disasters of Bosnia, Somalia, and Rwanda" (Cockell 2003: 183) and the continuing frustrations of a non-legitimated US intervention in Iraq and continuing genocide in Darfur are among pressing present problems. Winning, rather than preventing, the global "war on terrorism" seems more important to some of the Security Council's permanent members and their allies than either the meliorist goal of conflict management or the transformative goal conflict. Many "realists" see competition for hegemonic supremacy and great power as historical, natural and inevitable. Despite this, the UN World Summit of September 2005 unanimously affirmed an expanded preventive mandate that "each individual State has the responsibility to protect its population from genocide, war crimes, ethnic cleansing and crimes against humanity" (United Nations General Assembly 2005: paragraph 138).

Former UN Secretary-General Kofi Annan has recently argued that although "prevention is now understood as central to the mission of the [UN] Organization, system-wide strategic leadership in this area is still weak" (Annan 2006: paragraph 94). Referring to an earlier General Assembly resolution, he admits that "no specific progress has been made" regarding "early warning, collection of information and analysis" and that despite a variety of related activities within the UN system, a "comprehensive repository for the knowledge gained in its diverse conflict-prevention activities" is needed (ibid.).

Below, I shall first analyze two current frameworks for identifying preventive objectives and socio-historical factors that have led conflicts towards or diverted conflicts away from violence will be analyzed. The recommendations in the UN Secretary-General's Report on improving the capacities of states, societies and the UN system for realizing these preventive goals will be summarized. Macro-political, systemic, operational, and institution-specific perspectives will be considered in the analysis of preventive capabilities within the UN system. Then this chapter will offer a plausible, transformative vision of significantly stronger early warning, analysis and response capacities within the UN system for dealing with potentially deadly conflicts. At the time of publication we have been celebrating the 60th anniversary of the United Nations. The vision discussed in this chapter will be aimed at another 60 years into the future, approximately 120 years after the founding of the United Nations.

Two Frameworks for Response-Oriented Early Warning Information Collection and Analysis

Two recent UN-relevant schematizations of early-warning-early-response and conflict prevention analysis2 are useful as a concrete introduction to the conceptual and evidentiary richness of the early warning analysis and response problematic. They also operate well as background material for better understanding the Secretary-General's potentially far-reaching reform proposals. The first comes from a late 2005 "Early Warning & Early Response Handbook" (CPR Network 2006); the second from a contribution to an "Early Warning and Preventive Measures" (EWPM) joint project of the UN Department of Political Affairs (now considered the United Nations' lead agency for conflict prevention) and the UN Staff College3 (Cockell 2003). If the latter is evidently UN-centered, the former is somewhat broader in its orientation, being the work of "an informal network of senior managers of bilateral donor countries and multilateral agencies dealing with the complex issues of conflict management and response" including several of those entities sponsoring or contributing to the former study (CPR Network 2006:3-4). These include a post-conflict reconstruction manual from the US Army and a USAID planning and performance monitoring manual, a "Compendium" of "Operational Frameworks" of Peacebuilding Donors, the Forum on Early Warning and Response (FEWER), the West Africa Network for Peacebuilding (WANET), the European Commission, the World Bank, OECD, and various other national research centers and UN departments and agencies (ibid.).

Conforming to the operational imperative of "putting it all on one page" for busy decision-makers, the Conflict Prevention and Post-Conflict Reconstruction (CPR) Network's "Conflict Diagnostic Framework" is schematized in Table 1, below.

The Handbook itself mostly outlines the use and revision of such a framework in seven steps: after an overview, the next three steps suggest

Table 1
Conflict Diagnostic Framework*

(P) Political	(E) Economic	(S) Social	(SEC) Security	(I) International/Regional
Peacebuilding Objectives Optimal: Contingency:				
Conflict Factors	Peace Factors	Stakeholders	Strategic Issues	
Manifestations •	Ongoing Peace Efforts •	Actions •	Conflict Synergies •	
Proximate Causes •	Structures/Processes in Place •	Agendas/Needs •	Peace Synergies •	
Root Causes •	Peacebuilding Gaps •	Alliances •	Stakeholder Synergies •	
Scenarios: Best Case – Middle Case – Worst Case –				

* Early Warning-Early Response Handbook, v2.3 September 2005 - A CPR Network Resource, p. 7.

lengthier outlines and definitions for constructing entries to Table 1. These steps begin with assessing conflict-exacerbating and peace-promoting factors, what are called "stakeholder dynamics," and continue with a process of filling out different scenarios and defining "peacebuilding objectives." The final two steps "help define strategic issues and choices, as well as key entry points for response" (CPR Network 2006: 5).

Because they represent an important difference between the frameworks of the CPR Network and the EWPM project, the explicit treatment of the actions, agendas, needs, alliances and synergies of stakeholders in Table 1 and "stakeholder dynamics" throughout the CPR Handbook deserve special attention. Defined as "primary, secondary, and external parties," individuals or groups "with a stake in maintaining the conflict and/or building peace," stakeholders are profiled in order to understand their "potential and actual motivations" and "the [peace or violent conflict promoting] actions they may take to further their respective interests." Urging attention to the "relative importance of the various actors and interrelationships," the Handbook and Table 1 tell us to study both conscious and unconscious "synergies," in particular note that the "combined effect of stakeholders can produce an effect that enhances, or reinforces, the effect of individual actors" (CPR Network 2006: 12).

Leading figures in shaping the earlier conflict analytical frameworks of the FEWER network, David Nyheim and Kumar Rupesinghe, have commented revealingly about the importance of attending to stakeholders in an earlier essay which appears to underlie and explain Kofi Annan's potentially radical, almost anti-interventionist, advocacy of fostering "home-grown self-sustaining infrastructures for peace" (Rupesinghe et al. 2001: 410). The guiding principles for the locally led and implemented early warning networks these authors discuss are: urging that local perspectives on causes, dynamics and solutions to violent conflicts are heard by other (often non-local) policymakers; promoting inter-organizational synergies with (more quantitatively and computationally oriented, often far away) monitoring efforts in North America and Europe; and linking warnings to appropriate responses and a peace "owned by" local, regional and international stakeholders (ibid.). Arguing against an "interventionist paradigm" and those seeing only local perspectives as biased4 they conclude that "top-down or select interventionist approaches do not work… [E]ffective responses to conflict require integrated action, and action that is owned by communities in conflict prone/affected areas," resulting in a need to communicate local perspectives upwards and outward (Rupesinghe et al. 2001: 418f). A detailed and concrete example of such assessments, based on insights from both global and local organizations in the Georgian Republic (of the former Soviet Union) is given for the Javakheti region of the former Soviet Union (see also Ivanov and Nyheim 2004). Decentralized power-sharing considerations are clearly implied by such an emphasis on local perspectives and interests. Also, a contemporarily relevant concern with sustainable peacemaking seen as often antithetical to politically motivated short-term Great Power or Security Council-legitimated interventions in far away places, I find the distributed, extended network character of a globally effective knowledge repository of this sort visionary, as well as mind boggling, and shall say more about it below.

Although much more could be said about the CPR Handbook's framework and its construction and implementation, I want now to discuss a second framework, basing my discussion of John Cockell's excellent, detailed account of the EWPM project (Cockell 2003). His paper attempts to get beyond the paralyzing view that early warnings too often fail to produce timely and effective responses entirely because of failures of political will. The UN's capacities also need improving. He outlines "the basis for an organizationally specific redefinition of conflict prevention" pointed towards its needed "strategic and proactive application in situations of protracted internal conflicts" (Cockell 1003: 182).5 Like the CPR Handbook, a document of similar length, Cockell's article is focused on providing concepts and an analytical language for a nine—step process of multi-sectoral, inter-organizational applied policy planning, beginning with early warning analyses (not the earlier, locally-oriented information collection issues discussed above) and ending with strategically chosen action responses. Cockell's nine basic steps are (Cockell 2003: 189):

1) Analyze key causes of conflict and conflict dynamics.
2) Prioritize sectors for strategic and comprehensive responses.
3) Define specific operational objective(s).
4) Identify range of potential preventive measures for each operational objective.
5) Assess the UN's comparative advantage.
6) Determine required combinations of preventive measures.
7) Integrate participation of key UN departments and agencies.
8) Coordinate operational implementation of preventive measures.
9) Monitor preventive action and determine exit criteria.

Beyond the obvious (and less obvious) similarities of this action-oriented, applied-planning framework, and with that of the CPR Handbook, I see that the most distinctive difference is this list's intentional emphasis on the United Nations' central, non-local, organizational specific requirements. Stakeholders are not explicit or important parts of the picture although, of course, they are part of the "required combinations of preventive measures." Items 5 ("the UN's comparative advantage"), 7 and 8 ("integrating and coordinating the activities its departments and agencies"), and item 9 ("monitoring actions and thinking hard about exit criteria") have a strategic, institution-specific character. There is nothing wrong with research projects focused on improving the United Nations' capacities, but as Annan synergistically recognized, success is interdependent with the enhancement of more national and local preventive capacities. Written with more input from conflict early warning NGOs, the CPR Handbook focuses much more centrally on local, regional (and international) stakeholders, mostly both short-term and long-term players rather than what appears to be the promotion of more efficient successes and the diminution of resource-and-legitimacy-depleting failures of the United Nations.

But a conceptual reorientation with both reformist and transformative implications is also visible here. These success and failures appear to be judged relativistically, vis-à-vis other organizations, agencies and individual great powers trying to achieve semi-anarchic adaptive success in an evolution-like struggle for survival. This thematic concept helps to motivate the following discussion of accelerating the intelligent; the partially synoptic redesign of global conflict prevention capacities up to the point where new species of preventive early warning, analysis and response are born.

Kofi Annan's "Progress Report on the Prevention of Armed Conflict"

Attempting to articulate a potentially realistic longer-term vision, it is prudent to start with expert judgments of the directions of feasible reform, even if one's goal is to articulate a more fundamentally transformed world. Based on wide consultations among those seriously interested in conflict prevention, Kofi Annan's impressive "Progress Report on the Prevention of Armed Conflict" is a timely place to start (Annan 2006). Within this more inclusive text, we shall focus on those features that seem most directly relevant to our discussion on early warning, analysis and response. Surely the previously mentioned "catch-all" character of the recommendations should also be evident. Table 2 summarizes the mostly incremental recommendations at the end of the report.

Elements of a More Comprehensive Vision

But there is more going on within, and in the preparation of, the Secretary-General's Report than its obvious character as a multi-agency,
multi-programmatic review. Many things are unsaid, or stated in cautious and unclear terms. What would a more comprehensive vision of
improved early warning and early response practices and systems look
like in another 60 years, circa 120 years after the founding of the United
Nations? Several more radical elements of such a vision are suggested by
the previous discussion, Table 2, and the rest of Kofi Annan's report.

First, I stress the transformative potential of a world where a multi-
level "culture of prevention," seen as derivative from the "responsibility
to protect," had significantly upstaged the "culture of reaction" now
characterizing most member states' conception of the United Nations'
role as well as most of the major Security Council actions of the United
Nations' first 60 years. Part of the realism of both the CPR Network's
and the EWPM project, and the Carnegie Corporation's project before
them, was their recognition of the reactive "conflict management" rather
than "conflict prevention" orientation of much of the Security Council's
actions.6 Thus, all of these studies, like others, conceptualize conflict dynamics in cyclical terms, involving earlier escalatory and later, hopefully,
de-escalatory phases; the effectiveness of different coping mechanisms
is seen to depend on suitability for particular phases in a conflict, and
perhaps even its history of phase sequences. Encouraging de-escalation
and preventing re-escalation are as important as preventing escalation
at all in the discussions of most of these cases. That the United Nations
authorized (as a "first") the UN Preventive Deployment Force (UNPRE-
DEP) for the Former Republic of Macedonia in December 1992 is so
regular and lonely a citation of a genuinely preventive orientation of UN
action, that one is correct in emphasizing the dominance of more reactive
peace-bringing actions.

Think what a difference a multi-level commitment to a global culture
promoting the peaceful resolution of disputes and crises would mean.
Patriotic heroism—the highly gendered willingness to kill, die, or commit
suicide for one's buddies, family, community, nation, state, religion or
way of life, would be redefined and redirected towards global, regional
and local preventive practices and authorities7. At least for significant
minorities in all regions of the globe, war, still glorified by so many as
the highest form of human antagonism and service, would have to be
devalued vis-à-vis a global mix of peaceful, life-and-dignity-preserving,

Table 2
Kofi Annan's 2006 Recommendations for Improving Conflict Prevention

A. Actions addressing tension sources and promoting pacific norms & institutions
1. Global, systemic actions: 98. Member States (hereafter MSs) should support private-sector initiatives on conflict-sensitive business practices, curtail illicit flows of small arms, find common ground against nuclear, chemical and biological weapons use, fight HIV/AIDS, environmental degradation, focus on the prevention-migration nexus, try harder to attain Millennium Development Goals, and strengthen respect for human rights. 99. MSs should support international human rights, humanitarian, etc, legal instruments facilitating the prevention of armed conflict. 100. The international community as a whole should embrace the "responsibility to prevent" via peaceful means, as a way of living up to their obligations to protect their populations (the responsibility to protect).
2. Country-specific structural actions. 101. In accord with their Charter obligations, with UN support, Governments should strengthen their capacities for peaceful dispute/conflict resolution by strengthening their capacities to address structural conflict risk factors. 102. A better approach is needed to assist the building of democracy, constitutional capacities and election conduct. The SG hopes that the two main related intergovernmental efforts—the movement of new or restored democracies and the Community of Democracies—will work together in these directions. Increased support for the UN Democracy Fund is also requested. 103. MSs, with support form the UN and other external sources, should consider creating elements of a national infrastructure for peace. Especially important for this purpose are the potentials for inclusive national dialogue and consensus-building processes, reflecting the views and voices of indigenous groups and women.
3. Operational actions. 104. The SG urges more creative and constructive use of fair and clear sanctions. For example, the tracing and re-channel of natural resource exploitation revenues to meeting the legitimate needs of a population, as has been suggested by a Group of Experts on the Democratic Republic of the Congo. 105. The SG urges active and early use of Charter-mentioned means for dispute resolution and the prevention of conflict escalation.

B. Acting in Concert with actors from civil society and individual governments.
106. All relevant actors, from civil society, individual Governments, regional organizations and constituent parts of the UN system should accept and act upon the principles of shared vulnerability and mutual responsibility, thus facilitating support at all levels for the preventive actions proposed in this Report.
107. UN organs, including the new Human Rights Council and the Peacebuilding Commission, and MSs should likewise deepen their engagement with civil society and other actors important for conflict prevention, as by inviting civil society representatives to provide regular briefings to pertinent bodies. 108. The SG calls for speedy implementation of the UN system-wide action plan re SC Resolution 1325 (on the roles and needs of women in security and peace relevant processes and gender sensitivity), and for more attention by MSs and the UN system to preventing gender-based violence.

C. Enhancing UN capacities to meet its obligations and commitments
110. The UN needs more resources for a strengthened capacity to prevent conflict, and support for developing a related, system-wide, strategic vision. 111. He calls for Member States to support joint conflict prevention efforts of the wider UN system

Table 2 (cont.)

involving its development, humanitarian, human rights and political arms. Especially the increase of developing MSs' mediation and prevention capabilities. 112. As a way of supporting MSs' integrated strategies for addressing root causes of potentially violent conflicts, the SG invites these States to support the Interdepartmental Framework for Coordination (of efforts vs. structural sources of violent conflict). 113. MSs should consider deploying integrated offices for enhancing national capacities for conflict prevention, as in Sierra Leone, and, perhaps, Burundi. 114. Bearing in mind the experiences in Haiti, the Central African Republic, Guinea-Bissau and Timor-Leste, the SG urges MSs not to end UN peace operations prematurely, since peacebuilding can prevent conflict relapses. 115. He requests more financial support for UN humanitarian responses to avert crises and subsequent conflict, especially involving food security, the health and needs of children, refugees and the internally displaced. 116. He calls for Member States and the UN system to launch regular dialogues on conflict prevention, especially re. their joint efforts to build relevant national capabilities. 117. Following upon the 2005 World Summit Declaration, more support is needed for the good offices of the Secretary-General and related mediation partners, including an already approved start-up mediation support capacity. 118. MSs should consider predictably supporting conflict-prevention-activities with, say, 2 per cent of the annual peacekeeping budget.

Source: (Annan 2006: paras. 98-118) relabeled, summarized, quoted and paraphrased.

justice-approximating conflict management and resolution practices. Somewhat skeptically, if all the bloodshed and structural violence of the 20th century was not sufficient to convince large fractions of the world's populace about the superiority of a culture of prevention, it is hard to imagine what horrific acts of human carnage could, in the next half-century be likely to, bring about such a transformation.

Much of the systematic literature on long-term hegemonic competition within the European/World system sees the early decades of the 21st century as likely to witness either a full-scale hegemonic war or a fundamental transformation of the patterns of practice of the previous centuries (Goldstein 1988, Thompson 2001). Islamicist attacks on the United States and the United Nations represent one such threat to the United Nations and the current quasi-hegemon, the United States. Additionally, China is seen as a potential alternative source to insecurity. In a somewhat Spenglerian mood, Samuel Huntington has been plausibly concerned about the multi-decade threat to US interests and Western civilization of a Confucian-Islamic civilizational coalition (Huntington 1996). As is typical in other writings on early warning and early response, our choice of the two frameworks for discussion in an earlier section reflects that most of Annan's 2006 Report, except for a brief reference to weapons of mass destruction, focuses on smaller, local, development-linked conflicts. Perhaps it should also be said that Kofi Annan was courageous to incrementally introduce the categories of "systemic causes" and "systemic actions" (in the body of his Report and in its Recommendations, summarized in Table 2). To the extent that better, publicly demonstrated capabilities obviously exist, a half-century of such continued improvements and rethinking at the systemic level might incrementally produce significantly greater shared commitments among Member States to systemic changes in UN conflict prevention practices.

It should be recalled that the United Nations was born out of a determination of a generation of world leaders and publics to do better than the League of Nations had done in avoiding disastrous wars like World Wars I and II. It is perhaps necessary to say that the ultimately successful handling of this momentous transition is a necessary presupposition of the visionary stance of the present effort. Surely this is an optimistic, middle-term projection of the future of the next half-century or so, to make more plausible the shift in relative attention to a culture of prevention envisioned above.

Like the Carnegie Commission before him, the Secretary-General (Annan 2006: paragraph 4) talks counterfactually about the savings in conflict management and post-conflict rebuilding costs, in this case peacekeeping costs, made necessary because of inadequate, earlier, less expensive prevention activities. The closing recommendation (#118 in Table 2) of 2 percent of peacekeeping budgets regularly contributed towards prevention reflects this thinking. Both the frameworks for early warning, analysis and response we have reviewed above attempt to make such counterfactual arguments more plausible. But that is a very hard task, especially if it includes the development of analytically and politically persuasive action recommendations that will appeal across the many divisions in cultural, scientific and political orientations apparent in today's or tomorrow's world.

Persuasive analyses of approaching conflicts can improve the quality of expectations of what is likely to happen. This allows for some insight into which systemic, structural and operational causes and their level of success, effects, costs, savings, and side-effects are likely to occur. Despite the increase in sophisticated training programs benefiting from early-warning and response analytical frameworks associated with the UN system, there is not a globally-shared agreement on the best analytical (or interventionary) practices in this area7. As we have seen from the discussion of our two existing frameworks for strategic early warning and response analyses and recommendations, a key goal is the provision of timely, analytically and historically well-supported recommendations of best situation-specific mediation and intervention practices.

The construction and use of such knowledge repositories is an enormous task. It is necessary for my argument that the ability to discern the relative strengths and weaknesses of relevant analytic approaches would be shared among a much wider group of pacifically-oriented professional scholars than is the case today.

In one of his more potentially radical remarks, the UN Secretary-General argued: "If we are to enhance the impact of our efforts and address the root causes of conflict, the thrust of preventive work must shift—as indeed it has begun to do—from reactive external interventions with limited, ultimately superficial impacts to internally driven initiatives for developing local and national capacities for prevention ... [i.e., fostering] home-grown self-sustaining infrastructures for peace" (Annan 2006: paragraph 7). Obviously, the Secretary-General is concerned with the generation of what can be called, more generally, a global-cum-local (glocal) political will for peace. This suggests, though, incredibly rich informational and organizational requirements. If we are to gather preventively relevant information as a way of getting beyond "superficial" interventions directed by the central components of the international security system, the Great Powers, the Permanent Members of the Security Council, then this must mean going beyond our reliance on improved, strategically integrated, centrally-oriented information/data collection efforts by NGOs, UN agencies and observer missions.8 It suggests the need to increase our reliance on partly decentralized, multi-perspective information networks or digital formations9 as knowledge repositories working at the level of both local communities and global systems.

If one sees enhanced early warning, analysis and multi-sectoral, multi-integration response capabilities as a desirable goal (CPR Network 2005; Ivanov and Nyheim 2004), the need for greater financial and political support is still clear. I, therefore, argue the significant development within member states, UN departments and agencies, and associated actors, of a coherent set of commitments, and associated resources, for preventively oriented early warning information collection, analyses, and response recommendations. Tactfully but ambiguously, Kofi Annan similarly refers to a key feature of political will in terms of the need within and outside of the United Nations for strategic leadership in the development of relevant capabilities; a key task for that leadership would be the encouragement, sustained by and supporting a culture of prevention, of a global will to peace.

In a future when the hegemony of the United States and the alliance of Anglo-American powers may still exist or be seen as things of the past, it is uncertain exactly what the most likely and realistic prospects are for such a transformation in political capabilities, consciousness, and commitments. Moreover, the uncertainties concerning future power relations relevant to armed conflict prevention goals, and to related early warning, analysis and response capabilities and practices, are greater than that. If local stakeholders are to be empowered by their related efforts at communal, societal or national capability building, this would mean a radical, decentralizing change in order-producing capabilities even more significant than the many extant proposals for increasing different classes of Security Council membership and/or changing their voting rights.

Looking forward another 60 years, in a world of perhaps ten to twelve billion people and much fewer nonrenewable energy resources (except nuclear power, and hard to access coal and oil reserves), green-encircled cities or megacities may be the most "natural" population units seeking direct representation in some Third Tier of the United Nations' governing institutions. Functionally oriented regional and global networks are likely also to have greatly proliferated, hopefully including those related to the different but related tasks of preventing armed conflicts within a continuously developing world system.

Notes

1.   Hamburg 2004: 313, quoting Kofi Annan's citation of the Carnegie Commission on Preventing Deadly Conflict 1998 report. http://www.wilsoncenter.org/subsites/ccpdc/pubs/world/frame.htm.

2.   Although I have given citations indicating the recent tendency in UN system-related discussions to treat conflict early warning issues within the larger functional context of conflict prevention, I shall not attempt to review the history of the addition of early response to invocations of the need for early warnings concerning potentially large scale violent conflicts. Suffice it to suggest that early warners both on the fringes and at the center of the UN system were repeatedly frustrated by their relative success in calling attention to emergently dangerous situations, somewhat less worried about criticisms of having cried "wolf" too often, and frustrated by the resultant lack of adequately authorized and resourced, prompt, responsive, preventive actions. Hence, pointing to the focus on the need for political will in supporting early responses. The highly invasive and political nature of such early warnings has also contributed—along with the broader trend towards thinking of threats to the peace in terms of violations of basic human needs and human insecurities—to a sometimes confusing merging of more classical conceptions of early warnings about threats to the peace with related, often more general, preventive concerns with sustainable development, humanitarian relief or post-conflict reconstruction,

and the specific concerns of many different specialized UN agencies and/or their sectoral administrative branches. For evidence on this catch-all tendency, see the summary of Annan 2006's recommendations in Table 2 below and the website www.reliefweb.int, "the global home for time critical humanitarian information on Complex Emergencies and Natural Disasters". Michael Lund (2004: 302) has thus provocatively suggested an on-line "PreventNet" for focusing on the conflict prevention objectives more specifically.

3.   In addition to previously cited studies, I should also at least mention as highly relevant, but less content-revealing regarding my specific purposes here, the pioneering series of publications sponsored by the International Peace Research Association (Rupesinghe 1992; Adelman and Suhrke 1996; Jentleson 2000; Last 2003; Kirton and Stefanova 2004).

4.   In the formative discussions of the Conflict Early Warning (information) Systems (CEWS) project (Alker, Gurr and Rupesinghe 2001; Alker 2005) which I coordinated with Kumar Rupesinghe, there were repeated references by our contributors from Latin and Central America, Asia and Africa to the non-lasting, media-driven character of such foreign interventions. Methodologically, this meant that the "structured, focused comparisons" methodology of Alex George, relied on by many other Carnegie Corporation of New York projects and ably used by Bruce W. Jentleson (2000) was seen as too focused on single-dimension outcome variables manipulated from a distance, and therefore unacceptable as the general approach of our project. This encouraged me to propose a multi-stage, multi-paradigm approach to generating shareable categories for discursively, computationally and graphically representing conflict elements, phases, factors and interventions, and a more complex, peace-research methodology of "emancipatory empiricism" articulated earlier (Alker 1996). Here is the motivation for the interpretation just given of the CPR Handbook's linkage with the 2006 Annan Report on synergistically improving the conflict prevention capacities of both national communities and the United Nations.

5.   Cockell's explicitness on this point is most helpful, and largely corresponds to the CPR Handbook's similar focus, a far cry from the inter-state focus of much early UN and League of Nations activity and the state-building or peace-building nexus that recent American national administrations have been very ambivalent about. The emphasis on a document written primarily for strengthening the United Nations' conflict prevention capabilities in this area, seen as one of its "comparative advantages" vis-à-vis other international organizations or direct inter-state alliances and relationships clearly sidesteps the veto-hindered capacity of the United Nations for dealing peaceful with great power competition.

6.   After earlier work analyzing voting alignments, their contextual correlates and their coalitional politics, most of my own work on UN peacemaking has mostly followed Ernst Haas's "conflict management" orientation to the UN Collective Security System (see the discussion and citations in Haas 1993 and Alker 1996). This work has tended to show that a collective security system has existed, has undergone significant evolution in its operating rules, and made a limited difference even during the partial paralysis of the Cold War. It has thus argued against frequent American arguments denying value to UN activities, taking more of an incremental reformist orientation rather than a transformative perspective.

7.   See Alker 1993 and 1996; Stremlau and Francisco 1998: 42f; Davies and Gurr 1998; Adibi et al. 1998; Alker, Gurr and Rupesinghe 2001; King and Zeng 2001; Gordon 2004; Carment and Schnabel 2004; Wodak and Chilton 2005 for an incomplete but methodologically diverse overview of promising qualitative, quantitative and textually-oriented representational and analytic strategies.

8. Tatjana Sikoska and Juliet Solomon (Sikoska and Solomon 2004) suggest a particularly well-articulated framework for analyzing the gendered aspects of conflicts and conflict prevention practices.
9. David Last's chapter (Last 2003) is an excellent statement of how better staffed UN observer missions could help revolutionize systemic, structural as well as operational and instrumental information collection relating to conflict prevention.
10. For this sociologically sophisticated conception of emerging postmodern knowledge formations, see (Latham and Sassen 2005), which includes the most immediate precursor to the present article as a constructively oriented example of such formations (Alker 2005).

References

Adelman, H, and A. Suhrke. "Early Warning and Response: Why the International Community Failed to Prevent the Genocide." Disasters, 20(4) 1996: 295-304.

Adibi, J., H. R. Alker, M. Malita, and L. T. Vest Jr. "PARIS: A Prototype Action Recommender's Information Support System for Conflict Prevention." Romanian Journal of International Affairs, 4(1998): 75-108.

Alker, Hayward R. "Designing Information Resources for Transboundary Conflict Early Warning Networks." Latham and Sassen (eds), Digital Formations: IT and Digital Architectures in the Global Realm, 2005. New Jersey: Princeton University Press.

Alker, Hayward R. 1996. Rediscoveries and Reformulations: Humanistic Methodologies for International Studies. New York: Cambridge University Press.

Alker, Hayward R., T. Robert Gurr, Kumar Rupesinghe, (eds). 2001. Journeys Through Conflict: Narratives and Lessons. Lanham, MD: Rowman & Littlefield Publishing, Inc.

Alker, Hayward. R. "Making Peaceful Sense of the News." Merritt, Richard L., Robert G. Muncaster, and Dina A. Zinnes (eds). International Event-Data Developments: DDIR Phase II (1993). Ann Arbor: University of Michigan Press.

Annan, Kofi. "Progress report on the prevention of armed conflict: Report of the Secretary General." United Nations General Assembly A/60/891/. 18 July 2006. http://www.ipu.org/splz-e/unga06/conflict.pdf.

Axelrod, Robert, and Michael Cohen. 1999. Harnessing Complexity: Organizational Implications of a Scientific Frontier. New York: The Free Press.

Carment, David, and Albrecht Schnabel (eds). 2003. Conflict Prevention: Path to Peace or Grand Illusion? Tokyo: United Nations University Press.

Carment, David, and Albrecht Schnabel (eds). 2004. Conflict Prevention from Rhetoric to Reality, Vol. 2. Lanham, MD: Rowman & Littlefield Publishing, Inc.

Cockell, John G. "Early Warning Analysis and Policy Planning in the UN Preventive Action." Conflict Prevention: Path to Peace or Grand Illusion? (2003). Tokyo: United Nations University Press.

CPR Network (Conflict Prevention and Post-Conflict Reconstruction Network) "Early Warning & Early Response Handbook, Version 2.3," Pearson Peacekeeping Center, United Nations Department of Economic and Social Affairs (UNDESA), and West Africa Network for Peacebuilding (WANEP), downloaded in August 2006 from www.reliefweb.int.

Davies, John and Ted Robert Gurr (eds). 1998. Preventive Measures: Building Risk Assessment and Crisis Early Warning Systems. Lanham, MD: Rowman & Littlefield Publishing, Inc.

Goldstein, Joshua S. 1998. Long Cycles: Prosperity and War in the Modern Age. New Haven: Yale University Press.

Gordon, Andrew S. 2004. Strategy Representation: An Analysis of Planning Knowledge. Mahwah: Earlbaum.

Haas, Ernst B. "Collective conflict management: Evidence for a New World Order?" Thomas G. Weiss (ed), Collective Security in a changing World. Boulder: Lynne Rienner.

Huntington, Samuel P. 1996 The Clash of Civilizations and the Remaking of World Order. New York: Simon and Schuster.

Ivanov, Anton and David Nyheim. "Generating the Means to an End: Political Will and Integrated Responses to Early Warning." Conflict Prevention from Rhetoric to Reality, Vol. 2 (2004): 163-1776. Lanham, MD: Rowman and Littlefield Publishing, Inc.

Jentleson, Bruce W. 2000. Opportunities Missed, Opportunities Seized: Preventive Diplomacy in the Post-Cold War World. Lanham, MD: Rowman and Littlefield Publishing, Inc.

King, Gary and Langche Zeng. "Improving Forecasts of State Failure." World Politics, 53 (2001): 623-58.

Kirton, John J. and Radoslava N. Stefanova. 2004. The G8, the United Nations, and Conflict Prevention. Aldershot: Ashgate Publishing.

Last, David. "Early warning and prevention of violent conflict: The role of multifunctional observer missions." Carment and Schnabel (eds), Conflict Prevention: path to Peace of Grand Illusion (2003): 157-181. Tokyo: United Nations University Press.

Latham, Robert and Saskia Sassen (eds). 2005. Digital Formations: IT and New Architectures in the Global Realm. Princeton: Princeton University Press.

Lund, Michael S. "Conflict Prevention is Happening: Learning from "Successes" as well as "Failures." Schnabel, Albrecht and David Carment (eds), Conflict Prevention from Rhetoric to Reality, Vol.1 (2004): 289-304. Lanham, MD: Rowman & Littlefield Publishing, Inc.

Rupesinghe, Kumar and M. Kuroda (eds). 1992. Early Warning and Conflict Resolution. London: Macmillan Press.

Rupesinghe, Kumar, and David Nyheim with Maha Khan, "A Review of Research and Practice in Early Warning and Early Response," Journeys Through Conflict: Narratives and Lessons (2001). Lanham, MD: Rowman & Littlefield Publishing Inc.

Schnabel, Albrecht and David Carment (eds). 2004. Conflict Prevention from Rhetoric to Reality, Vol. 1. Lanham, MD: Rowman & Littlefield Publishing, Inc.

Sikoska, Tatjana and Juliet Solomon. "Introducing Gender in Conflict and Conflict Prevention: Conceptual and Policy Implications." Carment, David and Albrecht Schnabel (eds), Conflict Prevention from Rhetoric to Reality, Vol. 2(2004): 637-78. Lanham, MD: Rowman & Littlefield Publishing, Inc.

Stremlau, John, and Francisco Sagasti. 1998. Preventing Deadly Conflict. Report of the Carnegie Commission on Preventing Deadly Conflict. Washington DC: Carnegie Corporation of New York.

Thompson, William R. 2001. Evolutionary Interpretations of World Politics. New York and London: Routledge.

United Nations (Anand Panyarachun, Chairman). 2004 "High-Level Panel on Threats, Challenges and Change." A More Secure World: Our Shared Responsibility. New York: United Nations Publication.

United Nations General Assembly, "World Summit Outcome," A/RES/60/L.1, 24 October 2005.

Wodak, Ruth and Paul Chilton (eds). 2005. A New Agenda in (Critical) Discourse Analysis. Amsterdam and Philadelphia: Benjamins.

Towards a New Bandung: The Global Civil Society and the UN Multilateral System

Kinhide Mushakoji

Introduction

The future historians who will study the first century of the United Nations will compare how this multilateral institution developed through the two major crises of the Cold War and the War on Terror. The two "wars" challenged the multilateral governance born with the creation of the United Nations. In the first instance, this global institution had to survive under a bilateral hegemony receiving the support of the counter-hegemonic historical bloc created by the anti-colonial South at the Asian-African Bandung conference in 1955. Under the unilateral hegemony of the War on Terror, the same organization has to maintain the legitimacy of multilateralism, in an entirely new context where the Westphalian state system is itself put into question by the unilateral power. I ask, what may emerge as an anti-imperial institution comparable to the historical bloc, which emerged from Bandung?

The Year 2005 was the fourth anniversary of 9/11 and of the War on Terror. It was also the fiftieth anniversary of the Bandung Afro-Asian Conference (Mushakoji 2001). This gave the occasion for several intellectuals and social movements to reflect about Bandung and to hold small scale meetings celebrating the fiftieth anniversary of the emergence of an Afro-Asian Solidarity bloc of states, broadened later to include tricontinental regions including Latin America and the Caribbean region. The Government of Indonesia initiated a Second Bandung Conference in 2005, inviting some of the original participants. Several international and regional meetings were organized by popular movements calling upon the global South to organize a "people's" Bandung. They argued that the first Bandung conference was a meeting of the newly emerging states of Asia and Africa indispensable to build peace and development under the pressure of the Cold War, but that now, under the War on Terror, a broader alliance was needed—one in which the peoples of the South should participate alongside the anti-hegemonic nations. It was argued that due to the post-Cold War unilateral global hegemony, a larger counter-hegemonic alliance was necessary, whereas in 1955, only new nations that were agents of change formed the counter-hegemonic alliance at the Bandung conference.

This chapter first presents an overview of what Bandung meant to the emerging Third World during the Cold War, showing that it played an historical role in developing a process of counter-hegemonic activities. These activities developed political, economic and cultural projects that succeeded in ending the Cold War. The new hegemonic order which was formed at the end of the Cold War led to the emergence of a trilateral alliance between the United States, Europe, and Japan, which co-opted the major agents of Bandung. This is why a new Bandung has to propose a new project to form a new counter-hegemonic coalition.

This paper is not meant to present a complete picture of the historical and contemporary conditions that call for a second Bandung. It will only propose a few entry points for further dialogue among the social forces to be involved. It is assumed that intellectuals of the global South, and of some part of the North, will join organically to develop further the points made in this very preliminary discussion about a new Bandung under the War on Terror. We will ask what role this new historical bloc will have to play in order to sustain the multilateralism represented by the United Nations and its family of IGOs and NGOs.

The Bandung Conference in the Cold War Context

The Bandung Conference played a constructive role in mobilizing the counter-hegemonic forces of what was to become known as the Third World against the power bloc, which emerged post-World War II. The conference was the first manifestation by the newly independent nations of the Third World (called later "Nefo" by Sukarno, the host of the conference) to unite in the polarized Cold War period (Mackie 2005).

Created outside of the UN system, Bandung aimed to create a bloc of nations outside of the hegemonic competition between East and West. The participating nations shared a common interest in creating an anti-colonial international environment favorable to their nation-building efforts. They argued for a peaceful international environment able to provide resources for the development of the South rather than for the continuation of the East-West nuclear competition. Their efforts were thus channeled later into the UN system and led to the development of the Non-Aligned Movement (NAM) and of the G77 of developing nations, which have further played an important role in the General Assembly, due to the large numbers of "Third World" member countries. The legacy of Bandung, however, should not be assumed only to have initiated the NAM and the G77. Importantly, it was an occasion for a non-Western bloc of nations to formulate a project that had two contradictory, but also complementary aspects. On the one hand, Bandung based itself on the Westphalian principle that the international community was composed of independent states and built an alliance of the newly independent states, though the conference was later criticized for not including non-state actors. Bandung was also the first occasion for a non-Western civil society project in a time when development was seen to go hand-in-hand with Westernization. This complex view of modernity was formulated long before post-structuralist critiques questioned Western models of statehood and power.

The Bandung conference was based on principles representing their non-Western and anti-colonial identity. It proposed ten principles for the counter-hegemonic alliance of the newly emerging nations. The Pancha Sila, the five principles of peaceful co-existence that were originally proposed by China and India, were especially crucial. They were developed as an inter-state framework for all the counter-hegemonic nations to form an alliance in spite of their political, economic and cultural differences. These also became the rallying principles for the peoples of Asia, Africa, and later the Latin American states. The Pancha Sila principles represented an imaginative reformulation of the modern Western international political framework of the Westphalian system. They were imaginative in the sense that they had the potential for critiquing the Westphalian system. Though the principles did not undermine the sovereignty of states, they called for "peaceful coexistence" and a commitment to the principle of "mutual equal benefit." This was a non-Western ethical position (at least a position alien to the great Western modern cultural tradition of enlightenment) by stressing instead of individual freedom to compete for individual benefit, an ethical position based on mutual respect among different peoples, and equal mutual benefit in the place of the Western concept of the right to colonize uncivilized peoples.

It is important to realize the historical context within which these principles were adopted. "Peaceful coexistence," which had already been used within the Cold War context, meant the coexistence between socialism and capitalism in opposition to the orthodox Leninist thesis of anti-Imperialist revolution. The emerging nations used this concept in a cultural context far more radical than its ideological definition. It is especially meaningful that "peaceful coexistence" was first agreed between India and China, two new post-colonial states with long histories of colonization, accustomed to being at the center of a concentric world order of nations of unequal status, which were in spite of their inequality, basing their relations on mutual respect and mutual benefit. Obviously, two such orders could not co-exist without accepting living in a non-concentric world order recognizing the equality among its members, as the Westphalian order was proposing to them. Thus mutual respect of territorial sovereignty, affirmed mutual non-intervention, and non-interference in each-one's domestic affairs, first by India and China, and then by all the participant nations of the Bandung Conference was proclaimed.

The principle of "mutual equal benefit" combined with "peaceful coexistence" was a crucial principle to the post-colonial states. They agreed that among themselves, their political economic interactions should never lead them into new relations of dependence even when they had among them different stature, some more powerful or more wealthy than others. Economic competition among them should never permit new colonial relations and equality and mutuality in any transactions had to be maintained. The principle of "peaceful coexistence" had a civil society context in contrast to the prevailing Westphalian order and "mutual equal benefit" was a concept alien to the Western liberal concept of free market with a colonial periphery.

These two principles were of special relevance for the two Asian civilizations in overcoming prevailing conceptions of world order. They gave to the Pancha Sila an entirely new meaning to inter-state relations, by putting them in a cooperative framework instead of an adversarial one. "Mutual benefit" and "peaceful coexistence" were two principles, that were absent from the anarchic principles of the Westphalian system and of the free competition of the liberal economy of the West. They provided the ground for a community of the newly emerging post-colonial states, economically complementary and politically non-hegemonic.

The Final Communique of the Bandung Conference included ten principles called the "Dasa Sila Bandung" (Mackie 2005: 106) which included, alongside the Pancha Sila, principles of the respect of human rights and of the Charter of the United Nations, equality among all races and nations, abstention of exerting pressures on other countries, using peaceful means to settle international disputes, and respect for the rights of each nation to defend itself in accordance with the Charter of the United Nations. In this way, the Bandung Conference established itself firmly against colonialism on the basis of the multilateral institutional frameworks of the United Nations including human rights. This is an important aspect of the Bandung message that makes it relevant even today in coping with the unilateral hegemonic tendencies putting in danger the universality of human rights and the multilateralism of the United Nations. The principle of "peaceful coexistence" plus those linking Bandung to the United Nations were, and still are, important to any anti-colonial and counter-hegemonic alliance. Bandung refused any intrusion of the hegemon and of all the rich countries of the North in the Third World affairs, proclaiming their collective self-reliance and non-violent cooperation among them and with the United Nations. After fifty years, the importance of the Dasa Sila Bandung including the Pancha Sila has not decreased. The Bandung message has, nevertheless, been improved in the meantime by the further developments during the 1960s and 1970s. Also, some deficiencies of Bandung emerged and had to be corrected.

An increasingly globalized international political economy was accompanied, especially in the Third World, by the emergence of ethnic, religious, and other identity communities that challenged the state's legitimacy and power. The framework proposed at Bandung, assuming the infallibility of state sovereignty, is no longer viable. We will discuss later the reasons why Bandung has a powerful message for those who want to form a counter-hegemonic alliance under the quite different current and future conditions of the global age. The application of the Bandung principles is valid on the condition that it is re-conceptualized in full accordance with the new realities of this time of globalization and neoliberalism.

The Bandung message was affected by the divisive neo-colonial forces that characterized the Cold War. It was regrettable that the Sino-Soviet dispute, a socialist version of colonial North-South inequality between the Soviet Union and China, brought discord and division in the Afro-Asian Solidarity Movement. China opposed the criticism of the Soviet "new colonialism" in Eastern Europe made by the Delegate of Nepal, and yet later broke its alliance after facing Soviet pressures. The Afro-Asian Peoples' Solidarity Movement, which had accompanied the Bandung Conference, also lost its dynamism following this Sino-Soviet conflict of the end of the 1950s. The states that gathered in Bandung did not meet again, due to the difficulty in retaining the Bandung spirit under the divisive pressure of the Cold War. India and China were in conflict over borders and many leaders who gathered in Bandung were replaced, as was the case of Sukarno, the original host of the conference. Yet the Bandung message was clear and was further expanded by two new groups that were formed within the UN General Assembly, the NAM and the G77, both historical heirs and logical continuations of the Bandung conference and sensibility.

Through the NAM, Bandung triggered a process, which prevented a nuclear annihilation of humankind. The NAM played a precious role in the General Assembly of the United Nations against the nuclear arms race of the two nuclear superpowers. Truly enough, the two hegemonic powers preferred to negotiate the adjustment of their nuclear strategic policies, and the major agreements on nuclear arms control and disarmament were negotiated between them, excluding the UN General Assembly where the NAM countries were adopting resolutions opposing nuclear tests and nuclear arms race.

The Non-Aligned Movement was an inter-state movement within the United Nations, but its position was synchronized and reinforced by the broad popular movement against the bi-hegemonic nuclear arms race triggered-off by the Russels-Einstein Declaration and the Stockholm Appeal. The emerging non-state actors, such as the international peace movements trying to mobilize international opinion to prevent nuclear war, found in the NAM a precious ally inside the UN system.

The exacerbation of the Cold War seemed to have bypassed all the efforts made by the NAM, and nuclear arms race continued outside of the UN disarmament framework. The end of the Cold War came, however, when the Soviet Union recognized unilaterally the recommendation to start a process of disarmament proposed by the NAM countries and by the international peace movements, under the leadership of Gorbachev. The NAM position in the General Assembly and the peace movement initiatives in the international civil society arena helped this decision.

The end of the Cold War was due to the cooperation between the NAM states and the international popular movement, which involved not only organized parties and labor unions but also peace activists and pacifist groups internationally, especially in capitalist countries. It is important to take note of this fact, since the NAM, anti-hegemonic and anti-nuclear, was receiving large support in the civil societies of the global North, which was also the Cold War West. The end of the Cold War was, in a sense, the product of this large alliance involving Third World Non-Aligned states and the peace-loving sectors of nations from the global North and the global South.

The Bandung Afro-Asian Conference also instigated the development of the Third World economic platform, the G77. The G88 was formed later in the 1960s, by the tri-continental alliance demanding more equitable terms of trade between the rich industrial countries of the global North and the poor countries of the global South. The G77 demands led to the emergence of a new international economic order in the 1970s.

The formation of a tri-continental bloc played a key role in transforming the Bandung message of "equal mutual benefit" into an opposing force against neo-colonialism. It was in Latin America that the efforts of Raul Prebich developed into the theory of "dependencia" which played a crucial role in the development within the United Nations of CEPAL (Economic Commission for Latin America, ECLA) and later of the UN Conference on Trade and Development (UNCTAD). The unequal terms of trade between the North and the South were criticized because they were violating the principles of equal mutual benefit. Neo-colonialism was thus criticized in the General Assembly of the United Nations on the basis of principles emanating from the Bandung conference.

Truly enough, the demands of the G77 were often motivated by their neo-mercantilist position, aimed at preparing the ground for rapid industrialization, and their political leadership often led to the development of despotic states, pro-hegemonic in their attempts to obtain economic aid from the hegemons. This negative aspect of the G77 movement was, however, largely compensated by the fact that its demands triggered-off a broad based search for principles of alternative development by a large sector of the civil societies, both in the North and in the South. Thus, several versions of "new international orders" were proposed.

The campaign against neo-colonialism developed in the UN General Assembly emerging from the Bandung tradition was supported by a parallel trend in the international civil society during the 1960s and 1970s. Future historians will find an amazing synchronicity between the emergence of the Third World offensive in the United Nations and the civil rights movement in the United States. The same type of movement against neo-colonialism was emerging in the 1960s and '70s in the international forum of the United Nations and in wider international civil society. The fight against colonialism and racism, which began on the international level in Bandung, was continued on both the inter-state level in the United Nations, and internationally, beginning in the United States, whose hegemonic position was based in some ways on its constitutional tradition of racial equality in opposition to the socialist class-based hegemony.

The civil rights movement in the United States expanded into other human rights movements such as the native-American Wounded-Knee movement and the Latino movement. It spread to the feminist and to lesbian and gay emancipation movements. The anti-Vietnam War movement emerged internationally in universities, culminating in 1968. It was then-Secretary-General U Thant who proposed in 1969 the development of the UN University, in order to mobilize the energy of youth rebellion with different cultural backgrounds in reinvigorating the UN system and overcome its Western-centric institutional culture. The Bandung spirit was shared, so to speak, between international civil society and the United Nations also in this historical moment when the Third World was emerging as an important force in modern history.

The combined activities of this new global movement opposing colonialism and racism were indeed following the Bandung tradition. It was, however, going much beyond Bandung in several ways. Bandung, as we have already pointed out, was the manifestation of an anti-colonial agency built by emerging nation-states. The Bandung conference operated in a patriarchal framework and was organized by all male leaders. Bandung proposed peaceful coexistence among states and not between ethnic identity groups within states. Common mutual benefit was also proclaimed as a principle of inter-state relations and not as a principle of domestic socio-economic transactions involving minorities in delicate opposition with majorities, such as the overseas Chinese in South East Asia and overseas Indians in East Africa.

The Bandung plus fifty debates that took place in 2005 recognized these limitations of the Bandung conference and wanted to take stock of new developments in anti-colonial movements both in the United Nations and in international civil society. It was clearly stated by many participants of these debates that a new Bandung should be a people's Bandung, broadened to include anti-colonial and anti-racist social forces in the North, including the United States.

The Bandung spirit in itself was found to be insufficient in representing the broad-based movement that developed in the 1960s and 70s. It is only with hindsight that we can realize the scale of anti-colonial and anti-racist social justice movements developed around the United Nations by international civil society and in the UN-related sector represented by the NGO community.

The UN began to organize special sessions and conferences dealing with global problems. The 1972 Stockholm Conference on Human Environment opened the series of such conferences. It is generally believed that this conference, which dealt for the first time with ecology, was a consequence of the Club of Rome Report on the "Limits to Growth," which had nothing to do with the worldwide movement against colonialism and racism. However, another root of the ecological concern was closely related to the anti-neocolonial tri-continental movement. Having taken part in a series of consultations organized by the World Council of Churches, it can be said that the environmental issue came up in an entirely different context from the Club of Rome. It was in a consultation taking place in Montreal in 1969, under the chairmanship of Maurice Strong, who was later appointed as the secretary-general of the Stockholm Conference, that the Latin American participants argued that the present interpretation of development based on transfer of funds and technology from the North to the South was contrary to true development which had to be a liberation of the people. This condemnation of the Western model of development was met by the participants from the North by a wise response. To oppose the ongoing development strategy in the name of "liberation" was too close to the communist propaganda, and a better argument against it was to point out to the environmental devastation of present-day development. Thus, Lady Jackson Barbara Ward, one of the participants of this consultation proposed the idea of the "global village."

The World Council of Churches began its activities in the field of environment and development, and Maurice Strong, a leading figure in the field, was appointed as secretary-general of the Stockholm Conference. Another forgotten aspect of this process of close cooperation between the NGOs and the United Nations is the fact that the tradition to have the global issue conference accompanied by an NGO forum was an invention of Strong in his attempt to force the representatives of the states to recognize the existence of environment pollution in their respective countries. The Stockholm Conference initiated a process where alternative development strategies became a main theme. Eco-development was proposed, putting into question the very validity of the economic development as proposed by the UN expert economist serving the interests of the states and corporate agents of the North. This was what the Latin Americans had wanted to say, when they claimed that development was "liberation," transforming the present colonialist and racist North-South relations.

This liberation of peoples would be seen as a dangerous support to communism, but the liberation of nature was not posing such political difficulties. The transformation of the present North-South relations was also promoted on the inter-state level within the institutional framework of the United Nations. The NIEO was proposed at the UN level, while alternative development was promoted in the NGO community. This synchronic evolution of the ideas represented twenty years before in Bandung was made possible by this close cooperation between the United Nations and the NGO community. The richness of the intellectual creativity of this process could be seen from my position in the United Nations University, where so many ideas about how to replace the present international order were discussed.

A New International Cultural Order, a New World Information Order, a New International Constitutional Order, and several other "new orders" were proposed, officially and unofficially. These projects raised serious questions about the hegemonic order supported by the North, and maintaining unequal post-colonial or neo-colonial economic, political and military relations between the North and the South.

Unfortunately, processes of globalization evolved in a completely opposite direction of these proposed international orders since the beginning of the 1980s, when the oil dollar boom was terminated with the major Third World nations incapacitated by their accumulated debts. Margaret Thatcher and Ronald Reagan initiated a new neoliberal era led by a global mega-competition bloc of states and multinational corporations. The US-led trilateral hegemony of "industrial democracies" succeeded in establishing firmly this post-Keynesian system through the Plaza Accord, and fructified, after the end of the Cold War, into the "New World Order" declared by President George Bush, Senior. This was a world order dominated by the North and a total negation of the NIEO demanded by the South. The last decade of the 20th century opened an anti-Bandung period, which still continues under the War on Terror.

The present global hegemonic order (or disorder) seems to have put under its effective control the developing nations, eliminating the political economic projects of the Third World originating in Bandung. The historical trend of globalization led to the present unilateral hegemony, under which the corporate sector of the trilateral regions prosper and the tri-continental regions are partly co-opted by and partly excluded from this global hegemonic alliance.

In spite of its apparent failure to implement its political-economic projects, the variety of myths, utopias, and alternative projects imagined in the 1970s, following the principles originated at Bandung, continue to provide a valid critique of the political-economic myths and projects of the neo-colonial hegemonic alliance at the turn of the century. We will study the present global hegemonic colonial structures against which a new counter-hegemonic alliance has to be built. This will become possible, we will argue, only on the basis of a new interpretation of the powerful message of Bandung.

The UN, the NGOs and the New Global Colonial (Dis)Order

The 1990s was a decade in which the neo-liberal and neo-conservative unilateral hegemony of the United States was established following the fall of the Soviet Bloc leaving the United States the only superpower. It was also a period of a close cooperation between the United Nations and the global NGO community. The former trend was definitely taking a new course promoting colonialism and racism. The latter was a trend taking again, in this new global age, the messages of the 1970s towards anti-colonialism. The Bandung message was thus present there with fierce opponents and ardent supporters.

Let us first look at the cooperation between the United Nations and the NGO community in the 1990s that reflected the principles of Bandung. For example, the decade of UN conferences dedicated to global issues were occasions for declarations and programmes of action aimed at correcting the course of the neoliberal and neoconservative globalization recommended in the 1970s. The NGO Forums provided occasions for global civil society to express its disagreement with the new world (dis)order developing under the unilateral hegemony of the United States.

The series of such conferences opened with the Rio Summit on Environment and Development of 1992. This summit launched the concept of "sustainable development" which was a strong anti-colonial principle related to environment proposed 20 years before at the Stockholm Conference on Human Development. This summit was followed by the Vienna Human Rights Conference of 1993. The principle that "women's rights are human rights" was a key concept preparing the 1995 Beijing Conference on Women held twenty years after the Mexico City Conference on Women. The 1974 Social Development Summit of Copenhagen saw the concept of "human security" proposed by the UNDP in its Human Development Report. This concept supported by Canada and Japan has since provided an important conceptual way to criticize of the neoconservative War on Terror unleashed by the United States in 2001. The Cairo Conference on Population was the occasion for "reproductive health rights" to be recognized as human rights. In 1996, Habitat II was held in Istanbul, defining crucial habitat rights especially relevant in post-colonial and global colonial contexts.

The last meeting closing the 1990 UN conferences on global issues was the World Conference Against Racism held in Durban in August/September 2001 immediately preceding 9/11, where the United States stepped out with Israel in the midst of deliberation claiming that the Conference had been "kidnapped" by the Palestinians, in a way declaring the War on Terror ahead of 9/11. Western media saw the Durban Conference and accompanying NGO Forum as a failure because of the disharmony it generated (Mushakoji 2003). This conference was nevertheless crucial in posing the problems of racism, colonialism and slavery in its historical context in the Bandung tradition, and thus provides a critical framework to analyze the post-9/11 neoliberal and neoconservative global governance regime and the War on Terror.

The different concepts proposed by NGOs at these UN conferences and formally adopted by the participating states all developed out of the debate on a new international order and on alternative development in the 1970s. They provided an intellectual and programmatic background for the United Nations and the NGO community to develop a systematic critique of the "new world order" promoted by the Unites States. The Bandung message evolved and was thus an important part of a counter-hegemonic movement at the turn of the century.

We will focus here on two the concepts of human security and sustainable development adopted by the United Nations and the NGO community in the 1990s. The two concepts will help us understand the colonial and racist nature of neoliberal and neoconservative globalization under the unilateral hegemony of the United States. The Bandung critical framework as represented in the critiques of colonialism and racism of the Durban Conference will be the basis of this analysis.

The Commission on Human Security Report of 2003 in, "Human Security Now," officially defined the concept of human security (Commission on Human Security 2003). The report relates human security to the protection and empowerment people in situations of insecurity, such as violent conflict, post-conflict situations, and refugees, trafficked women and children. Human security considers international stability and as depending on people-centered security such as development in addition to traditional forms of state-centered security. The report criticizes the War on Terror for ignoring state terrorism and allowing the labeling of legitimate political groups as terrorists by authoritarian governments.

The Report conceptualizes security in an entirely different way to the 2002 report on the *National Security Strategy of the US of America* (The White House 2002), outlining the official position of the Bush administration on the War on Terror. The report defines the present state of the world as most peaceful in history, in view of the fact that inter-state wars have been replaced by a world coalition of states united against terrorists and rogue states. The report proposes preemptive strike on rogue states in possession of weapons of mass destruction as a means of maintaining security and a basis of a world order where conflicts are prevented unilaterally by the top down application of the political and military power of the United States. The human security report, on the other hand, defines the present world as most insecure for the vulnerable peoples. Human security must be guaranteed within the multilateral context of the United Nations by coping with the complex causes of human insecurity, poverty, lack of basic education and health services and the failed representation of vulnerable people. It proposes a bottom up global alliance for human security to which citizens cooperate with states within the multilateral context provided by the United Nations. This is why we can use the concept of human security as a powerful tool for a critical analysis of the neoliberal and neoconservative global hegemony, especially of the War of Terror it uses to perpetuate its surveillance and control of the world.

The concept of sustainable development is also useful in critiquing the current global political economy. Proposed in the Bruntland Report on Environment and Development, sustainability is defined primarily in terms of ecological sustainability. It insists on the need to combine with it socio-economic sustainability. The Johannesburg Conference of 2002, ten years after the Rio Summit, launched a decade of sustainable development education, aimed at awareness-building on sustainable development, taking stock of the achievements of thirty years of environment education, which succeeded in creating a broad epistemic community in support of ecology. This community has infiltrated different agents, governments, business firms, media, international organizations, and social movements. An analysis of the present-day insecurity and unsustainability of the global political economy provides a useful framework for all projects and policies seeking to build a sustainable and secure alternative world order beyond the present economically neoliberal and political neoconservative hegemonic new world order.

Human insecurity is one of the basic characteristics of the present unsustainable global political economy. It is a consequence of the "new colonial global order" or "disorder." The contemporary world economy is global in the sense that it is in the final (global) stage of a capitalist economic expansion of the world system which has so far been able to feed its economic/technological growth by the exploitation of the surplus from the "colonies" or economic peripheries of the global South. The global economy is global in that it has reached a stage where such frontiers do not exist any more. So, the exploitation of the surplus can be done nowhere abroad and must be done everywhere possible since the global economy needs surplus for its mega-competition and for its speculative financial activities.

This global process of exploitation is in itself not only a source of human insecurity, but is structurally unsustainable. This is where we must analyze neoliberal and neoconservative global political economy by calling upon the concept of sustainable development, which is too often used in a narrow context of ecological sustainability, understanding it to include also socio-economic sustainability, as defined in many UN documents.

The polarizing and exclusionary processes of the global market creates insecurity for all the subaltern exploited social formations and all the peoples in the South and in the North who are in the excluded segment of the global structures. A variety of colonial relations of exploitation and exclusion cross-over in the surplus extraction from the South by the North, from women by men, from the rural by the urban sectors, from the local communities of each country by its urban center, from the ethnic minorities by the global majorities.

The neoliberal governance mechanism of this threefold structure of the global political economy is unsustainable in the long-term, because the neoliberal regulations encouraging the free market growth of the first global sector keeps widening the gaps between the first and the third sector, reproducing its workforce only thanks to the subaltern cooperation of the second. It is only until the small farmers, the small industries and the local communities cease to hope to be integrated in the global financial market that this system can continue to work sacrificing the third sector. The growing rich-poor gaps and the impoverishment of many sectors of the production economy, not only in the South but also in the North, suggest the unsustainability of the present neoliberal global political economy.

We must realize that these unsustainable structures are quite different from the North-South structure of the Cold War days that was critiqued at the Bandung conference. The global political economy has created a situation where the three segments exist in both the South and the North and where their difference lies in their relative proportion. This is why the counter-hegemonic alliance that was formed at Bandung cannot remain limited to developing countries. It should include non-state agents in the subaltern and the excluded segments of the trilateral regions, as well as support from social movements and non-state actors in the global North.

The above analysis may lead to the wrong conclusion that the historical bloc formed in Bandung is invalid under the current global colonial situation, which extracts surplus not only from the South, but also from the subaltern and excluded segments of the North. If the global hegemony had not developed a new exclusionary unsustainable structure between the trilateral North and the tri-continental South, we may not need to go back to Bandung in our attempt to build a new counter-hegemonic alliance.

However, the United States and its allies are creating a new divide between the North and the South in their efforts to strengthen security, both national and "human," by strengthening the human security of the trilateral "security community" (Mushakoji 2003B: 117-159) and by making "humanitarian" interventions in the tri-continental regions. In spite of the political-economic elimination of the borders between the South and the North, this divide still exists, as the security project of the "new global colonial order" both excludes and intervenes in the South. This creates a new North-South exclusionary structure with outposts of the North in the global South, where Bandung principles can be seen to be increasingly relevant for the building of a counter-hegemonic alliance. The South now divided within itself between a pro-North prosperous sector and an impoverished sector need to reunite in the face of vast disparities in human security caused by the new North/South divide.

The current economic political community is composed by one single "security community" in the global North which is built on a complex network of overlapping, inter-dependent security communities and a network of interacting fragmented security communities excluding and suspecting each-other, in the global South.

In the precarious global South, each security community perceives other's efforts to increase their security as a threat to their own security, unlike in the global North where all states do not fear that others would attack them militarily. The mega-competition that engages multinational corporations in the core of the world system often, in the South, takes the form of militarized competition among security communities, states, religious groups, ethnic minorities, and so on.

The present global political economy is peaceful in the North as far as inter-state and inter-firm competition is concerned. The societies in the North often hide, however, situations of tension and insecurity in the midst of their state security communities. Among others, the security dilemma between the citizens and the security communities of the migrant diasporas causes a chronic mutual insecurity to be sustained between the citizens and the migrant communities. This is why the "new global colonial order" has developed the concept of "global governance." This governance is colonial especially in that it is based on the tutelage of the South by the North which deploys eventually its military forces in high-risk regions, ready to intervene anywhere where the interests and values of the global market and of the hegemonic order is perceived to be threatened.

The trilateral hegemons (Gill 1990) from the global North intervene in the conflicts between different security communities designated as enemies of the global order that started these conflicts. Such intervention is in most cases arbitrary and lacks international legitimacy. The UN is expected to provide multilateral legitimacy to these interventions. UN reform as proposed by the hegemony is designed to allow for the legitimating of these interventions in the name of security.

The insecurity in the global South where non-state security communities are divided under pressure from the global market is genuine, and there are situations where a humanitarian intervention is the only hope for the security of vulnerable groups. This does not mean that interventions labeled as "humanitarian" can serve to legitimate colonial interventions. Here, the Bandung principle of non-interference in domestic affairs has to be seriously considered as a means to check the abuse of power by hegemonic states.

Human insecurity is, however, not only generated by interventions. It must be realized that conflicts are caused in most cases by pressures from the global neoliberal market economy, which forces each security community to maximize its power to grab resources trickling down from the North in order to achieve a minimum level of security and well-being. Their competition over the scarce resources is a zero-sum process where each community perceives others as competitors and potential threats. The only way to overcome these conflicts is to focus on inter-community relations. This is where the Bandung principles of "peaceful coexistence" and "equal mutual benefit" become indispensable, not only in inter-state relations of the global South, but also in all relations among the different types of security communities, whether they are based on gender, class, ethnicity or religion, and so on.

The principle of "non-interference in domestic affairs" should be applied; the North should cease to intervene on alleged humanitarian grounds when there is a hidden national interest.

A non-hegemonic system of governance must be built to replace the present global hegemonic security system, based on a strict application of the UN Charter as was stressed in the Desa Sila Bandung. The reform of the United Nations can benefit from a joint attempt to build a non-hegemonic system for human security in line with the project of a new anti-colonialist, "New Bandung" alliance. The UN should be capacitated in such a way as to cover the multilateral and multi-level needs of the "peoples of the United Nations." The states and civil society agents supporting the United Nations should cooperate with this institution to develop an integrated approach to cope with both security as well as economic issues. The Bandung principle of "mutual equal benefit" is useful in the regulation of mega-competition that favors multinational corporations and the principle of "peaceful coexistence" is necessary in conceptualizing an end to the vast global insecurities of the War on Terror and neoconservative global governance.

United Nations Reform and a Multi-Level Multilateral Alliance following Bandung

In face of the hegemonic bloc conducting the War on Terror, the formation of an alternative historical bloc reigniting the fire of the Bandung spirit in the contemporary context of global colonialism is indispensable. It will be a people's, bottom-up Bandung, organizing a counter-hegemonic alliance in full support of the multilateral initiatives of the United Nations. It will build an alliance between subaltern states, social formations and civil society internationally. This alliance will be made possible by the anti-colonial principles of Bandung. The alliance has to benefit from the long tradition of cooperation between the United Nations and global civil society.

Recent reforms of the United Nations suggest a mixture of hegemonic and counter-hegemonic influences. From a hegemonic point of view, the reforms were expected to facilitate the efforts of "humanitarian interventions" in support of the "War on Terror." Put simply, the trilogy of Human Rights Council, the Security Council and a Peace-Building Commission was supposed to make the United Nations an efficient multilateral institution supporting the unilateral projects of the United States.

The creation of Human Rights Council was recommended in order to improve on the present Commission, which was too broadly representative of states with poor human rights records, and too slow in reaching decisions. Reform of the Security Council was meant to add to its legitimacy by adding new permanent members, and a new Peace Building Commission was a new tool for the post-conflict reconstruction of territories devastated by humanitarian interventions.

These proposed changes were modified during the UN reform debate in a way unsatisfactory to the United Sates, especially as they did not allow for permanent membership to the Security Council. The reform of the Security Council is a case where UN reform may be directed towards strengthening the hegemonic system or improving multilateral decision-making by allowing better representation of the interests of the subaltern states. Whether to abolish the veto power, as recommended by the supporters of international democracy, or to strengthen it under the present US hegemony, is crucial for the future of the War on Terror.

The Peace Building Committee is another institution that has the potential to become a stronghold of neoliberal and neoconservative peace building. The participation alongside the NGO community of the corporate sector which participates and profits from peace building and reconstruction work is problematic, and reforms must emphasize the human security dimension of peace building where local citizens and communities are consulted in the development process.

UN reform however, must not be limited to modifying and creating institutions. It should be seen in connection with larger global processes where citizens and multitudes seek to cooperate with the United Nations. It is important to develop the contacts with cities and regional governments initiated at Habitat II. UNESCO has developed several Networks of Cities for peace, human rights, and anti-racism. The Decade of Education for Sustainable Development has been an occasion for UNESCO and the UN University to develop a network of Centers of Regional Expertise (CRE) in which citizens, universities, the corporate sector, and local administration participate. The UN, which started as an inter-state institution, should seek all possible links with non-state actors and wider civil society. The Bandung message can enable a variety of agents and agencies seeking to build an alternative world to come in support of UN reforms and the United Nations as an effective multilateral institution.

The principles of Bandung can provide a necessary framework for the organization of a counter-hegemonic alliance across cultures and traditions, a broad alliance of the civil societies of the South and of the North, incorporating excluded and marginalized peoples, women, peasants and workers, indigenous peoples, as well as the marginalized peoples in the informal sectors of both industrial and developing societies. This broad alliance should be organized in close cooperation with the United Nations, under the hegemony of the peoples of the Third World, who constitute a vast majority in the General Assembly.

If we take seriously the anti-colonial message of Bandung, broadened to include all peoples and not only states, a truly "human" security that would also be a "people's" security would be conceptualized. A truly human approach to security should be based on the rights to life and to development of each and every person and community. A truly sustainable model of human development should be endogenous, determined in consultation with local community actors and question the imposition of exogenous models. The principle of peaceful coexistence should be expanded to all human security communities, and non-interference in domestic affairs should be guaranteed to these groups, as well as to each individual in all human communities whose self-determination should be respected by the larger units, be it states, regional organizations or transnational corporations. The dialogue among civilizations on all levels, a key task of the UN University, should lead to such a multicultural peace.

The Bandung message can be used to oppose the current neoliberal global political economy. It should especially regulate the casino capitalism harmful to both the subaltern and excluded segments of the world. This is one of the most difficult tasks of the future Economic Security Council. The principles of Bandung should also be used to reject hidden hegemonic economic projects of global or regional neo-mercantilist nature, aiming at regulating the "global standards" imposed by the neoliberal economy. This regulation must guarantee working conditions internationally and the land rights of indigenous peoples should be regulated. Gender inequity and all other forms of discrimination intrinsic to the current global political economy should be eliminated from all aspects of economic life, production, reproductions, service and consumption.

New Bandung intellectuals have an especially important role in developing a civilizational dialogue, in and out of the United Nations, among all the participants of the counter-hegemonic alliance, as well as with the trilateral hegemonic alliance. The UN should play a key role in developing a global dialogue, between the Bandung intellectuals and the modernizing elites with a neo-liberal, technocratic vision of a Eurocentric progress of human civilization. The dialogue on how the United

Nations can guarantee sustainable human development eliminating all causes of human insecurity must be continued.

References

Commission on Human Security. 2003. *Human Security Now*. New York: United Nations.

Gill, Stephen. 1990. *American Hegemony and the Trilateral Commission*. Cambridge, MA: Cambridge University Press.

Mackie, Jamie. 2005. *Non-Alignment and Afro-Asian Solidarity*. Singapore: Editions Didier Millet.

Mushakoji, Kinhide. "Bandung Plusse 50: Appel a un Dialogue Tricontinental Face a 'Hegemonie Mondiale.'" *Alternatives Sud* 8:2 (2001): 141-156.

Mushakoji, Kinhide, "The World Conference Against Racism: A Great Failure or a Great Success" in Bernard Founou-Tchuigoua, Sams Dine Sy & Amady A. Dieng (eds.) *Critical Social Thought for the XXIst Century: Essays in Honour of Samir Amin* (Paris: L'Harmattan) 2003: 289-302.

Mushakoji, Kinhide (2003B) Ningen Anzennhoshou-Ron Josetsu: Global Fascism. ni Koushite (Kokusai Hoin).

The White House. 2002. *The National Security Strategy of the US of America*. Washington DC: White House Publications.

World Economic Forum. 2002. *The Global Competitiveness Report 2001-2002*. World Economic Forum.

Group of 77 and the United Nations Reforms

Bagher Asadi

Introduction

In the summer of 2005, the United Nations endured a heated debate in the General Assembly on the reform package proposed by Secretary-General Kofi Annan in his two recent reports, the report of "High-Level Panel on Threats, Challenges and Change" and "In Larger Freedom," a package containing mainly political ingredients. In the course of the months-long debate, the chairman of the Group of 77, representing the biggest negotiating bloc at the United Nations with over 130 members (including China), emphasized in numerous statements to the Assembly the centrality of, *inter alia*, development, genuine international cooperation, imperative of multilateralism, and the necessity of faithful implementation of all previous commitments made in the course of the United Nations' major summits and conferences. The essence of the G77 pronouncements pointed (sometimes poignantly) in the direction of the Group's dissatisfaction with the package proposal and the unfolding debate on it in the General Assembly. In casting doubt by questioning the relevance of the major political elements of the package under discussion to the most acute problems of billions of poor people in underdeveloped nations across the globe, the permanent representative of Jamaica, chairman of the Group of 77 for the year 2005, was not just playing politics for tactical negotiating purposes as might befit the image of the diplomatic representative of the heterogeneous bloc of countries still grappling with the woes of development and progress.

His challenge to the relevance of the proposed package reflected the Group's long-established tradition since the 1960s; it is vital to champion the cause of the developing world, and promote a new world order that would achieve development and justice possible for the ever-growing numbers of poor people in the world community. His words of critique, even dissent, might have been found extremely unsettling to those very few countries, headed by the United States, bent on keeping the Draft Outcome Document[1] confined for all practical purposes to a number of political reforms and away from any substantive provisions in the economic and development fields. There was even opposition to any reference to the Millennium Development Goals (MDGs) adopted by the Assembly back in September 2000.

Regardless of how laborious the discussions were at the Assembly, horse-trading within the multilateral forum resulted in a somewhat compromised document. The document was definitely unsatisfactory to any of the major blocs, and prominent players such as the United States, and even to the secretary-general. It is important to examine the rationale behind the critical outlook and positions of the bloc of developing countries, as represented by the Group of 77, in the course of these UN discussions. It would be difficult to arrive at a realistic understanding of the critical outlook, political-diplomatic demeanor, and conduct of the developing world at the UN General Assembly discussions in 2005 without a relatively good grasp of where the Group of 77 began and how it has developed over the past four decades. This essay tries to shed light on the Group's genesis, evolution, and how it has adapted itself to changing times and circumstances. It has endeavored to remain faithful to its original outlook. The essay will also attempt to look into the future of the Group. Based on historical hindsight, it is not a foregone conclusion that the representation of the developing world in the United Nations, and its multilateral processes, will continue and persevere as long as there are countries and peoples aspiring towards development, progress, and a more equitable world order.

The Context for the Group's Formation[2]

The Group of 77 came into being, on 15 June 1964, through the "Joint Declaration of the Seventy-Seven" issued at the end of United Nations Conference on Trade and Development (subsequently known as UNCTAD I), which was held in Geneva between 23 March and 16 June 1964. The Geneva Conference was the first major North-South conference on development questions. It had its immediate roots in the 1961 decision of the UN General Assembly designating the 1960s as the "United Nations Development Decade"[3] and the concurrent resolution on "International Trade as the Primary Instrument for Economic Development." It was fourteen years after the failure of the 1949 Havana conference on world trade,[4] after the formation in 1961 of the Non-Aligned Movement (NAM—an offspring of the Bandung Conference of 1955), and after the 1962 Cairo "Conference on the Problems of Economic Development" (a non-UN gathering with the participation of 36 countries from the three continents) that the developing countries made the first serious attempt to coordinate their international economic policies. Furthermore, it was then that the General Assembly could muster the necessary political support to call for the convening of the first session of UNCTAD. In line with the established practice that has persevered ever since, a Preparatory Committee was established with the mandate of drawing up of the agenda of the conference and preparation of the necessary documentation (Sauvant 1981: 1).

The distinctive interests of the developing countries, within the overall framework of the predominant bipolar world, began to take form during the work of the Preparatory Committee. These interests manifested themselves at the end of the second session (21 May to 29 June 1963). In the "Joint Statement," the developing countries stated to the Committee, "they summarized the views, needs and aspirations of the Third World with regard to the impending UNCTAD session." This statement, in whose advancement and preparation Yugoslavia had played an important role, was submitted later the same year to the General Assembly as a "Joint Declaration" on behalf of 75 developing countries, which were then members of the United Nations. This was the cornerstone for the establishment of the Group of 77, manifested a year later in the "Joint Declaration of Seventy-Seven" in Geneva.

The Joint Declaration regarded UNCTAD I as "an event of historic significance" and emphasized their "own unity" as the "outstanding feature" of the Geneva Conference. The Declaration stated that:

> This unity has sprung out of the fact that facing the basic problems of development they have a common interest in a new policy for international trade and development... The developing countries have a strong conviction that there is a vital need to maintain, and further strengthen, this unity in the years ahead. It is an indispensable instrument for securing the adoption of new approaches in the international economic field. This unity is also an instrument for enlarging the area of co-operative endeavor in the international field and for securing mutually beneficial relationships with the rest of the world.

The seventy-seven developing countries, on the occasion of this declaration, pledge themselves to maintain, foster and strengthen this unity in the future. Towards this end they shall adopt all possible means to increase contacts and consultations among themselves so as to determine common objectives and formulate joint programs of action in international economic cooperation.

It should be added that the dominant outlook throughout the preparatory process was largely inspired by the conceptual work of Raul Prebisch, then executive secretary of the Economic Commission for Latin America (ECLA), who became the first secretary-general of UNCTAD (1964-1969). Through this process the developing countries came to form and formulated, for the first time since the establishment of the United Nations, an overall outlook and a comprehensive set of policies and measures towards "creating a new and just world economic order." The aspiration for the "new order" arose from the "dissatisfaction of the developing countries with the liberal economic order instituted at the end of World War II" (Williams 1991: 18). The liberal economic order was centered on Bretton Woods Institutions, including GATT (superseded by WTO in 1995) which is nominally part of the UN system. In reality, it was more in tune with the interests and policies of the advanced Western economies. The "new order" as espoused by the Third World, did, in fact, reflect the preponderant Prebisch/ECLAC thinking in early 1960s and the subsequent UNCTAD analysis, outlook and policy. It was premised on "a new international division of labor"; "a new framework of international trade"; and the "adoption of a new and dynamic international policy for trade and development." The latter was expected to facilitate the formulation of new policies by the governments of both developed and developing countries towards meeting the needs of developing countries (Sauvant 1981: 3). It was regarded as necessary that the new political machinery "serve as an institutional focal point for the continuation of the work initiated by the conference," and it was manifested in the General Assembly Resolution 1995 (XIX), later in the year, which decided to institutionalize UNCTAD as a permanent organ of the General Assembly to "deal with trade and the related problems of development as well as trade among countries with different economic and social systems" (Kousari 2005: 7). Thus, UNCTAD became the main forum for global development discussions (until mid-to-late 1970s) as well as the focal point of the activities of the Group of 77,[5] whose membership continued to grow over time even though for "symbolic reasons" the original name has been maintained to this date."[6]

The point begs to be made at this juncture that the Group of 77 was, from the very beginning, a loose coalition of countries aspiring to achieve development, or "underdeveloped" countries as they are called. The "Seventy-Five" of the General Assembly in 1963, the "Seventy-Seven" of UNCTAD I in 1964, the "122" in 1980, and the current "133," are all composed of a wide range of countries vastly differing in size, population, and natural and human endowments: "historical experiences; political, economic and social systems with vastly different cultural and religious identities" (Behnam 2004: 265); level of development; and of no less importance, greatly different, even opposing, orientation in foreign policy. The Group that has been aptly called an "informal, formal coalition" that "has never had a written constitution nor a legislative foundation or rules of procedure," never developed a permanent secretariat [7] or a leadership structure,[8] and has yet to develop into a credible, enduring negotiating force for the community of developing countries (Williams 1991: 165; Behnam 2004: 268). As observed and commented by various analysts and observers, the Group's inherent, ever-deepening, expanding heterogeneity and the difficult, time-consuming, problem-ridden process of achieving full in-group consensus—not an easy feat by any means within multilateral framework and process[9]—have, in fact, contributed to the very points of strength of the Group. The sense of solidarity within the coalition was based on a "common perception—the inequitable nature of the existing economic order and the overriding need to change it and in the need for improved management and functioning of the world economy" (Behnam 2004: 265). The Group's unity from the outset, despite inherent divergences and ever-present centrifugal pressures,[10] and the realization that "united we stand, divided we fall." This could be considered as the overriding reason for the perseverance of the Group of 77. As surmised by an activist G77 ambassador: "developing countries left their differences at the door step outside the meeting rooms as if they were personal baggage."[11]

The Group of 77—Champion of the Third World: Ascendance and Declining Fortunes

The circumstances leading to the formation of the Group of 77 as well as its original loci of activity, as briefly discussed in the preceding section, came to have a catalytic influence over its subsequent development. Throughout the remainder of the 1960s and early 1970s, the Group, while gradually gaining articulation in different aspects, including institutional aspects (Williams 1991: 82-86), developed a very organic relationship with UNCTAD. With UNCTAD commanding global development discussions, the Group served as "one of the most important agents for the socialization of the developing countries in matters relating to international political economy, and established itself as the Third World's principal organ for the articulation and aggregation of its collective economic interest and for its representation in the negotiations with the developed countries."[12]

The onset of the 1970s, however, ushered in quite a substantial change in the developing countries' outlook. For one, having witnessed the widening gap between North and South, there was a growing dissatisfaction with the performance of the post-WWII international economic system among the least developed among developing countries. Economic development came to be regarded, within the South as well as in such institutions as UNCTAD, as a necessary complement to political independence that had been won by many developing countries during the previous two decades (Sauvant 1981: 4). Considered as "low politics," the development issue generally moved more towards the center and occupied a much higher profile. This significant change was, in fact, the result of Non-Aligned Movement (NAM) efforts in the early 1970s, which had elevated the issue to the highest level of its meetings and accorded it priority on their agenda. The growing weight of the NAM politics and activities, further enhanced with OPEC's newfound clout (indicated by the quadrupling of oil prices in the wake of October 1973 Arab-Israeli War), finally led to the adoption in May 1974, by the Sixth Special Session of the UN General Assembly, of the "Declaration and Programme of Action on the Establishment of a New International Economic Order (NIEO)."[13] Later that year, the Group of 77 was actively engaged in the process for the negotiation and final adoption of the Charter of Economic Rights and Duties of States. Although it was another significant document for the developing world, it was equally given the cold shoulder, as was the case in NIEO, by the Western bloc, the only difference being that the Charter was put to a roll-call vote both in the Second Committee and subsequently in the General Assembly.[14]

Although radical restructuring of the international economic system was originally conceived and spurred by NAM,[15] it was the Group of 77 that became the flag-bearer of NIEO and the Charter from 1974-75 and onwards. It was particularly the General Assembly whose membership had risen substantially and steadily during the 1960s that enjoyed absolute majority of developing members. And, in its Second Committee, the Group also had come to play a more prominent role in discussing development issues. As a matter of fact, it was the preparatory process for the Sixth Special Session that galvanized the constituent regions of the Group of 77 and led to the emergence of an active G77 in New York.[16]

G77 initiatives in the earlier part of the 1970s also led to the creation of such new UN institutions as United Nations Industrial Development Organization (UNIDO) and International Fund for Agricultural Development (IFAD). Ever since the adoption by the Assembly, the establishment of NIEO, a radical overhaul of the world economy and its major constituent elements, became a fundamental rallying cornerstone of the developing world, and its main politico-diplomatic representative, the Group of 77. The Group also played a very active, effective role in the successful negotiation of the Generalized Scheme of Preferences (GSP) and the Integrated Programme for Commodities, including the Common Fund—both were regarded as major UNCTAD achievements at the time. Active pursuit of NIEO dominated the agenda in UNCTAD IV (held in Nairobi, 1976), UNCTAD V (held in Manila, 1979) and the Group's various meetings throughout the 1970s. The G77's persistent endeavors through these years towards further articulation of the changes needed for the establishment of the "new order" finally led to the adoption, by its Fourth Ministerial Meeting in Arusha, Tanzania, in February 1979, of the "Arusha Programme for Collective Self-Reliance and Framework for Negotiations" (Sauvant 1981: 5). "The developing countries had clearly taken the initiative in their hands in trying to bring about negotiated changes to … institutions governing international economic relations" (Kousari 2005: 9). The developments and trends of the next decade proved that the success was short-lived and, more importantly, had remained largely at the level of "soft law" international agreements, inclusive of the Programme for Commodities and the Common Fund for Commodities. The same destiny befell the Brandt Commission and its report, notwithstanding the highly respected caliber of its members and a high profile meeting in Mexico.

Contrary to the steady progress for the Group and UNCTAD during the 1970s, the onset of the 1980s brought a series of developments with substantial negative effects and repercussions. If considered retrospectively from the vantage point of the developing world, it could be said with certainty that while progressive political economy and Third World radicalism held sway at the United Nations and in multilateral processes during the 1970s, the 1980s began with the assertion of power by resurgent conservatism both in the United States and UK. The Reagan administration's hard-line, blatantly anti-globalist attitude and policies, matched and reinforced by that of Margaret Thatcher's prime ministership, were instrumental in steering the 1981 Cancun Summit towards pushing forward the North-South dialogue, and hence, NIEO discussions

were relegated to the backburner.[17] Even as early as 1979, the UNCTAD
V meetings showed the emerging strains of the North-South dialogue
(Behnam 2004: 271). This incipiently negative trend witnessed a similar
debacle in the same year during the launching of "global negotiations" in
New York under the auspices of the General Assembly which involved
all the key aspects of North-South relations.[18] As far as the world
economy was concerned, the onset of global recession, the debt crisis,
and the consequent focus on the industrialized economies, practically
sidestepped political economy discussions of the 1970s and weakened
position and clout of relevant institutions, UNCTAD and G77. At the
international level, the previous East-West rivalry during the 1960s
and 1970s had also somehow declined. While the Soviet Union was
enmeshed in the Afghan quagmire and simultaneously experimenting
with glasnost and perestroika, which resulted at the end of the decade
with the whole system collapsing, the Western bloc, led by the United
States and an energetically ideological President Reagan, was gaining
pace in its multi-pronged offensive. The damaging effect of the Iraqi
war against Iran (September 1980) and the consequent eight-year-long
armed conflict between the two important OPEC members can hardly
be discounted (Kousari 1981: 10). The net result at the end of the decade for the developing countries was that, while in deep disarray, the
developing countries lost quite a significant source of support for their
demands on the Western industrialized economies. The heydays of the
1970s were gone.

   The change in the overall balance of power on a global scale also
changed the dominant discourse on economic issues at the United Nations. The earlier debate on the need for radical change was substituted
with the focus on the need for domestic reform within the developing
countries (Behnam 2004: 273). A concurrent and corresponding change
in the approach and policies of the Bretton Woods Institutions (BWIs)
vis-à-vis developing countries, which came to be known as "conditionalities." "Structural adjustment programmes,"[19] and the neoliberal policies
known as the "Washington Consensus" also signaled the drastically
changed times, as well as the declining fortunes of the Third World during the 1980s. The Group's Ministerial Declaration in 1984, in which
the ministers expressed "grave concern at the critical stage of the world
economy," catalogued a litany of the challenges facing the developing
countries and was quite indicative of the negative changes in the overall
external environment, on the ground, and on the home front (ibid.: 273).
"[The ministers] also deplored the continuing impasse in international

economic negotiations resulting from some developed countries not living up to their commitments. They particularly regretted attempts to erode the international consensus for development that had existed and attempts, in some areas, to deny such a consensus" (ibid.). They emphasized that sustained growth of the international economy required "an equitable adjustment process."

The assessment of the situation in mid 1980s by a British analyst is quite telling[20]:

> Many enthusiasts for international organization now find themselves sunk in despair about future prospects and are inclined to dismiss as utterly futile many of the go-ings-on at which UN delegates spend so much time and effort. Few doubt that the current scene in New York or Geneva or other places where members foregather is depressing and its future prospect dim.

Almost a decade of North-South "dialogue" (so-called) seems to have reached a point where neither side has any more to say to the other. North and South are like two people in a Harold Pinter play: there they both sit talking right past one another, repeating to themselves and for their own satisfaction the words and phrases they have already used to each other countless times before. After the clarion call of the Brandt Commission for a great new effort to tackle the fundamental problems of international economic disorder and discontent, there has followed a deathly silence.[21]

The work of the United Nations as the 1990s set in were shaped and determined by the cumulative impact of "the end of the Cold War, the upsurge of globalization, and reaction to the lost decade of the 1980s, which had exacerbated the problems of poverty in most countries of the developing world."[22] The quite perceptible change in the political environment at the United Nations and the possibility of forging inter-national consensus on important issues was instrumental in initiating a new trend by focusing, for the larger measure, on human rights and good governance—the latter being a new entrant into the UN discourse and literature.[23] Within this overall framework and an emergence of seri-ous doubts, due to increasing impoverishment and deprivation in many parts of the developing world, about the efficacy of the predominant neoliberal policies of the 1980s, interests for poverty reduction and human development were revived.[24] They led the United Nations to organize a series of major conferences and summits in a wide range of social, economic and cultural areas, which was practically impossible to organize prior to the demise of the Soviet Union, the never-ending mutual bickering between the two rival poles of power, and the effective filibustering at the General Assembly by the socialist-Third World alliance.[25] The point hardly needs to be emphasized that the new trend was being pushed, in a very concerted manner, by the post-Cold-War Conquistadores. The concept of development, not as perceived, defined and debated in the 1960s and 1970s, but defined in the 1992 Rio Earth Summit as sustainable development and in the United Nations (UNDP) with the "human" qualifier was somehow revived on the international agenda.[26] The launching of the Report on "An Agenda for Development" in 1993 by Secretary-General Boutros-Ghali, following "An Agenda for Peace" in 1992 as part of the reform process during his five-year tenure, was to be seen and judged within this general trend.[27] It has to be added that the Group of 77's active engagement in the negotiations that followed on the Agenda for Development in New York helped to reinvigorate and revive the Group's role. However, its role was partial compared with that of the 1970s, when it was considered the negotiating arm of developing countries. Notwithstanding this trend, UNCTAD's position and profile, its work procedures (group-based negotiations), its original *raison d'être*, and its mandate as a principal forum for consensus-building negotiations and rule-making remain under attack. Due to such attacks, ongoing since the '80s, UNCTAD never regained its earlier stature and function. It did not evolve into the International Trade Organization (ITO) as initially indicated in the 1964 General Assembly resolution (1995/XIX), and subsequently reinforced in the UNCTAD IV Resolution 90 (Institutional Issues), rather it was gradually and systematically reduced to "a knowledge-based institution devoted almost entirely to policy dialogue and capacity building," where "there is resistance even to any form of "soft agreement" such as agreed conclusions or chairman's summary" (Behnam 2004: 283).[28] In a candid assessment of the state of North-South dialogue in mid-1990s, South Centre (a Geneva-based developing countries think tank) commented that "unlike in the earlier period when the G77 was the main source of proposals, it is the North which now holds the initiative. The developing countries often appear unable to make a counter proposal or put forward credible alternative proposals of their own in international gatherings. At best, they resort to a limiting damage strategy."[29] The Group's failure to participate collectively in the Uruguay Round of trade negotiations (1986-95), leading to the establishment of the World Trade Organization (WTO), could be considered a telling gauge in the state of affairs at the time.

Reform Process at the United Nations—G77 Outlook

A. "Renewing the United Nations: A Programme for Reform"—1997

In mid-July 1997, just few months after taking office, Secretary-General Kofi Annan, issued his report entitled "Renewing the United Nations: A Programme for Reform" (A/51/950, 14 July 1997, referred to as "Report" hereinafter). The Report, premised on an analysis of the then-existing world situation and the status of the United Nations within the international system as well as of the challenges it faced in carrying out its mandate, proposed a number of reform measures. The proposed measures covered administrative, structural and programmatic areas: establishment of the post of deputy secretary-general; review of the mandate and work programs of UNCTAD and the UN Department of Economic and Social Affairs (UN/DESA); strengthening of ECOSOC; establishment of the UN Development Group (UNDG); reform of the ECOSOC subsidiary bodies; reform of the Secretariat; establishment of governance of the funds and programs; creation of a "dividend for development'; and reform of the financial aspects and procedures.

The Report was welcomed by the developed members of the organization and recommended to be adopted as a package and as a matter of priority.[30] Conversely, the developing community, as represented for political and security issues by the NAM and for economic and development issues by the Group of 77, while diplomatically welcoming the secretary-general's initiative, took a more cautious position, a non-committal attitude, and as is customary, called for its in-depth discussion at the General Assembly. The open-ended consultations of the General Assembly Plenary on Agenda Item 157, United Nations Reform: Measures and Proposals, took a good number of months before the final outcome could come up for action in the Assembly in December 1997, just a few days before the end of the main part of the 51st Session of the General Assembly.

The Group of 77, focusing mainly on management and financial issues, as well as the economic and development aspects of the Report, did not seem comfortable at all with the underlying presumptions of the Report, nor with its analysis of the global situation and the international system, and much less specifically, with the way development aspects and issues had been addressed.[31] The Group, in its formal pronouncements in the course of the open-ended consultations on different proposals/recommendations,[32] opted for a detailed dissection of various proposals, queried the relevance and rationale of others, rejected still some others, and sought further clarification from the secretary-general on a number of proposals. In late September 1997, the Ministerial Declaration of the Group[33] addressed, *inter alia*, the question of reform at the United Nations, and in particular the secretary-general's Report. The Declaration emphasized the following principles on reform—which lay at the basis of the Group's subsequent negotiations in the GA consultations:

- the UN, as the most universal world organization, is the most credible body for performing developmental tasks. The reform process, therefore, must strengthen the UN's ability to fulfill its role and functions in the development field;
- the developmental tasks of the Organization are of fundamental importance and may not be treated as secondary to its peacekeeping, human rights and humanitarian functions;
- the UN must carry out its mandated, comprehensive role in the economic and social areas, which includes policy analysis, consensus building, policy formulation and coordination, and delivery of technical assistance to developing countries;
- the General Assembly's role in the area of macro-economic policy formulation and coordination has to be strengthened and the core economic issues must be restored to the top of the UN's agenda;
- the functions of organizations within the UN system, which do not fully observe democratic norms, should be comprehensively reviewed. The decision-making process of the Bretton Woods Institutions should be reformed to allow for greater democracy, universality and transparency;
- all reform proposals must aim at giving greater effect to the principles of transparency, pluralism, and democracy, which are the unique strengths of the UN. This means ensuring the availability of multiple perspectives/analyses on critical socio-economic issues and the strengthening of democratic decision-making;
- managerial measures to reduce overlap of functions, eliminate redundancies and minimize fragmentation are exceedingly important, but must be subservient to the larger goals of the reform process, and reform of the Secretariat should be undertaken in accordance with the relevant UN resolutions; and
- a primary pre-requisite for enhancing UN effectiveness is to have stable, predictable and adequate financing for the UN. Member States must fulfill their legal obligations to pay their contributions promptly, in full and without conditions, in accordance with Article 17 of the Charter, and take concrete actions to clear their arrears within a reasonable and defined time-frame and without any conditions.[34]

As can be easily seen, the Group's principles in the secretary-general's Report and the reform process clearly reflect the traditional outlook of the

Group of 77 with respect to the work of the UN system, its constituent bodies, and Bretton Woods Institutions. The centrality of development for the agenda of the UN system, the imperative of democratic governance at the international level, and the primacy of the role of the General Assembly in the UN policy and decision-making processes are all part and parcel of the same familiar developing countries discourse since the 1960s—it resonated in very clear and lively fashion in the Group's outlook on the reform proposals. It would be extremely difficult, if not almost impossible, to try to assess the degree of the Group's success in influencing the final outcome of the General Assembly discussions on the secretary-general's Report and its reform proposals. As it is usually the case in the United Nations and multilateral negotiating processes, perhaps more often would be closer to reality, what came out of the General Assembly in the form of adopted measures was less than satisfactory to any of the major players involved. The most concrete decision was that the secretary-general ended up with a deputy which soon found actual manifestation in the person of a mellow, soft-spoken Canadian, Louise Frechette.[35] Agreement was also reached on devising a singular United Nations Development Assistance Framework (UNDAF), and a few other administrative and even policy-related measures and actions, which could be celebrated by the new secretary-general as achievements. It was also sold to the US Congress (which was holding off on the payment of US dues and arrears) as proof of solemn commitment to the actual reform of the world organization.[36] The developing countries could also feel, at least partially, pleased that they had prevented the worst from occurring. There was enough for everybody to go around and nothing particularly substantial or far-reaching that could be expected to have a critical impact on the betterment of the work and performance, or the final output, of the organization. Lack of tangible progress in the actual creation, operationalization, of the Development Fund could perhaps provide a measure of objective assessment of the degree of success of the reform package.[37]

B. Further Attempts at Reform: 1998-2004

The reform process continued during the two terms of office of Kofi Annan. In September 2000 the Millennium Summit was held in New York, in the course of which a Millennium Declaration was adopted. The high point of the Declaration was to be found in the Millennium Development Goals (MDGs)—a set of eight goals, 18 targets and 48 indicators. The eight goals, based on an analysis that "globalization and the interconnectedness of individuals and countries have synergistic effects with the world's economy and social development" were to be completed by the year 2015.[38]

In his September 2002 annual report to the General Assembly on the work of the Organization, entitled "Strengthening of the United Nations: An Agenda for further Change," Kofi Annan presented a reassessment of previous reforms and proposed new ones. The report, which was divided into six topics[40] and recognized in its introduction the age of "interdependence and integration," asserted the tenuous dichotomy between opportunity and danger for the future as a result of globalization—it called for the strengthening of cooperation at the United Nations to "forge a common destiny in a time of accelerating global change."[39] Among the six topics, "working better together" addressed the question of coordination within the organization and the roles and responsibilities of various actors and agencies. The section also emphasized the priority of addressing collaboration between the United Nations and civil society, and called for the creation of a High-Level Panel to look into the matter and make recommendations to further promote the relations between the two. It was this specific proposal that was followed up in earnest, first at the General Assembly through its adoption as part of the reform resolution, and subsequently in February 2003 through the actual establishment of the secretary-general's Panel of Eminent Persons on United Nations-Civil Society Relations. The Panel was composed of 12 members (six men and six women), representing different expertise and backgrounds with due respect for geographical representation[41], and chaired by Fernando Henrique Cardoso, former president of Brazil (known afterwards as Cardoso Panel). The Cardoso Panel submitted its report to the secretary-general in early June 2004. The report, entitled "We the Peoples: Civil Society, the UN and Global Governance" (A/58/817, 11 June 2004), called for the United Nations to become a more "outward-looking organization" and contained 30 different recommendations consisting of both organizational/structural as well as substantive nature. While calling on the United Nations to embrace a plurality of constituencies, inclusive of civil society and non-state actors in addition to the established intergovernmental body, it also called on the organization to strengthen democratic structures through global governance and accountability.[42]

The Cardoso report, complemented by a note from the secretary-general containing his own reflections and preferences on the proposed recommendations, mostly from the vantage point of practicality and also acceptability to the intergovernmental body, came up for discussion in early October 2004. While the report received generally strong support from the Western countries, it received equally strong criticism from the ranks of the developing community, and interestingly enough, generally critical response from the NGO community and civil society organizations.[43] As mentioned earlier, it is the NAM rather than G77 that deals with political or non-development, non-economic matters and issues, in the General Assembly. In this case as well, in addition to individual developing country delegations, it was the NAM that took a critical group position on the general tenor of the report and the key recommendations, which was regarded to be in some ways undermining state sovereignty at the United Nations as enshrined in the letter and spirit of the Charter.[44] The net result was that the strong negative reaction from the developing community seems to have cowed the president of the General Assembly into sending the pending matter to the backburner.[45] Moreover, the matter was soon overshadowed completely by the unfolding heated debate in the assembly on the politically sensitive report of the UN High Panel on Threats, Challenges, and Change. The Report, entitled "A More Secure World: Our Shared Responsibility." The Panel, established by the secretary-general in late 2003, had been tasked with generating "new ideas about the kinds of policies and institutions required for the UN to be effective in the 21st century."[46]

C. The Millennium Review Summit (2005)

The High-level Panel report identified six "clusters" of threats that the world faces in the future.[47] Based on the understanding of the threats as such and the necessity of UN's change to meet them, the Report suggested the revitalization of the General Assembly and ECOSOC, restoration of credibility to the Commission on Human Rights, creation of a Peacebuilding Commission, and improved collaboration with regional organizations.[48] The report also called for the reform of the Security Council towards increasing its credibility and effectiveness.

In March 2005, Kofi Annan issued another major report, entitled "In Larger Freedom: Towards Development, Security and Human Rights for All."[49] The Report was intended to serve as blueprint for the Millennium Review Summit, scheduled for September 2005. While recognizing that the "imbalance of power in the world is a source of instability"[50] as well as the decline of public confidence in the United Nations, the Report also observed "there was growing belief in the importance of effective multilateralism." In the secretary-general's analysis and view[51]:

> Each developing country has primary responsibility for its own development—strengthening governance, combating corruption and putting in place the policies and investments to drive private-sector-led growth and maximize domestic resources available to fund national development strategies. Developed countries, on their side, undertake that developing countries which adopt transparent, credible and properly costed development strategies will receive the full support they need, in the form of increased development assistance, a more development-oriented trade system and wider and deeper debt relief.

Soon afterwards, a debate on the secretary-general's reports commenced in the General Assembly, a several-month-long marathon of plenary meetings for official statements and long drawn-out sessions of informal consultations and negotiation on the Draft Outcome Document, originally submitted by the president of the General Assembly. In the course of the general debate, major groups and individual country delegations expounded, in a number of successive sessions and reflecting on the state of play, their respective analyses and positions on various aspects of the secretary-general's reports and the evolving draft under discussion. The Group of 77 and the NAM, both representing the developing community, each addressed, according to their respective focus, certain aspects and areas. The Group of 77, in accordance with the long-established practice and its economic- and development-oriented outlook, focused on these aspects, and dealt with political issues and aspects in so far as they concerned, one way or another, directly or indirectly, development and its requirements.

The Group's statements,[52] some dealing more with principles and the overall outlook and some others focusing on specific areas and proposals/recommendations, addressed the most salient aspects of the issues and areas under discussion and lay out, in very clear terms, the outlook, positions, preferences and priorities of the developing community. The following represents a highly condensed and amalgamated summary of the Group's pronouncements[53]:

- The conceptual underpinning of the Report sees development in the context of addressing prevention of terrorism and organized crime as questionable. This rather narrow and restricted approach diminishes the importance of development which in itself represents one of the major challenges of our time;
- Recognition of the inter-connectedness of the threats and challenges and mutual vulnerability of Member States, and that these challenges cannot be met by any State acting alone and thus require international cooperative action;
- Development has to be considered in a comprehensive manner, in the context of a principal concern with human dignity and human

welfare. Hence, rejection of any notion that development should be viewed through the prism of security and the fight against terrorism. Such a narrow, conceptual framework would limit the scope for substantive treatment and meaningful action. The premise of the analysis of the link between security and development should not alter the balance of responsibilities between the various organs of the system, nor should it be used as a basis to strengthen the role of the Security Council vis-à-vis the other Principal Organs of the UN—the General Assembly and the Economic and Social Council;

• Rejection of any proposal that would lead to weakening of ECOSOC and its role in giving prominence to economic and social issues within the UN. The role of ECOSOC, as envisaged in the Charter, should be strengthened and not reduced to one of administrative coordination and to research and analysis of the economic and social threats to peace and security;

• Concurrence with the powerful conclusion in paragraph 56 of the High-level Panel Report that existing global economic and social governance structures are woefully inadequate for the challenges ahead. The imperative, therefore, to address systemic inequities in the international economic system to redress the historical balance against the developing world. Hence, the need for better management of the global economy and for better arrangements within the multilateral institutions for co-ordination and for the formulation of policy guidelines to ensure coherence, including more specific institutional prescriptions which envisage a role for the UN in decision-making in global economic policies, as well as reform measures and mechanisms to open up the way for developing countries to exercise greater influence on the formulation of policies affecting global economic relations;

• The imperative to move away from the policy conditionalities restricts policy options of developing countries. The enforcement of conditionalities and coercive measures should never become accepted as the price for economic co-operation;

• The international community should continue to focus on the fundamental underlying cause of current problems—the persistence of underdevelopment. It should be considered as a basic and fundamental issue in all its dimensions, not simply as an economic and social threat to peace and security. Such a narrow and restricted approach to development issues is untenable;

• International co-operation must, based on the principle of inclusivity, taking into account the concerns of all states/countries, reflect a partnership, which preserves the rights and interests of all parties. The terms on which co-operation is conducted should not endanger sovereign rights or restrict the development options available to developing countries, with the understanding that there is no single sustainable model for development and that developing countries need the policy space to select their own options in development policy to formulate their development strategies in keeping with national development policies and strategies that reflect national priorities and are responsive to the particular circumstances of each country. Rejection, therefore, of ideological prescriptions concerning economic organization, free markets or the role of the state;

- The Review Summit should seek to adopt a development agenda which can provide the basis for sustained economic growth for developing countries by the removal of imbalances and disequilibrium which promote impoverishment and impede the full implementation of the MDGs and other inter-governmentally agreed goals and commitments reflected in the outcomes of all major UN summits and conferences. The need, therefore, to create an enabling international environment in which the collective concerns of the global community are addressed adequately;

- The developing countries will support the recommendations and decisions geared to strengthen multilateralism, to uphold the principles of international law and policies, which promote equity and protect the rights and interests of all states. The international community should seek to have a stronger UN with improved institutional arrangements and the political orientation to deliver programs and policies to advance welfare throughout the world, in all its constituent parts, without the application of selective and discriminatory criteria;

- The focus of the whole process must be on broad development needs and objectives, and not simply on the creation of MDG-based national strategies. The MDGs represent an important aspect of the overall policy framework for development but they do not represent the full development agenda. Moreover, policies and strategies for attaining the MDGs and other internationally agreed development goals must uphold the principles of good governance at both the national and international levels;

- The imperative of striving in all of these deliberations and processes for action-oriented proposals and for significant decisions and substantive outcomes.

Having made this rather long catalogue of positions and priorities, do's and don'ts, admonitions and exhortations, hopes and expectations, known in the course of the General Assembly deliberations and informal consultations, the representatives of the Group and most prominently, the chairman, also made it known to the intergovernmental body that "for all of this, there is no better place than the United Nations"—the Group of 77 is committed to the "objective of strengthening the role of the UN in advancing economic co-operation to promote development and to advance the welfare of our peoples." In so far as progress in the actual negotiation on the Draft Outcome Document was concerned, the chairman of G77 opened his statement on 28 July 2005, with an expression of appreciation to the GA president and the co-facilitators: "there have been significant improvements in the text ... [and] the development cluster has been given increased coverage." He went on to add that the comments contained in his statement then were "with a view to further improve the text."

The process of negotiation in the Assembly on the Draft was then enmeshed in a controversy arising from about 750 unwieldy amendments from the US delegation (53), the essence of which was vehement opposition to any and all "language" unacceptable to Washington. The American delegation, led by then-newly appointed Ambassador John Bolton, had made it known that it was willing to negotiate and make progress only in three areas: peace and security, terrorism, and human rights. Rejection of any reference in the text to MDGs, as surprising as it might have looked and sounded to everybody given the agreed status of the Goals, was featured among the American amendments. The US challenge engulfed the process for a number of weeks, during the interminable plenary sessions and informal consultations, and put in peril the very possibility of producing a clean text before the heads of state and government arrived in New York for the Summit. Last minute, intensive, and high-wire diplomacy, principally led by an embattled secretary-general anxious to save the day and the much celebrated event, finally managed to churn out an agreement of sorts that was "full of platitudes and generalities"[54] and fell short of everybody's expectation. secretary-general's tongue-in-cheek words, on and off the podium, on the final outcome were quite telling. Other leaders, from both developed and developing countries, were more outspoken in expressing dismay at the meager result.[55] The Ministerial Statement of the Group of 77, adopted on 22 September 2005, two weeks after the end of the Summit, "noted that while the development cluster of the 2005 World Summit Outcome fell short of the expectations of the G77 and China, there were positive elements which could be used as a platform for actively promoting the implementation of commitments made in previous UN summits and conferences and decided that special efforts would be made during the current session of the General Assembly towards advancing these objectives."[56] The Group was partly satisfied that they had succeeded in convincing the General Assembly in reaffirming, once more and at the summit level, that past commitments—a fundamental element in all G77 negotiations in the United Nations and all multilateral processes—are not allowed to be diluted or undermined.[57]

Concluding Remarks

Anchored in the Past—Looking to the Future

The discussion in the preceding pages has tried to depict a realistic picture of how and why the Group of 77 emerged on the multilateral scene in 1964 and how it has since performed as the spokesman of the coalition of developing countries. The essay has, for the most part, endeavored to elaborate, albeit in a wide brush, on the why aspect; that is, why the Group came into being in the first place, and more importantly, why it has persevered over the past four decades notwithstanding all the changes that have taken place in the world and at the United Nations.

The Group of 77 asserted clearly, in the "Joint Declaration of the Seventy-Seven," its first official pronouncement at the end of UNCTAD I on 15 June 1964, two basic and fundamental points as the very *raison d'être* for its formation. The developing countries had achieved unity, as an outstanding feature of UNCTAD I, and the unity had sprung out of having to confront the basic problems of development and a common interest in a new policy for international trade and development. The developing countries, signatories of the Joint Declaration, further asserted that they had a strong conviction that there was a vital need to maintain, and further strengthen, their unity in the years to come. The discussion here has, in the author's view based both on analysis and personal direct experience, borne witness to the correctness of the understanding, and analysis, of the developing countries back in 1964.

The world of 2005-06 is no doubt quite a different world from that of mid-1960s. In so far as the ideals and expectations of G77 and UNCTAD (up to mid-and late 1970s) are concerned, they are different from those of the 1970s. Gone are the days of Raul Prebisch—the early years of UNCTAD when the NAM-G77 pioneered the call for a new and just economic order and succeeded in convincing the UN General Assembly to adopt the "Declaration and Programme of Action on the Establishment of a New International Economic Order" and the "Charter of the Economic Rights and Duties of States." As we all happen to know, these two valuable UN documents in the economic and development field, along with a whole series of other inter-governmentally agreed and adopted documents addressing the wide and ever-increasing gamut of economic and development issues since mid-1970s, have remained for the most part, and in some cases totally, un-implemented. Far from being sarcastic, this appears to be the fate of almost all declarations that have emanated since 1945, from the General Assembly—the most universal intergovernmental body within the entire UN system, and all other UN forums, inclusive of the Economic and Social Council and all UN major summits and conferences with the exception of the Security Council (whose mandate and functions do not fall within the ambit of economic and development field and, hence, beyond the purview of this essay). Gone also are the days of the Cold War era, whose bipolar world and active superpower rivalry and jealous wooing of developing countries, in and out of the United Nations, made possible, *inter alia*, the adoption of such substantive, radical documents as NIEO and the Charter. The fast globalizing world of the early twenty-first century with the unchecked trend of expanding and deepening poverty; the marginalization of people; the resulting un-fathomable human suffering across the developing South (not to mention the HIV/AIDS pandemic or rampant, elusive violence of all sorts); the still reigning unilateralism *a la* Newconite Washington, whose immediate reverberations are felt in very tangible terms at the United Nations; and the multilateral institutions and processes are determined by the combined impact of the power of the gun and the purse. This realization does not seem to depict any promising picture on the horizon.

Notwithstanding this rather stark, gloomy assessment, on a global scale and at the level of the United Nations, the author fully concurs with the words of K. D. Knight, minister of foreign affairs of Jamaica, at the turnover ceremony of the chairmanship of the Group of 77 on 25 January 2005: "Against the background of increasing wealth and increasing poverty, evolving political and economic alignments and growing dominance of major power centers, the underlying policy rationale which inspired the formation of the Group of 77 and China has essentially remained unchanged." Given the reality for billions of people across the globe, especially in the bigger part of humanity that we call the developing world, and the certainty that poverty, deprivation and human suffering on a grand scale will still be part of our collective life on the earth for quite some time to come—the yearning for development, justice, progress, welfare, general prosperity, and for a new international order, at least a new international economic order as advocated by groups like the Group of 77 since mid-1960s, is bound to persevere. It would be very difficult, in fact, impossible, to presume otherwise. This reality has enlivened and been driving the Group for over four decades and will, in the years and decades to come, continue to blow wind into the sail of any coalition formed by countries considering themselves, or considered by others, as underdeveloped or developing. Inevitable change in the number of members, as some members of the coalition may move from the lower side of the development divide to the higher side and as the internal dynamism of the coalition continue to experience the rather inevitable trend of fragmentation due to the emergence of smaller group interests, may or may not affect the future name of the group.

What is important, instead, is that with the benefit of hindsight and historical discretion, multilateralism, in its broadest sense, will most probably triumph over the prevailing unilateralist trends and tendencies. For lack of a better reason, the mere fact that continued existence, if not further exacerbation, of the wide range of problems we human beings continue to face in our collective life, in our respective societies and in the global community, lead us, inevitably, to seek collective solutions for common problems. This is the very crux of multilateral enterprise, which will persevere. And for the enterprise to persevere there should be players, which will, in the author's perspective, abound. In so far as aspiration for development would continue to energize countries, societies and peoples in the coming years and decades, the Group of 77, or its reincarnation under whatever name or shape, will still have a role to play and function to perform.

Notes

1. The text presented by the president of the General Assembly as the working document for negotiation.
2. For the first two sections of the essay, dealing with the formation of the Group of 77 and its outlook, dynamism and role at the United Nations and in multilateral processes up to the end of 1980s, I have drawn extensively on the following two sources:
    *   Sauvant, Karl P., The Group of 77: Evolution, Structure, Organization, New York, Oceana, 1981, Williams, Marc, Third World Cooperation: The Group of 77 in UNCTAD, London, Printer Publishers, 1991, and also for the same period as well as for the 1990s, I have drawn—in alphabetical order - on the following sources:
    *   Awni, Behnam, "Developing Countries in the Group of 77: a Journey in Multilateral Diplomacy, 1964 to 2004" in R. St. J. Macdonald and D.M. Johnston (Eds.), *Towards World Constitutionalism*, The Netherlands, Koninklijke Brill BV., 2005.
    *   Gosovic, Branislav, *UNCTAD: Conflict and Compromise; The Third World's Quest for an Equitable World Economic Order through the United Nations*, Leiden, A.W. Sijthoff, 1972.
    *   South Centre, Recalling UNCTAD I at UNCTAD XI, May 2004, Geneva. This is a publication issued by the South Centre, a developing countries think tank based in Geneva, on the occasion of the 40th anniversary of United Nations Conference on Trade and Development (UNCTAD). UNCTAD I was held in Geneva from 26 March to 16 June 1964. UNCTAD XI was held in Sao Paulo, Brazil, from 13-18 June 2004.
    *   South Centre, *The Group of 77 at Forty; Championing multilateralism, a democratic and equitable world order, South-South Cooperation and Development*, June 2004, Geneva.
    *   South Centre, The Future of the Group of 77, A Background Paper issued on the occasion of the Ministerial Round Table of the Group of 77, Midrand, South Africa, 28 April 1996.

3.   Interesting, but ironic, that the call came from the US President John F. Kennedy in early 1961 following the launching of his Alliance for Progress plan for Latin America. The US-sponsored draft resolution on the "Development Decade" was passed unanimously by the General Assembly. The approach and policy at the time seems to have been rooted in the American desire to counter the attraction of Soviet ideology and prevent its further spread—following the Cuban example—in Latin America. Contrary to an unmistakably intransigent attitude and policy that in later years came to be a hallmark of the US attitude and practice towards economic discussions at the United Nations, "increasing flexibility was shown in working through the UN on economic development issues." Kamran Kousari, The Political Economy of Reform in the UN Economic and Social Sectors, *International Conference on UN Reform*, Tehran, Iran, 18-19 July 2005, p. 5.

4.   Since the US Congress did not ratify the Havana Charter, it never went into effect. Ibid., p. 3.

5.   It is important to note that that the group system that developed in the course of the preparatory process for UNCTAD I, and subsequently became part of its working modalities (and preserved ever since, even though weakened gradually since 1980s), played a pivotal role in the "consolidation of the Group of 77 as an effective interest group because it introduced certain institutional pressures for co-ordination and co-operation" (Sauvant, p. 10). It is also noteworthy that Raul Prebisch personally "played an important role in fostering and nurturing the Third World solidarity which culminated in the Joint Declaration of the Seventy-Seven Developing Countries. In his capacity as the secretary-general of the Conference he produced a report, *Towards a New Trade Policy for Development*, which exercised an enormous degree of influence over the conference proceedings. The report largely determined the agenda of the conference ... and it became the manifesto of the developing countries" (Williams, ibid., p. 43). It is equally important to note that the symbiotic relationship between UNCTAD and G77, and the latter's dependence on the former's secretariat for both organizational and policy support, gave rise to the rather prevalent impression within UNCTAD that the secretariat was biased in favor of the developing countries. Years later, Kenneth Dadzie, the fourth secretary-general of UNCTAD, defended the close working relationship and described it "as a development perspective that the organization necessarily needed to maintain" (Kousari, p. 7).

6.   Gosovic, ibid., p. 271. As of 2006, the membership of the Group of 77 has increased to 131. Moreover, The People's Republic of China—China—is also considered a member of the Group. While the official name and emblem of the Group solely refers to "77", G77 representatives usually make their official pronouncements/statements in the name of the "Group of 77 and China".

       For a good review of the relevant discussions on the membership of the Group, especially in its formative years, including discussion on the criteria for membership, see Sauvant pp. 10-16 and also Williams, pp. 78-82.

7.   For a detailed review of the relevant discussions, for and against, the proposal for the establishment of a permanent secretariat for the Group, see Sauvant, pp. 44-54 and also Gosovic, pp. 275-6.

8.   Since the early years of the formation of the Group, the principle of rotating leadership—coordination—among the three constituent regions (Latin America, Asia and Africa) came to be accepted and practiced. The annual chairmanship of the Group at UN Headquarters in New York, which came to be recognized over time as the *primus entre pares* (first among equals) of all G77 Chapters, was initially for the entire length of a General Assembly Session (September to September). Since mid-'70s, this annual tenure came to start in early January of each year and continued

for a whole year. It has become customary since 1977 that following informal consultations within the region through which the coordinator/chairman is agreed upon, and with the tacit understanding that the regional choice is acceptable to the whole Group, the formal designation of the coordinator/chairman is done by the meeting of ministers of foreign affairs of the Group. This meeting usually takes place in the latter part of September during the high-level segment of the General Assembly Session. Also see Gosovic (pp. 276-79 and pp. 286-91) for a concise analysis of the questions of leadership and decision-making in the early years of the Group.

9.   Needless to say, the Group's traditional and still valid requirement for full consensus within the Group "can result in a paralysis by allowing one or few countries to bloc action or in a policy position at such a low common denominator that it wholly frustrates the effort of the great majority of membership." South Centre, The Future of the Group of 77, op. cit., p. 10.

10.   For a brief analysis of the inherent cleavages within the Group in its early years—that were either preserved or even deepened due to, *inter alia*, increasing membership over time, see Gosovic (pp. 279-86), and also Williams (pp. 99-101).

11.   Ambassador Anthony Hill (Permanent Representative of Jamaica, UN, Geneva), as quoted in Behnam, op. cit., p. 266.

12.   Sauvant, op. cit., p. 3.

13.   The final resolutions on the Declaration and the Programme of Action were both adopted by consensus, but with strong reservations from the developed market economies (Sauvant, p. 75)—reservations which, as expected, were detrimental in their subsequent lack of interest in any meaningful effort for their implementation.

14.   Belgium, Denmark, Federal Republic of Germany, Luxembourg, the United Kingdom, and the United States of America voted against the Charter—both in the Committee and the Assembly (Sauvant, p. 96).

15.   As evidenced by consecration of a working committee at all NAM meetings to economic matters, and hence a separate part for economic matters in all NAM documents, the Movement's interest in economic and development issues has persevered up to this very date, even if overshadowed, for all practical purposes, by political and security issues. The point needs to be made, however, that the political significance and clout of NAM—the political NAM—suffered substantially in the wake of the demise of the bipolar world in early 1990s, albeit somewhat reversed in more recent years as a result of the changing circumstances, mainly due to the composite impact of unbridled globalization and ascendant unilateralism of the United States.

16.   This process, and the intricacies involved in the span of almost a decade, is an interesting aspect of the internal dynamism of the Group. For an analysis of the issues involved at various time periods see Sauvant (pp. 74-79) and Williams (pp. 82-90).

17.   "The importance of the US in negotiating and implementing change creates a situation where other leading states are unlikely to push ahead with reform efforts when the US is opposed…" (Williams, p. 167).

18.   It is also of interest to note that in the eyes of observers at the time what was seen as the emergence of "conflict and competition between the New York and Geneva economic arms of the UN, and the difficulties encountered by Governments in their efforts to coordinate their policies within these multilateral institutions reduced the effectiveness of the UN" (Behnam, p. 271). Also see Diego Cordovez, Diplomacy for Development, Multilateral Diplomacy, Kluwer Law International, The Netherlands, 1998.

19. Kousari, op. cit., p. 12, also pp. 13-4.
20. Susan Strange, The Poverty of Multilateral Economic Diplomacy, in Diplomacy at the UN, edited and introduced by G.R. Berridge and A. Jennings, Leicester University, Macmillan Press, 1985.
21. According to Kousari (p. 12), a US delegate to one of the preparatory meetings of the Trade and Development Board had said that he would rather take a walk along Lac Leman than attend UNCTAD VII, being then held in Geneva. According to the delegate, the sterile debates in UNCTAD were not procuring an extra plate of food for starving Africans. In Kousari's rather pointed remark, "Open markets, reduction of the role of the state in the economy, privatization, deregulation and the unleashing of the entrepreneurial spirits were seen as the path to economic salvation" (ibid., p. 12).
22. Richard Jolly, Louis Emmerij, Dharam Ghai and Frederic Lapeyere, UN Contributions to Development Thinking and Practice, United Nations Intellectual History Project Series (UNIHPS), Indiana University Press, Bloomington and Indianapolis, 2004, pp. 169-70.
23. Ibid., p. 169. For a detailed analysis of the relevant issues and discussions at the time see John Toye and Richard Toye, The UN and Global Political Economy, United Nations Intellectual History Series, Indiana University Press, Bloomington and Indianapolis, 2004, especially Chapter 10 (The Conservative Counterrevolution of the 1980s).
24. Ibid., p. 170.
25. Child Summit (1990, New York); Human Settlements (1991, Istanbul); Environment and Development (1992, Rio); Second World Conference on Human Rights (1993, Vienna); Population and Development (1994, Cairo); Social Development Summit (1995, Copenhagen); and Fourth World Conference on Women (1995, Beijing). Starting with 1996, the five-year review conferences of these conferences and summits were held. For a brief discussion and analysis of the context for these conferences see Jolly et al., ibid., Chapter 7 (The 1990s: Rediscovering a Human Vision), and in particular pp. 169-72 (The Development Context) and pp. 180-84 (the Impact of World Conferences).
26. During Ghali's tenure, the UN increased its "technical assistance" portfolio, a dozen operating units were abolished, and the UN Center for Transnational Corporations was dissolved. He trimmed both the staff of the UN and the budget, and presented two key documents on peace and development. James, A. Paul, UN Reform: An Analysis, 1996, as referred to in South Centre, Meeting the Challenges of UN Reform: A South Perspective, p. 5 (see note No. 30 below).
27. In the analysis of Jolly et al., "Second, the end of the Cold War further eroded the declining influence of the developing countries, as the great powers no longer felt the need to court their support. Among other consequences, this reinforced the decline in the development assistance, belying the hopes of those who expected that some dividends from the disarmament process would flow into development assistance. On the positive side, interest in issues of human rights and democracy revived." Ibid., p. 170.
28. "With the creation of the WTO in 1995, doubts were already being raised about the usefulness of maintaining UNCTAD, particularly as its negotiating mandate in the area of trade had been completely eroded owing to the far-reaching negotiations in the context of the Uruguay Round and the establishment of the WTO." (Kousari, ibid., p. 13). In Behnam's assessment, UNCTAD has, nevertheless, maintained certain intellectual independence and through its flagship publications challenges orthodoxy (p. 283).
29. South Centre, The Future of the Group of 77, op. cit., p. 10.

30. "The Report appears on the whole to have been successful in addressing the views emanating from key countries in the North. It was promptly acclaimed and given support by the developed countries. The developing countries, on the other hand, while generally welcoming the Report, were disappointed that the reform package did not always appear to take sufficient heed of their views, sensitivities and concerns." South Centre, A Commentary on "Renewing the United Nations: A Programme for Reform", A policy brief prepared at the request of the Group of 77, Geneva, Fall 1997, p. 1.

31. South Centre, "Meeting the Challenge of UN Reform: A South Perspective." The paper, to be completed and issued in early fall 2006, has been consulted—and used—by the author in its draft form.

32. See for example statements made on behalf of the Group on 14 and 29 October 1997. See the Group's Website at "g77off@unmail.org", Statements and Declarations, 1997.

33. Adopted at the Twenty-First Annual Meeting of the Ministers for Foreign Affairs of the Group of 77 on 26 September 1997, New York, G77 Website, ibid., 1997. It should be added that prior to the First South Summit (April 2000, Havana), the annual ministerial meeting in New York on the sidelines of the General Assembly Session was considered the highest [annual] forum of the Group where the most pressing issues before it, as well as the major issues before the General Assembly Session, were addressed and the Group position/analysis formulated. The annual ministerial meeting has since (2000 and 2005 Summits) continued to function as previously.

34. This is a condensed version of the Group's principles on reform. For the full text see Annex to South Centre Policy Brief, op. cit., p. 17.

35. Canada's Permanent Representative in New York in early 1990s and subsequently deputy defense minister.

36. In the words of an American critic of the US policy towards the UN, Kofi Annan's reform package also sought to "disarm [US] Congressional attempts at unilateral leverage over UN policy." Ian Williams, Default in Ourselves, *The Nation Magazine* (11-18 August 1997, as referred to in South Centre, Meeting the Challenges of *UN Reform: A South Perspective*, Op. Cit., p. 5.

37. 30- The new "Fund" was expected to accumulate about $200 million resulting from administrative and overhead cost savings through reducing non-essential meetings and documents. According to a report submitted to the Fifth [Budget] Committee (GA/AB/3663, 17 March 2005), as of early 2005 UN member states "still remained skeptical of the funding level allocated to it," leaving the actual Fund pending.

38. The eight goals were the following: eradicate extreme poverty and hunger; achieve universal primary education; promote gender equality and empower women; reduce child mortality; improve maternal health; combat HIV/AIDS, malaria and other diseases; ensure environmental sustainability; and develop a global partnership for development. South Centre, Meeting the Challenges of UN Reform: A South Perspective, op. cit., p. 7.

39. UN, Strengthening of the United Nations: An Agenda for Further Change (A/57/387, 9 September 2002), paragraph 2.

40. The topics were the following: strengthening of the United Nations; Doing what matters; Serving Member States better; Working better together; allocating resources to priorities; and the organization and its people.

41. The author was a member of the Panel—one of the two diplomats on the Panel, the other being Ambassador Andre Erdos, then Hungarian ambassador to France.

42. South Centre, Meeting the Challenges of UN Reform: A South Perspective, op. cit., p. 9.

43. For complete statements see "http://www.globalpolicy.org/reform/initiatives/panels/cardoso". It is noteworthy that part of the criticism from the NGO community was related to the inclusion of private sector/entities in the definition of civil society. As argued by a major developing country development-oriented think tank, such inclusion placed the United Nations in danger of being overpowered by the influences of private businesses. The Cardoso Report on UN-Civil Society Relations: A Third World Network Analysis, August 2004.

44. For a detailed account of the two-day debate in the General Assembly see UN, General Assembly Statements: General Debate on UN-Civil Society Relations, 4-5 October 2004.

45. As per established practice, once a major report is debated in the GA Plenary, the president of the Assembly establishes an ad hoc committee—chaired by a seasoned, respected senior diplomat and in recent years usually co-chaired by two such diplomats representing both North and South—to undertake informal consultations in order to prepare and negotiate the draft resolution for subsequent action at the Plenary. Despite efforts for some time by a number of delegations, including Brazil for totally understandable reasons, no such committee was established by the GA president.

46. UN, *A More Secure World: Our Shared Responsibility*, A/59/565, 2 December 2004, Executive Summary. See http://www.un.org/secureworld/report.pdf.

47. The "clusters" of threat were the following: war between states; violence within states, including civil wars, large-scale human rights abuses and genocide; poverty, infectious diseases and environmental degradation; nuclear, radiological, chemical and biological weapons; terrorism; and transnational organized crime.

48. UN, *A More Secure World,* op. cit., paragraph 263.

49. UN, *In Larger Freedom: Towards Development, Security and Human Rights for All*, A/59/2005, 21 March 2005, based on the mandate given to the Secretary-General in GA resolution 58/291 to prepare a comprehensive report as a basis for the consultations leading up to the High-Level Plenary meeting [Review Millennium Summit] in September 2005.

50. Ibid., paragraph 8.

51. Ibid., paragraph 32. The point needs to be made, however, that the language of the text as it pertains to what is expected of developing and developed societies, respectively, is unmistakably different. It calls on developing countries to adopt and execute certain strategies/policies as part of their primary national responsibility for development. But, conversely, it enjoins the developed countries to extend assistance to those developing countries that adopt such strategies and policies. In other words, the assistance of developed countries is conditional. The question of conditionality—political conditions for extension of development assistance—drew strong criticism from G77 and was rejected in a number of its pronouncements.

52. G77's Website—g77off@unmail.org—Statements and Declarations, 2005. See in particular statements made on 25 January 2005 (at the turnover ceremony of the chairmanship of the Group); 27 January; 22 February; 6, 18, 25 and 27 April; 21 June; and 28 July, in the course of the debate in the Assembly or consultations under the co-facilitators designated by the president. The Statements on 21 June and 28 July, given the rather advanced stage of debate and negotiation, also contain proposed/alternative language on specific parts/recommendations in the Draft Outcome Document.

53. South Centre, Meeting the Challenges of UN Reform: A South Perspective, op. cit., p. 14.

54.   Thalif Dean, *UN Summit World Leaders Under Heavy Fire*, Inter Press Service News Agency, 14 September 2005.
55.   Within the framework of the "political" cluster, despite strenuous efforts during the preceding months on the two options presented in the High-Level Panel report, the decade-old debate on the expansion of the membership of the Security Council continued in a state of impasse in Summer 2005. Council reform was not even mentioned in the final outcome. However, two other proposals in the Draft Document embraced success; the creation of a Peacebuilding Commission and the establishment of the Human Rights Council. Both measures were subsequently discussed in the course of the 60th Session of the General Assembly and the necessary resolution, for each, was adopted.
56.   See Website of the Group of 77—g77off@unmail.org, Statements and Declarations, 2005, Ministerial Statement for the Twenty-Ninth Annual Meeting of Ministers, 22 September 2005, New York.
57.   The author's personal experience over the years—both as an active 2nd Committee delegate and later Chairman of G77 (2001)—bears witness to the Group's consistent policy in endeavoring to save previously "agreed language" and "past commitments" in the face of onslaught by negotiators across the "development divide."

References

Behnam, Awni. 2005. "Developing Countries in the Group of 77: a Journey in Multilateral Diplomacy, 1964 to 2004." Macdonald, R. St. J. and D.M. Johnston (eds). *Towards World Constitutionalism*, The Netherlands, Koninklijke Brill BV.

Kousari, Kamaran. 2005. "The Political Economy of Reform in the UN Economic and Social Sectors." *International Conference on UN Reform*, 18-19 July 2005. Tehran, Iran.

Sauvant, Karl P. 1981. *The Group of 77: Evolution, Structure, Organization*. New York: Oceana.

Williams, Marc. 1991. *Third World Cooperation: The Group of 77 in UNCTAD*. London: Printer Publishers.

Contributors

Hayward R. Alker was Professor of International Relations at the University of Southern California and an Adjunct Professor at the Watson Institute for International Studies, Brown University.

Ambassador Bagher Asadi, an Iranian career diplomat, is currently serving as Senior Expert at the International Department, Ministry of Foreign Affairs, Tehran. He is the former ECOSOC Ambassador of the Iranian Mission to the United Nations (New York, 1996-2002), he was Chairman of the Group of 77 in 2001.

Kevin P. Clements is a Professor of Peace and Conflict Studies and Foundation Director of the Australian Centre for Peace and Conflict Studies at The University of Queensland, Australia.

Sovaida Ma'ani Ewing is the author of *Collective Security Within Reach* (George Ronald Publications 2007). She is a UK barrister-at-law, a US attorney-at-law, and former Attorney-Advisor International in the Office of the Legal Advisor of the US State Department.

Richard Falk is Albert G. Milbank Professor of International Law Emeritus, Princeton University and, since 2002, Visiting Distinguished Professor, Global Studies, University of California, Santa Barbara. He is also Chair of the Nuclear Age Peace Foundation. His latest book is *The Costs of War: International Law, the United States, the United Nations, and World Order after Iraq* (2007).

Daisaku Ikeda is the President of Soka Gakkai International. This is UN Proposal written on August 30, 2006.

Kinhide Mushakoji is the director at the Center for Asia Pacific Partnership, Osaka University of Economics and Law. He is also the president of International Peace Centre, Osaka; president of Asia Pacific Human Rights International Centre; and vice chair of the International Movement Against All Forms of Discrimination and Racism.

Ved P. Nanda is Vice Provost and John Evans University Professor, University of Denver, and Thompson G. Marsh Professor of Law and Director, International Legal Studies Program at the University of Denver Sturm College of Law.

Ralph Pettman is Director of the Master of International Politics program at the University of Melbourne. He held the foundation Chair of International Relations at the Victoria University of Wellington.

Majid Tehranian is Director of the Toda Institute of Global Peace and Policy Research and Adjunct Professor at Soka University of America.

Printed in the United States
by Baker & Taylor Publisher Services